WITH COURAGE
AND DELICACY

Civil War On The Peninsula

WOMEN AND THE U. S. SANITARY COMMISSION

Nancy Scripture Garrison

DA CAPO PRESS

A MEMBER OF THE PERSEUS BOOKS GROUP

Cataloging-in-Publication data for this book is available from the Library of Congress.

ISBN 0–306–81291–6

First Da Capo Press edition 2003
First published by Savas Publishing Company in 1999

Published by Da Capo Press
A Member of the Perseus Books Group
http://www.dacapopress.com

Da Capo Press books are available at special discounts for bulk purchases in the U.S. by
corporations, institutions, and other organizations. For more information, please contact
the Special Markets Department at the Perseus Books Group, 11 Cambridge Center,
Cambridge, MA 02142, or call (800)255–1514 or (617)252–5298, or e-mail
j.mccrary@perseusbooks.com.

1 2 3 4 5 6 7 8 9—07 06 05 04 03

FOR FRED

CONTENTS

FOREWORD
i

PREFACE
iii

CHAPTER ONE
A MISSION SHARED
1

CHAPTER TWO
PERSPECTIVES AND PERSONALITIES:
THE SANITARY COMMISSION IS BORN
9

CHAPTER THREE
WASHINGTON, 1861
41

CHAPTER FOUR
TO THE PENINSULA, 1862
61

CHAPTER FIVE
WHITE HOUSE
95

CONTENTS, CONTINUED

CHAPTER SIX
"LET NO ONE PITY OR PRAISE US"
119

CHAPTER SEVEN
DEPARTURES
141

CHAPTER EIGHT
LEGACIES
171

CHAPTER NINE
EPILOGUE
189

NOTES
205

BIBLIOGRAPHY
229

INDEX
237

ILLUSTRATIONS

GEORGEANNA MUIRSON WOOLSEY
In Her Nursing Costume
Courtesy of the MOLLUS Collection (Mass. Commandery)
Photographic Archives, U. S. Army Military History Institute
Carlisle Barracks, PA. 20

ELIZA WOOLSEY HOWLAND
Courtesy of the MOLLUS Collection (Mass. Commandery)
Photographic Archives, U. S. Army Military History Institute
Carlisle Barracks, Pennsylvania. 24

JOSEPH HOWLAND
Courtesy of Photographic Archives,
U. S. Army Military History Institute
Carlisle Barracks, Pennsylvania. 25

THE SEVENTH NEW YORK VOLUNTEERS
Marching down Broadway, Manhattan, in April 1861
Watercolor by George Hayward
Museum of Fine Arts, Boston, Massachusetts. 28

LOUISA LEE SCHUYLER
Courtesy of the MOLLUS Collection (Mass. Commandery)
Photographic Archives, U. S. Army Military History Institute
Carlisle Barracks, Pennsylvania. 32

DOROTHEA DIX
Courtesy of the MOLLUS Collection (Mass. Commandery)
Photographic Archives, U. S. Army Military History Institute
Carlisle Barracks, Pennsylvania. 33

GEORGE TEMPLETON STRONG
Courtesy of the MOLLUS Collection (Mass. Commandery)
Photographic Archives, U. S. Army Military History Institute
Carlisle Barracks, Pennsylvania. 48

FREDERICK LAW OLMSTED
Courtesy of the National Park Service,
Frederick Law Olmsted National Historic Site
Brookline, Massachusetts. 49

KATHARINE PRESCOTT WORMELEY
Courtesy of the MOLLUS Collection (Mass. Commandery)
Photographic Archives, U. S. Army Military History Institute
Carlisle Barracks, Pennsylvania.   71

DR. ROBERT WARE
Courtesy of the MOLLUS Collection (Mass. Commandery)
Photographic Archives, U. S. Army Military History Institute
Carlisle Barracks, Pennsylvania.   76

HOSPITAL STEAMER *DANIEL WEBSTER Number I*
Courtesy of the National Library of Medicine
Bethesda, Maryland.
and
STEAMER *SAMUEL SPAULDING*
Photograph by Mathew Brady
Courtesy of the National Archives Still Picture Collection.   80

TRANSPORTS AND DOCKS ON THE PAMUNKEY
Photograph by Mathew Brady
Courtesy of the National Archives Still Picture Collection. 88

TRANSPORTS AT WHITE HOUSE
Photograph by Mathew Brady
Courtesy of the Library of Congress, Washington, D. C. 96

WHITE OAK SWAMP
Photograph by James Gibson
Courtesy of the Library of Congress, Washington, D. C. 99

THE VILLAGE OF MECHANICSVILLE
Photograph by James Reekie
Courtesy of the Library of Congress, Washington, D. C.   106

FEDERAL LINES FACING RICHMOND
Above, Redoubt Number Five near Fair Oaks Station.
Below, more of the Federal works before Richmond.
Photographs by James Gibson.
Courtesy of the National Library of Medicine
Bethesda, Maryland.   108

AFTER THE BATTLES OF FAIR OAKS/SEVEN PINES
Sketches by Alfred Waud.
Courtesy of the Library of Congress, Washington, D. C.   112

OUR HEROINES
Lithograph courtesy of the National Library of Medicine
Bethesda, Maryland.   131

AFTER THE BATTLE OF GAINES' MILL
Above, the Union field hospital at Savage's Station.
Photograph by James Gibson.
Below, the retreat to the James.
Ink and wash drawing by Alfred Waud
Courtesy of the Library of Congress, Washington, D. C. 155

VIEWS OF BATTLE: MALVERN HILL AND GLENDALE
The Seven Days draw to a close.
Sketches by Alfred Waud.
Courtesy of the Library of Congress, Washington, D. C.   159

HENRY WHITNEY BELLOWS
and
THE OFFICES OF THE U. S. SANITARY COMMISSION
IN WASHINGTON, D. C.
Courtesy of the MOLLUS Collection (Mass. Commandery)
Photographic Archives, U. S. Army Military History Institute
Carlisle Barracks, Pennsylvania.   178

ARMORY SQUARE HOSPITAL, WASHINGTON, D. C.
and
U. S. SANITARY COMMISSION RELIEF STATION
Courtesy of the National Library of Medicine
Bethesda, Maryland. 183

McCLELLAN AT HARRISON'S LANDING
Sketch by Alfred Waud.
Courtesy of the Library of Congress, Washington, D. C. 193

KATHARINE WORMELEY'S SUMMER RETREAT
Courtesy of David Hewitt and Anne Garrison,
Architectural Photographers. 198

CHAPTER HEADING VIGNETTES

CHAPTER ONE
Seal of the United States Sanitary Commission

CHAPTER TWO
The Bombardment of Fort Sumter
From a print, courtesy of the Library of Congress,
Washington, D. C.

CHAPTER THREE
The Capitol at Washington D. C., shown as it was
after the Civil War. In 1861 and 1862, when the Woolseys
served as nurses, its dome was not yet completed.
Courtesy of the author.

CHAPTER FOUR
Brig. Gen. Philip Kearny leads a charge in rain and wind
at the Battle of Williamsburg.
Wash drawing by Alfred Waud
Courtesy of the Library of Congress, Washington, D. C.

CHAPTER FIVE
Transports lying off shore at White House.
Wash drawing by Alfred Waud.
Courtesy of the Library of Congress, Washington, D. C.

CHAPTER SIX
Detail from a lithograph, *Our Heroines.*
Courtesy of the National Library of Medicine
Bethesda, Maryland.

CHAPTER SEVEN
Detail from *The Battle of Gaines Mill.*
Drawing by Alfred Waud
Courtesy of the Library of Congress, Washington, D. C.

CHAPTER EIGHT
The Three Women
Courtesy of the author.

EPILOGUE
Col. Joseph Howland, Sixteenth New York Volunteers.
Courtesy of Photographic Archives,
U. S. Army Military History Institute

MAPS

THE PENINSULA
A basic overview of the areas described.
64

THE RICHMOND AREA
A view showing the Pamunkey River, White House,
the Richmond, West Point & York River railroad line,
and the sites of the Seven Days Battles.
The battlefields of Fair Oaks and Seven Pines, not
specifically indicated here, lie just east of Richmond.
100

THE BATTLEFIELD AT GAINES' MILL
This view shows the relative positions of Confederate and Union
forces during the Battle of Gaines' Mill, and indicates
the position of the Sixteenth New York Volunteers as they
attempted to retake two hotly contested batteries which changed
hands several times during the day's action.
150

THE SEVEN DAYS BATTLES
A view showing the terrain covered during the Seven Days Battles,
with locations of each engagement defined.
The route of the Sanitary Commission transports in
their exodus from White House to Yorktown, and then up
the James River to Harrison's Landing, is also traced.
158

FOREWORD

In a modern American military surgical unit, the arrival of the wounded is heralded by the roar of helicopters. Medical technicians rush for the stretchers handed down from the fuselage doors, the brilliant operating room lights snap on, bags of plasma are hung up, and with masked faces and gloved hands, the surgeons and nurses prepare to save a dozen shattered soldiers.

Imagine the same scene in the late spring of 1862, during George McClellan's mammoth Peninsula Campaign. It is two days after the Battle of Fair Oaks. The sky is pouring rain onto White House Landing, the earth is a sea of mud, and into this scene of misery pulls an entire trainload of wounded men. And another. And another, the dead and the maimed stacked together in freight cars, shattered bones grinding with every jolt of the iron wheels. Many of those still conscious are screaming with pain. At this moment of crisis, the U.S. Army has no provision for these men. No food. No beverage. No medicines. No bandages. The government boats tied up in the river have no kitchen facilities for providing food suitable for the sick; everything and almost everyone is in a state of confusion.

Yet out of the darkness, comes help. Fresh fires light the path from the train to the hospital tents. Men and women enter the cars with lanterns and flasks of brandy and wine. Iced lemonade is offered to men who have been tortured by thirst for hours or days. Gentle hands carry the wounded to the tents, brush maggots from the wounds, arrange surgery for those who need it, and distribute quinine to the malaria-wracked majority of these neglected victims. And who brings this comfort, this beacon of hope in a landscape of sorrow and despair? The United States Sanitary Commission, a volunteer, civilian, self-funded organization brought into being to do the things the army should have done, and might have done, had it not lain so long under the control of penurious and senile career men, and an equally penny-pinching United States Congress.

The army regulations of 1861 contain such guidelines as this: "The senior medical officer of each post will on June 30 make requisition for supplies for the coming year, if stationed on the upper lakes, upper Mississippi River or west of the Mississippi River. All other posts will submit their requisitions on September 30." The utter irrelevance of these regulations for the Civil War, where 18,000 men might be wounded in a single day (as at Antietam in September of 1862, for example), give a hint as to how the old army doctors regarded the Sanitary Commission. They saw them as busybodies, ill-informed interlopers, well-meaning, perhaps, but basically useless. However, these amateurs were visibly better organized, better equipped, and better administered than the army itself. They were so clearly helpful and so obviously needed and loved by the soldiers that the army, however reluctantly, absorbed enough of these lessons to make the Sanitary Commission eventually unnecessary.

At White House Landing, on the Pamunkey River, near Richmond, Virginia, three upper-class Yankee women, all part of the Sanitary Commission, played a crucial role in organizing medical care and nursing the wounded, a role which transformed the women as well as the army. Author Nancy Garrison has taken the letters of one of these pioneers and, through loving interpolation of family, military and geographic information, turned the raw material into a seamless exposition of these women's private lives. Included here are their views of General McClellan, their evaluation of their own place in the overall history of the war, their fortitude in a sea of blood, pus and mud, and their ability to transcend pain through humor and comradeship amid disaster. The women's culturally-conditioned and, to us, amusing reluctance to relinquish hoop skirts—and their eventual enthusiasm for more liberated garb—remind us of their growing independence. Finally it is the revelation of a true vocation which separates these compassionate adventurers from their wealthy, stay-at-home sisters.

Nancy Scripture Garrison has crafted a compelling narrative of a dramatic moment in our nation's rebirth. It is not Women's History; it is American History—at its finest.

Thomas P. Lowry, M.D.
Woodbridge, Virginia

PREFACE

Some years ago, before we were married, my husband brought me for the first time to an old house set high and remote on a hillside in the White Mountains of New Hampshire. Resting on a shelf of meadow with forest rising steeply behind, ledges and hemlocks form a protective guard to its rear, and a small rill runs through stands of birches on its right side. In front of the house, at the edge of its sloping lawn, a ravine drops away and ranges of mountains stand sentinel in the distance. The building itself, a shingle-style Victorian, sits four-square behind its columned verandah, gazing out across the valley through large, benevolent windows.

We arrived at this house on a September evening, and as we stood momentarily on its porch before going in, the muted colors of a stained and leaded panel—a diamond-shaped coat-of-arms patterned in translucent ruby and citron—fell across my coat, streaming out to me from the lights within. As the door swung open, a long, high room drew me forward and a graceful fireplace stood before me, gilt numerals carved above it marking the building's date as 1891. In that moment it seemed I was absorbed, with ease and familiarity—and within a tick of time I felt a coming-together with someone already known. Such feelings are not easily explained.

Since that first evening the hillside house has become, intermittently, my home. I have come to know it intimately, though somehow respectfully and with a certain awe. I have learned its moods, its secrets, its hidden delights; and from the beginning I've sensed also that it is a rare space fraught with influences and presences undefined. Such an aura clings about old summer houses, abandoned and long alone through windswept nights and trackless winter storms, solitary in their hidden clearings, turning in upon themselves, dreaming in the chill, distilling their mysteries. And in such houses, for whatever reason, proprietary presence leaves its mark long after it has gone, not simply in possessions but through—possession.

This house has had three owners—all women—and has changed
hands only twice since 1891; first in 1912, once again in the mid- '40s.
Prizing its unique beauty, not one of these successive chatelaines has
cared for cosmetic renovation, and today, save for functional modern-
ization of kitchen and bathroom spaces, the house remains proudly
unchanged. Late Victorian furniture, pictures, rugs and china occupy
the places they have graced unmoved for the past century. A complete
set of Balzac's novels line the book shelves of a landing halfway up the
stairs. Twain, Hawthorne and Dickens rest in their places by the
mantle piece, positioned just there by the woman whose notion it was
to create this refuge for herself. And, because there is a sense here of
time suspended, it has never seemed surprising to me that I should
experience this first owner as palpably as the books she left behind,
or, within my mind, perceive her as visibly as the watercolors she
once hung above my bed. Upstairs she walks between her writing
room and the bedroom where we sleep. She moves silently in the summer afternoons and chilly dusks of autumn. She is Katharine Prescott
Wormeley, the woman whose presence I feel strongly on each returning to her house, and it is her adventure that I recount once more in
the short history which follows. I emphasize "once more," for it was
she herself who, long ago, became the initiator of her own chronicle.

For me, visits to Katharine's house became a ritual; and through
them, as I came to know her better, I discovered that, although she
was an aging woman when she first came to the mountains, with
quiet years behind her, she had known, for a time, an interlude of
color and great challenge. Born in 1830, she was young at a unique
moment in our history when her special talents placed her at the center of tumultuous events beyond the pale for most well-bred women of
her time. In 1862, during the second summer of the Civil War, allying
herself with the newly-formed United States Sanitary Commission,
Katharine went as a volunteer nurse to Virginia, there to survive a
stern testing and come to terms with the realities of war as it then
was.

In that summer she recorded her awakenings gracefully through
the medium of letters as was her custom. Through those pages to
mother, sister and "Dear Friend" move a procession of memorable

figures: Frederick Law Olmsted, Katharine's mentor and leader on the Peninsula; Eliza Howland, sweet, brave and determined, with her heroic husband, Colonel Joe; tall Captain Curtis, whom Katharine christened "our extensive hero"; saintly Dr. Robert Ware, and kind Captain Sawtelle, the quartermaster who favored mint juleps and cheered the little band of transport nurses through their darkest times. Emerging most vividly of Katharine's associates is the extraordinary Georgeanna Woolsey, a woman whose strength and humor defined her own liberation and a new professional ideal. Living on shipboard with these exceptional companions, Katharine worked as she had not worked before, suffered privation, laughed, wept and confronted life as few women then were free to do.

Katharine Wormeley understood the importance of her letters, and, even as she wrote, asked that they be saved by their recipients. Soon after the war those remaining were collected and published sparingly as memoirs of a conflict whose passions and sacrifices were still keenly felt. A second edition, titled *The Cruel Side of War,* followed in 1898. Though few of these books still survive, one small volume stood in its place at Katharine's hillside house, and it was there, on rainy summer afternoons, I came to read its owner's story.

In 1995, at graduate school, distanced from days of lazy dreaming, my own life altered course and focus. A long-held interest in 19th century American History had deepened and become defined, and as I considered several projects relevant to that subject, the story of Katharine's wartime career returned to me in all its fascination. It seemed a natural next step now to re-examine it as basis for my own writing, and so, in due course, a proposal was made and approved, the research begun, and in 1996 a paper completed. When finished, it presented a defensible argument—as theses must—yet, once done I put it away and moved on to whatever might come next; the project behind me, or so I thought.

This was not to be, however. Once evoked, Katharine did not subside gently. A year had passed in writing; still, as I reviewed the project, I realized that somehow I had not presented her story quite as I had wished to do, and so, within a month, reopening her file, I added and refined, deleted and discarded, cut and pasted, working again—yet this time without the pressing need for argument. Now it was important only that Katharine speak for herself, with no interpretations on my part supporting a position. Abandoning all thought of being "the writer," I became a conduit, channeling paragraphs from her small book of letters, setting myself the task of weaving diverse elements together so Katharine's voice might flow, and thereby the story of her companions and the U. S. Sanitary Commission might be told again. On this second round of research I broadened my reading to include more fully the volumes of letters written by members of the Woolsey family which further elucidated and reinforced Katharine's own tale. This time also a wider range of secondary sources were accessed. An important narrative link was forged on the day we encountered, in the archives of the U. S. Army War College, a regimental history detailing the career of Katharine's tall hero, Captain Curtis, and placing him unequivocally within the Sixteenth New York Volunteers, an infantry regiment commanded by Col. Joseph Howland, Eliza Woolsey's husband. This discovery placed five of Katharine's principle figures in close juxtaposition, and supplied a story line in which events described by any or all players might seamlessly be integrated.

In two years the new work was completed—or, more accurately, a deadline was at hand which could no longer be deferred. As a sometime writer of fiction I had found the conventions and proscriptions of history satisfying, the telling (or in this case retelling) of a story exciting, without manipulation of character or plot. For me, the contrivances of fiction had paled beside the rich allure of history.

There are many reasons why Katharine's tale came to absorb me, all distilled in her progressive voice: the courage of what she did, how she viewed her work, and the manner in which she wrote about it. In her era it was assumed that the preponderance of "history" dealt with men and affairs: exploits of statesmen and soldiers, wars, politics, economics and power. History was written by—and about—the individuals who orchestrated these masculine realities. For a woman to comment upon military strategy—albeit through the gentle medium of letters—and for female nurses to be present in a male preserve, were, though not unknown, novel departures in 1862.

Katharine's letters are fascinating because, to cite but one aspect of their virtues, they present a woman's view of male-controlled events, yet portray women and men fulfilling equally their overlapping roles within a common arena. She is easy and knowledgeable with war because she sees her presence valued within a vital endeavor. Her summaries compare favorably with those of male contemporaries, and her appraisals of personalities and events are no less accurate (or in some cases no less *inaccurate*) than those of more seasoned critics. If she and her companion nurses were not physically involved in combat, they *did* stand close behind the lines, and were full contributors in a common effort. Katharine saw, she listened and she wrote with unusual perceptiveness. When read concurrently with more familiar accounts, her work provides dimension and specifics not recorded elsewhere. As she lived it, she recorded it: a very individual history not to be categorized as "women's" per se, nor to be trivialized for its gentle manner or frame of reference.

The retelling of Katharine's adventure is done. The cycle of discovering and uncovering is closed. I think about the hillside house, and Katharine in it, and know that there must be a time in winter when the sun in afternoon angles across the mountains to cast an image of her ruby crest against the wall. The rooms are quiet then, the summer voices still, the brook silenced. In the aftermath of one cruel battle Katharine wrote of dreams—nightmares—of horror and unimaginable sadness which, she believed, would come to her in illness from her experience of war. I think perhaps such dreams did return in the house she called the Säter, and that even now we hear their echoes. But time has gentled every pang. Today there are no presences abroad in those woods and meadows save peaceful ones. Katharine's legacy is one of intellect and perseverance—and a dash of daring. She and her friends of 1862 have left their mark; others have retold their tale, and so it becomes, in turn, a shadow of that old passion—revered canon or national legend—our collective memory of Civil War.

Nancy Garrison
January 1999

ACKNOWLEDGMENTS

This book could not have been written without the help of many people. Among those who assisted me from the outset were Carol Demos and Daphne Harrington of the Beatley Library at Simmons College, and Virginia Smith of the Massachusetts Historical Society. Librarians at Radcliffe's Schlesinger Library, the Houghton and Widener Libraries at Harvard, The Library of Congress, the Library of Military History at Carlisle Barracks and the National Library of Medicine also offered valuable assistance, as did resident historians at the Olmsted National Historic Site, the National Park Service National Battlefield Park in Richmond, VA, and the Newport Historical Society. In the final stage of the design process, technical consultant Jennifer Smith offered unstinting support and encouragement. I thank all of these talented professionals for their patience and expertise. I am indebted also to Henry W. Longnecker, who shared family letters and memorabilia pertaining to Katharine Wormeley which otherwise would have been unavailable to me.

The primary sources which inform this account are the wartime letters of Katharine Prescott Wormeley, Georgeanna Muirson Woolsey, and Eliza Woolsey Howland, written during the years 1861 and 1862. They are, in themselves, pristine and needed no elaboration. These cultured women thought and expressed themselves with the ease and fluidity of polished Victorians, yet with a simple forthrightness which avoided the embellishments and literary affectations of their time. They wrote directly and clearly, leaving a moving testament which easily stands alone. This book is dedicated to them.

Of equal importance were the insights provided by more recent historians. I am especially grateful for the work of several scholars who have written of the same, or similar, persons and events in a manner which clarified my thinking. Most important among these are George T. Fredrickson and Nina Bennett Smith, both of whom I cite often, and whose thoughtful views on the United States Sanitary Commission and the position of female nurses in the Union Army, respectively, have influenced and instructed me. Kristie Ross and Lori Ginzberg presented facts and insights which further informed my perspective. Also invaluable was the work of biographer Anne L. Austin, who examined the lives of several generations of Woolseys during the nineteenth century.

My professors and colleagues at Simmons College provided essential support, guidance and humor during the initial stages of this work. First among them is Susan Porter, a mentor and friend whose high standards of scholarship demand her students' best efforts and lasting respect. Her promptings emerge on every page that follows. It is my good fortune to have worked with her. I am grateful also to my publisher, Theodore P. Savas, for granting me an unprecedented degree of freedom in the creation of this book. His confidence has warmed me through the months we've worked together.

Finally I acknowledge with great affection the friendship and encouragement of Ann Levin who has shared my journey, and I give thanks for the good humor of friends and family who have cheerfully survived my preoccupation. I am especially grateful to Tim Garrison for his patience and willingness to solve the many technical problems which beset me along the way. Most of all, I recognize the blessings of time, gentleness and laughter so freely given by my husband, editor, and research partner, Fred Garrison, who picked up the domestic pieces as I remained for three years at the computer. I offer this book to him in love and gratitude.

"They say that a lady must put away all delicacy and refinement for this work. Nothing could be more false. It is not too much to say that delicacy and refinement and the fact of being a gentlewoman could never *tell* more than they do here."

Katharine Prescott Wormeley
June 14, 1862

Chapter I

A MISSION SHARED

The United States Sanitary Commission, proposed as an innovative concept in the spring of 1861, evolved to become an intricately organized civilian endeavor which would provide health care and other humanitarian services to Union soldiers throughout the Civil War. Its efforts would confront an entrenched military hierarchy to efficiently coordinate the disorganized outpourings of Northern generosity to the end. As historian Allan Nevins wrote, "the Sanitary Commission remained absolutely indispensable. All told, it raised not less than twenty-five millions in money, goods, and personal help. . . . In a nation which had no medical association, no nursing schools, no apparatus for meeting a sudden strain on hospital facilities, it mobilized the best talents available for the war emergency."[1] It was a radical plan, conceived by conservatives, implemented at an historic juncture.

For an ambitious and spirited cadre of women who rallied to its cause, the Commission was also a transitional institution which, as it deliberately abandoned the sentimentality of Victorian benevolence, incidentally served to create a framework within which they might exchange prescribed domesticity for independence and challenge. As their accomplishments were transposed into wartime settings, female Sanitarians expanded the limits of middle- and upper-class propriety to accommodate their active patriotism. Although it neither promoted nor espoused a women's rights stance, the Commission became an important outlet for women's energies and administrative talents. By war's end it would prove itself as an organization in which women, especially well-connected women, could function in positions of authority and could construct a prototype for later efforts in social reform. Affluent Protestant women like Katharine Prescott Wormeley and the Woolsey sisters of New York served the Commission as equally-valued participants. Their insistence on practical efficiency rather than pious rhetoric hastened the evolution of private benevolence from individual, church-based charity to an all-inclusive model of secular volunteerism. The Commission's leadership, both male and female, combined idealism with a specific vision of orderly system. Its founders, professional men of privilege like the Rev. Henry Whitney Bellows, Frederick Law Olmsted and George Templeton Strong, were articulate proponents of this vision, as were their female counterparts. Yet although the Sanitary Commission has been noted often, and at some length, in various Civil War histories, there have been few works devoted to it as a separate entity—and none except Katharine Wormeley's and the Woolsey sisters' collected letters that have succeeded so well in recreating the unique experience of female Sanitarians on campaign in Virginia "at the heels of the army."[2]

What follows is their story, as they told it, and the story of their companions on board the water-borne hospital transports of the Peninsula. As such, it seemed natural to include, as its second theme, a partial history of the Sixteenth New York Volunteers during 1861 and through July 1862. This infantry regiment, whose personal associations and fortunes in battle would keenly affect the women's lives and sympathies, becomes integral to their experience; for the regiment exemplifies the military narrative of officers and men who served with Gen. George B. McClellan's Army of the Potomac during the Peninsula Campaign of 1862. As we trace this unit's progress, the fullness of the campaign, as well as the nurses' tale are further illuminated. Their endeavors intersect and complement on many levels and are, to the end, inextricably linked.

The Sanitary Commission was originally designed to fulfill two missions, the first of which necessarily would be the systematization of individual generosity through the collection and distribution of donated supplies. These accumulated stores were to be meticulously inventoried and allocated where needed. Donations included food of all descriptions, wine and spirits which eased pain and cheered the weary, vast quantities of clothing and bedding, and—perhaps most importantly—the funds necessary to purchase drugs and other medical supplies. The Commission's vast network converted acts of random compassion into reliable resources which were used to reinforce the Union army throughout the war and channel Northern benevolence through a pattern of disciplined management which historian Lori Ginzberg has called a "passion for efficiency."[3]

The second mission of the Sanitarians was the improvement of daily life for Lincoln's army through the new "science" of sanitation—a revolutionary departure for most military planners at the time. In response to the horrifying circumstances of disease and death suffered by the British army in the Crimea only six years earlier, American Sanitary Commissioners in 1861 determined to adopt a variety of sanitation measures and to educate a wary military establishment in their implementation. These measures outlined the improvement of campsite drainage and the construction of latrines, bathing and cooking facilities. They also detailed improved routines of discipline, diet, dress, and personal hygiene for soldiers in camp and on campaign. But despite their good intentions and efforts at reform, the Sanitarians encountered resistance on all levels from the Secretary of War and Surgeon General in Washington to regimental and company commanders in the field. Even Lincoln, as he signed the instrument which would make the Commission "official," referred to it as a "fifth wheel."

Yet, with persistence, the Sanitary Commission prevailed to a remarkable degree, persuading military personnel from the regimental level up, and eventually using sophisticated political manipulation to accomplish its ends. American Sanitarians adopted many of the measures outlined by Florence Nightingale in her crusade for nursing and health care reform, and it became instrumental in the design and construction of the famous "pavilion hospitals" of the Civil War which revolutionized the care of military casualties through their insistence on fresh air, sunlight, central heating, convenient plumbing and laundry facilities all under one roof. In the summer of 1862, during the Peninsula Campaign, the Sanitary Commission set up an operational model which proposed to attain its highest expectations. For Frederick Olmsted, the Director who personally supervised the Commission's work in Virginia, this was a fresh and energetic time— a cresting wave of optimism and idealism. To the extent that Sanitarians on the Peninsula were allowed to distribute their supplies as planned, and minister to the ill and wounded as they were prepared to do, their operation of mercy was highly effective. However, the work of the Commission was limited by the exigencies of battle and, more importantly, by the dissonance of two systems at odds: the Army Medical Bureau's hidebound structure and the Commission's painstaking methods.

Important as the overall work of the Sanitary Commission ultimately proved to be on all fronts for the duration of the war, it is this mission to the Peninsula, and the adventure shared by a specific group of young women, which emerge as perhaps its most exciting, and most poignant, interlude. The story of that flawed campaign as told by Katharine Wormeley, Georgeanna Woolsey and Eliza Howland, is a revealing and very human testament which complements and expands the scope of military histories when the two are read in conjunction. Their journals and letters, written on board the hospital transports of the York, James and Pamunkey Rivers offer rare insights into the day-to-day realities of sheltered women who chose this environment of danger. Sharply perceptive, frequently amusing, they furnish arresting glimpses of the men for whom they cared and with whom they served, including a handful of military leaders whose feats—and foibles—have become legendary.

While these very personal accounts only suggest the motivations which may have compelled such women to pursue high adventure, their observations are unfailingly fresh and filled with growing wisdom. As they assumed new roles, Wormeley and the Woolseys entered and, to a degree, appropriated a male world —often deliberately transforming themselves as they ministered to the sufferings of others. As their nursing and management skills increased, they conformed to, yet at the same time rebelled against, the prevailing sentimental imagery of their time. Their notes, often jotted in moments of exhaustion or anguish during the nine intense weeks of the Virginia sojourn, recount the fundamental adjustments—social, physical and emotional—that helped them maintain a perilous equilibrium. They suggest grace under pressure, but also reveal women suspended between two worlds in both of which, paradoxically, they thrived. It was a setting that extended their reserves of stamina, humor and compassion, and at the same time offered a sense of purpose and justification unlike anything they had experienced in their privileged lives—or would experience again.

The women's adventure unfolds within a dual framework: that of the ever-present Sanitary Commission ideology, and the tactical realities of a full-scale military campaign. To appreciate their journey we place ourselves within these parameters and, as essayist Carroll Smith-Rosenberg has suggested, know their text not only in terms of the environment and time for which it was written, but in terms of our own retrospection and experience, linking the physical world which surrounds with the emotional, perceptual world of both writer and reader.[4] The women's great adventure, the "new life" so eagerly embraced in the spring of 1862, embodies cultural and emotional elements both foreign and familiar to us, and we must absorb the specific challenges imposed upon them by the Campaign itself. We must also grasp the peculiar significance of their role as Sanitarians—along with the conflicting loyalties implicit in that role. Letters and journals, reflecting a series of external events—often deeply shocking—and long-ingrained internal perspectives, witness the shaping of their self-discoveries. Physical terrain and military maneuvers define their transport service; distinctive social and personal convictions inform it. These periphery merge to become the story and the awakening.

Yet there is a further dimension to be sensed in the enormity of the women's undertaking. The new behavioral flexibility they now experienced was not only welcome but overdue. Feminist historian Nina Bennett Smith has noted that such privileged young women were, for all their material assets, "trapped in a peculiar bind," at once restricted and free, "educated but with nothing formally devised to employ that education other than child-rearing and charity. . . . [for them] the way to a wider life beyond the domestic model was simply to go out and find something one could do well, and *to do it despite all opposition.*"[5] Katharine, Eliza and Georgeanna grasped this challenge eagerly, responding with distinction, creating new significances for themselves while serving a greater cause.

Finally we must understand that, for the men and women who would establish and conduct the work of the Sanitary Commission, any such endeavor would necessarily proceed within a self-fulfilling certainty of class superiority. The cultural climate of their era affirmed and supported this assumption. Aristocratic gentlemen felt justified in advising Cabinet Members; elite women who volunteered as Sanitary Commission nurses considered themselves specially qualified for their work. There were many reasons for these attitudes, and they invariably reflected class-consciousness and a self-assurance born of position. Katharine Wormeley insisted that unique qualities of refinement, orderliness and forbearance were prerequisites for "a lady's" presence in the male environment of war; she also implied that such qualities were the natural consequence of gentility as well as womanhood.

From its inception, and for its time, the Sanitary Commission demonstrated a rare fusion of men's and women's energies, equally valued, coming together in common cause. A congregation of affluent women first articulated the necessity for humanitarian aid, and a group of similarly placed men assisted them in molding it into a working machine. The Commission's success was insured through its orderly management and with the enthusiastic adoption by women *and* men of a superior corporate paradigm. As Nevins has written,

It was clear that women could write a lustrous page in
public affairs. Partly from the foresight of one feminine organization—the Women's Central Association of Relief in New
York—was born a body which finely typified the possibilities
of private endeavor: the United States Sanitary Commission.
This body faced a rough road ahead, but nothing quite like it,
in its combination of specialized skill, sturdy common sense,
and consecration to a great aim, had previously been known
in American annals.[6]

The Commission was indeed historically unique, and Nevins'
summation is accurate. No scholar has seriously attempted to disparage this record of achievement. Yet any close examination of the organization inevitably poses certain provocative questions. Was there, in
addition to altruism, a more subtle agenda of power that sought to
extend beyond the immediate emergency? Historian George
Fredrickson has suggested that the elite men who founded the Sanitary Commission manipulated a benevolent cause on behalf of private goals connected with conservatism and influence. To a lesser extent it seems evident that elite women also used the opportunities of
wartime volunteerism to enhance powerful identities that were personally rewarding rather than truly progressive towards the advance-
ment of women in the largest sense. For despite the securely privileged "equality" which female Sanitarians achieved for themselves, it
is undeniable that many of the most successful remained indifferent,
even hostile, to the cause for suffrage after the war. And it is significant that although the ladies of the Sanitary elite utilized their status
to make important contributions in areas of postbellum reform, these
were predominantly conservative not feminist; individual never universal. It is a legacy that has, over time, generated its own contradictions.

Chapter II

PERSPECTIVES AND PERSONALITIES:

The Sanitary Commission Is Born

It could be said that the initiatives of efficiency and order which would frame and undergird the United States Sanitary Commission evolved over night in the mind and words of one man; yet in fact they comprised a vision shared by many, which waited only on an instigator to set them in motion and see them swiftly consummated.

On Sunday April 14, 1861, the Rev. Henry Whitney Bellows, pastor of All Souls Unitarian Church in Manhattan, stood before his congregation with mixed emotions and some disquietude. Throughout the previous night he had inwardly debated the sermon he knew he must preach this morning, and had examined his own compelling need to arouse in his parishioners that passionate level of Union loyalty which for him burned so fiercely. By nature a man of peace, Bellows was deeply troubled—yet at the same time exhilarated by the anger which had risen within him during the darkening winter and spring of Southern secession. Now he could suppress his feelings no longer, and was prepared to address issues of duty and patriotism in a manner which might, he knew, be received as offensive or alienating by many of his parishioners. As he looked out across the waiting flock, he understood that, for them, outright civil strife could imperil not only the futures of their friends and loved ones, but the material stability of their prosperous lives; and he realized that to whatever degree he challenged them, he must lead with compassion as well as with fiery exhortation.

Bellows was well aware that the majority of these affluent New Yorkers were neither passionate abolitionists nor political progressives—and he knew also that many of them viewed their financial involvement with the business of the South as a practical necessity rather than a moral dilemma. Law-abiding and upstanding citizens, pillars of the church, their routine investment of Northern capital in Southern commerce remained largely unquestioned; an essential fact of business reality.[1] While men of substance might prudently express disapproval of slavery as an institution, many of them were at the same time engaged in enterprises which benefited the Southern cotton empire. Bellows understood the ambivalence, even resentment, implicit in this position, and he knew that his friends might well reject pious rhetoric on behalf of the Northern cause.[2]

With this conflict in mind, Bellows began to speak, but had progressed barely halfway through his sermon when the explosive news of Fort Sumter's surrender swept through the church on a sibilant wave of excitement. His biographer noted that "the sermon was half over and was being received in ominous silence when the pastor became aware that some important news was spreading throughout the congregation." Bellows himself remembered that "suddenly the hook and line of my discourse, which had hitherto hung loose and free, were nibbled at as by an eager school, and then seized and pulled as if by some voracious fish, until I could feel the whole weight of the hearts and minds for which I had been fishing with apostolic hope fastened to the rod."

Bellows' biographer described the extraordinary scene, as together the congregation experienced an emotional sea-change:

> At first whispered quietly, one to another, word of Fort Sumter's fall was received at length in a burst of full significance by every parishioner who came to All Souls Church that morning. The moment Bellows concluded his sermon the people rose and with one voice asked the choir to sing the national anthem, united in a general sentiment of indignant patriotism and determination to avenge the insult the nation had received."[3]

The pastor's dilemma was now resolved as his congregation closed ranks with him in passionate commitment. The prophetic sermon he preached that morning would be remembered as a significant prelude to events which followed. Among his parishioners were privileged women and men who would ignite to his words and join with him to become the nucleus of the United States Sanitary Commission, fashioning through their cooperation an unprecedented undertaking which would come to define the effective response of private citizens in a time of public crisis.

Although these and other well-intentioned New Yorkers had no clear plan of action before them in the days immediately following Fort Sumter's surrender, they recognized the time as one of opportunity. Women especially were accustomed to rallying to domestic crises, and in this instance they responded promptly to the challenge of immanent mobilization. Within ten days, ladies of Bellows' congregation joined with women from similar Protestant parishes, gathering at New York's Infirmary for Women to launch an effort which would support patriotic local men as they answered President Lincoln's call to enlist. The specific goal of this meeting, organized by Dr. Elizabeth Blackwell, was to create a Soldiers' Aid Society—and to accomplish this she had astutely used her own social connections to invite a powerful group of the city's wealthiest and most influential women. Blackwell, a respected physician and associate of Florence Nightingale, realized that these determined ladies would be prepared to commit considerable resources of time, energy and funds to an independent project of compassion which they would consider their own.[4]

For American women, the *cachet* of Florence Nightingale carried great weight. The so-called "Angel of the Crimea," famous for her humanitarian achievements in England, was an inspirational icon: a formidable woman of aristocratic background and impeccable associations who nonetheless abjured the label of "reformer" to perform the humble duties of a nurse. During the Crimean conflict, a debacle in which thousands of once-magnificent British fighting men were decimated within the space of one winter, Nightingale had employed delicacy and a will of steel to successfully effect change within the hidebound Army medical hierarchy at the British hospital base of Scutari during 1854 and 1855.[5]

Although she had been sentimentally envisioned as the "lady with the lamp" of Henry Longfellow's poem, Nightingale was, in fact, a much more significant figure; a pragmatist of tireless determination who had stood firm against an authoritarian military establishment and used her social and political connections to instigate sanitary reform.[6] Hers was the ideal upon which female Sanitarians would soon model themselves, and her insistence upon revised sanitation procedures for both camp and hospital would provide the paradigm which the U. S. Sanitary Commission would strive to emulate.

Before Nightingale's crusade, the horrors of wartime military hospitals were largely unknown to British and American civilians, and until the Crimean war they had never been universally—nor graphically—publicized. But in this most important aspect of her work Nightingale had benefited from the power of the press. As her biographer noted, "England rang with the story of Scutari because with the British Army was the first journalist to become a war correspondent: William Howard Russell of *The Times,*" a reporter whose methods presaged a new era of journalism. Just as the Civil War photographs of Mathew Brady would imprint horrific images upon the American mind, thereby arousing public consciousness to the stark face of battle, Russell's daily dispatches from the Crimea shattered a long silence and deeply shocked the sensibilities of his British countrymen. As they detailed appalling hospital conditions of cold, filth and misery, Russell's reports awakened national outrage and forced the realization that radical improvements in sanitary standards were essential. Through this process Nightingale's crusade became dramatized in a manner she had not forseen.[7]

In September 1854, now officially named "Superintendent of the Female Nursing Establishment of the English General Hospitals in Turkey," Nightingale left England bound for Scutari with a party of thirty-eight hospital nurses, "ladies," and religious sisters from both Anglican and Roman Catholic orders; an historic deputation which established a precedent for women determined to serve as nurses in military hospitals, and became the model for respectable female Sanitarians as they entered a male environment previously forbidden to them. Within weeks a "Sanitary Commission" composed of influential gentlemen and highly-placed civilian doctors was also sent out from England to "investigate the sanitary state of buildings used as hospitals." It was this Commission, according to Nightingale, that "saved the British Army"—for through its advocacy, and her own unrelenting activism, sanitary conditions in the hospitals *did* gradually improve; the death rate among British soldiers at Scutari falling from 293 men per 1,000 in July 1854 to a mere 25 men per 1,000 by January 1856. The British Commission became the prototype upon which Bellows and Olmsted would create their own, more elaborate organization six years later. But American Sanitarians in 1861 would discover, as had their British counterparts before them, that the struggle to institute sanitary reforms against the obduracy of an entrenched military establishment was a delicate and trying process.[8]

As she had hoped and anticipated, the first of Dr. Blackwell's meetings brought out an impressive array of New York's social leaders, a number of whom were congregants of the Reverend Henry Whitney Bellows. It seemed natural that these Unitarian ladies would look to their pastor to provide leadership—and although their unquestioned assumption of male authority would seldom prevail within this group again, it must be said that Bellows set forth an inspired initiative in the project he proposed. This was scarcely a surprise. The minster was a man who exuded power, described at this period of his life as "successful"—and that success, "having come to him easily and early, had given him a manner ebulliently confident and guilelessly self-satisfied; he enjoyed turning phrases, and his speech was mellifluous and elaborate. . . . he was a man of driving energy, quick to turn it to social purposes and brilliantly successful in engaging others in them with him, though not businesslike in handling the routine of the enterprises he inspired."[9]

Advising the women to invite *all* New York churches, schools and similar associations to join them in a systematic plan to supply necessities to the Union army, Bellows urged that they, as a group, adopt the concept of centralization, a concept which would come to define the Sanitary Commission as it, too, went on to construct its linked, but independent, organization. The decision to centralize administrative control, and to distribute donated supplies on a broad rather than regional or individual basis, was an historic one; for it would professionalize these joined undertakings and set them above all other volunteer efforts in terms of efficiency.

Thus well begun, Dr. Blackwell sent out a second round of notices without delay—again bearing a roster of socially imposing names—to *all* interested women, inviting them to meet together to continue the process already initiated. And so on April 29, barely two weeks after the fall of Fort Sumter and Lincoln's declaration of war, more than two thousand women gathered at New York's Cooper Union to form the Women's Central Association of Relief, hereafter known as the WCAR, an organization which would become a groundbreaking example of consensual leadership and efficient structure, as well as a life-saving mercy for fighting men on both sides of the conflict.[10]

Pleased to take part in an organization composed equally of women and men, a balance virtually unknown in 1861, female Association leaders were both clever and altruistic enough to harness the power generated by Bellows and his associates for the common good, even as they appropriated symbolic male authority to advance their own agendas. Astutely, the women would later instruct spin-off societies *always to invite a man* to preside at founding meetings, for such a "formality," they reasoned, would publicly emphasize seriousness of purpose and would impress upon impulsive volunteers the necessity of regularity and discipline. In so doing they reinforced the impression of efficient system and enhanced their own reputation as smooth administrators.[11] Yet although they may have used male power in the initial stages of organization, the WCAR and its satellite women's groups often reserved full control of decision-making and implementation functions for their female officers—and for women like Katharine Wormeley and the Woolsey sisters, these early leadership positions provided excellent training for subsequent hospital service. For them, administrative experience would be transposed to settings where chaos routinely threatened order, and where cool, trained heads would prove essential. These women were feeling their way in an entirely new medium, and it is exciting to contemplate how truly radical their experiment came to be as they tested their growing professionalism and exercised newly-developed executive skills.

As well as being gender-balanced, the WCAR was strikingly patrician; from its very origins an association of the elite. As such it is relevant to note how perfectly its first—and only—Corresponding Secretary exemplified her fellow-volunteers, for she would epitomize and affect the Association's legacy long after the organization itself ceased to exist. Louisa Lee Schuyler was a descendent of

Alexander Hamilton and Revolutionary War General Philip Schuyler. Born to old wealth and discreet social prominence, her executive talents would become legendary and her views would influence a generation of social reformers in the years after the war. The position she occupied at the WCAR would expand far beyond the normal parameters of a secretary's responsibilities, and her authority would be unquestioned as her power increased. For Schuyler, the Sanitary Commission would become the first step in a life distinguished by philanthropy, setting the tone for other affluent reformers as they set themselves to the work of benevolence. Generally her legacy would be seen as positive; in some aspects controversial.[12] Yet this remarkable career began quietly enough. Years later, as she recalled the first months of her wartime service, she wrote, "we began life in a little room which contained two tables, one desk, a half dozen little chairs, and a map on the wall. We sent out circulars, wrote letters, looked out the window at passing regiments, and talked about our work, sometimes hopefully, sometimes despairingly."[13]

And indeed Schuyler's volunteers had much to contemplate and a good deal to despair of in those early days, for they were met with resistance on many fronts. Typical of their discouragements was the outright hostility with which their first and most ambitious project was denied—a plan to train an elite and disciplined corps of female nurses to assist over-worked army medical personnel in military hospitals. This was a plan so eminently practical that WCAR leaders were confident of its acceptance in the current emergency. As it happened, Army medical officers thought otherwise, and, unprepared for any such female incursion upon their preserve, they refused the offer out of hand, denouncing it as unworkable, if not frivolous. But though rebuffed, the plan did not die; and as April turned to May, a small but growing number of determined women ignored official rejection to volunteer as nurses and hospital visitors. Among the first of these was Georgeanna Woolsey, whose extraordinary talent for nursing would come to symbolize the excellence of Sanitary Commission intervention throughout the war.

Woolsey, like Louisa Schuyler, was forceful, young, well-connected and well educated. She was the fourth of seven daughters in a progressive, women-centered family whose widowed matriarch set an example of philanthropy and social consciousness, and from the very earliest days of the war she was suffused with an eagerness to engage. Georgy, as she was invariably called by family and friends, was born in England in 1834 and christened George Anna in honor of paternal English grandparents. As a child she was impulsive, bright, and a bit wild—with a clownish sense of humor that often tried the patience of her more sedate elder sisters. As she became more mature, these energies were gradually tamed and focused, so that by the spring of 1861 Georgeanna appears to have evolved as the perfect war-nurse candidate: energetic, fearless, disciplined and intelligent.[14]

The Woolsey women were all firm advocates of anti-slavery, and indeed the eldest sister, Abby, was respected as a passionate and outspoken abolitionist whose commitment was nourished by a steadfast religious piety. With her mother and sisters, Georgeanna had been an active participant in the work of the WCAR from its inception—yet although their duties with the newly-formed Association could never be described as passive, they *could* be seen as "awaiting" or "fulfilling," and for Georgy this was not enough. She soon outgrew such tasks as letter-writing, coordinating and inventorying—essential functions of the WCAR—and from the first days of the war exhibited an overwhelming need to place herself at the center of action—a position for which her cool head and good humor suited her well.

In May of 1861, as she commenced training to become one of the first volunteer nurse-superintendents in a profession considered risky and even shocking by many, Georgy faced not only the disapproval of her own family, but the stern scrutiny of a selection

committee who came armed with a set of daunting criteria. Writing
with characteristic humor of her initial interview, she noted,

> It was hard getting myself acceptable and accepted.
> What with people at home saying "Goodness me! a nurse!
> all nonsense! . . . and what with the requisites insisted upon
> by the grave committee, I came close to losing my opportu-
> nity.
>
> First, one had to be just so old, and no older; have
> eyes and a nose and mouth expressing just such traits, and
> no others; must be willing to scrub floors, if necessary, etc.,
> etc. Finally, by dint of taking the flowers out of my bonnet
> and the flounce off my dress; by toning up or toning down,
> according to the emergency . . . [I was] at last sat upon by
> the committee and passed over to the Examining Board.[15]

Among the requirements which governed the acceptance of well-
bred WCAR nurses were the following: candidates were to be no
younger than thirty years of age nor older than forty-five, they must
possess good health, an exemplary character, the grace to submit to
firm discipline, and the willingness to wear a very plain regulation
nursing costume. Dr. Blackwell and Miss Dorothea Dix, soon to assume jurisdiction of female nurses for the Union Army, prudently
accepted for training only those women who were strong physically
and morally. They also rejected those whom they thought likely to
excite the romantic fantasies of their patients. To this end they insisted that aspiring applicants abandon hoop skirts, ruffles, curls
and tightly-laced corsets so that they might present a suitably so-
ber appearance—though Blackwell, unlike Dix seems not to have
dictated that her nurses be "plain to the point of ugliness." In Georgy's
case, this leniency of Blackwell's proved fortunate in light of subsequent events; for had she been denied on grounds of attractiveness,
the transport service would have lost one of its most effective nurses.
Much later, addressing the Woolsey nieces and nephews from the
vantage point of mature age, Georgy referred briefly to the potential problem of her appearance, imagining her young relatives

"amazed to know that your aunt was considered by some of the committee as too young and too pretty to be sent to the front in those days—though of course that was thirty-seven years ago. . . ."[16]

Draconian as these restrictions must have seemed to novice professionals in an age which favored the appearance of femininity, they were, in fact, dictated by logic. Physical hardiness as well as strength of character were *de riguer* for women in hospitals who were required to move easily within a confined space and expected to lift heavy burdens—often the patients themselves.[17] Although at twenty-eight Georgy was younger than the age deemed appropriate by administrators, she pressed for acceptance with spirited determination and was eventually admitted as a nurse-trainee. "The Board was good to me," she noted wryly, "it had decided upon my physical qualifications, and so, having asked me who my grandfather was, and whether I had had the measles, it blandly put my name down, leaving a blank where the age should have been - and I was launched, with about twenty other neophytes, into a career of philanthropy more or less confused."[18]

This acceptance did little to counter maternal resistance, however, and despite the remarkably enlightened and progressive notions Mrs. Woolsey shared with her daughters, Georgy would have to endure family skepticism for some time to come. In May she managed to enroll in a rigorous month-long training program being offered at New York Hospital, but this seems to have been accomplished only through a measure of subterfuge. In a letter to her sister, Eliza Howland, she complained of "family opposition," and cautioned Eliza to say nothing about the hospital opportunity: "I don't want to have to fight my way through the course," she wrote, "and then be badgered by [relatives] generally, besides giving a strict account of myself at home." But although Mrs. Woolsey remained negative toward the nursing scheme for a time, by June her resistance seemed to have softened, for it was then that she defined the rules which would, in the end, govern her daughter's wartime career: "Georgy is more earnest than ever about being a nurse for the

Georgeanna Muirson Woolsey
In Her Nursing Costume

soldiers," the mother wrote to an absent elder sister. *"I shall never consent* to this arrangement unless some of her own family goes with her." Mrs. Woolsey had announced her terms, and so it was to be.[19]

On successful completion of the hospital course, Georgeanna was ready for assignment by Dorothea Dix.[20] But despite the enthusiastic ambitions she shared with her colleagues, the mission these women undertook was fraught with hostility and unforeseen indignities. Often barely tolerated by doctors and military personnel, the "lady-nurses" persevered, sustained by the mitigating devotion of their patients from harassments from above. It was a difficult time of testing survived by only the most resolute. As she completed her hospital training, and for the first time came into contact with army medical personnel, Georgy recalled that "hardly a surgeon, of whom I can think, received or treated [us] with even common courtesy."[21] These doctors objected *not* to the idea of female medical assistants per se, for the obedient sisters of Roman Catholic nursing orders had traditionally been welcomed in army hospitals. Instead, they feared the incursion of well-educated Protestant women whose self-confidence would present a challenge to their own professional—and male—authority. The fact that the new nurses were careful *not* to conduct themselves in a threatening manner generally went unnoticed in the atmosphere of paranoia created by their presence, for in their new role the women lived and worked among hastily-recruited civilian doctors who were typically defensive about their own competence.[22]

These were stern realities for hitherto sheltered, well-bred women to suffer, yet as Georgeanna's career gathered momentum she withstood them with grace, demonstrating a degree of professionalism which would, over time, enhance the perception of women as dependable workers in surroundings not only "indelicate" but emotionally and physically stressful. Frederick Law Olmsted, who would be her colleague on the Virginia Peninsula, greatly admired women of her initiative and high courage. He wrote of Georgy that "[she] would, upon orders, take command of the channel fleet, arm, equip, man, provision, sail and engross the enemy, better than any landsman I know."[23] Beloved by patients, eventually respected by even the most despotic doctors, Georgeanna emerges from the memoirs of her contemporaries as a woman perpetually strong, humorous and unruffled. As such she personified an ideal quite unlike the self-effacing "angel of mercy" romanticized in the sentimental fiction of her day, a stereotype which she and her colleagues deliberately resisted throughout their service.

As the WCAR gathered momentum, and as small cohorts of women trained to become nurses, the Union army, to whose care these women would dedicate their sustaining efforts, swelled rapidly in number. Military regiments throughout the North formed, and, like the fledgling nurses, underwent basic training in a new and unfamiliar profession. Near Albany, men of the Sixteenth New York Volunteer Infantry—drawn predominantly from Hudson River Valley farms and villages—mustered and gradually cohered into a unit which, its officers hoped, would embody a sense of mission and *esprit de corps*. The path upon which these young men now embarked would touch and join the Sanitary Commission nurses' journey at many points during the painful summer of 1862 when both groups would work and survive together under conditions which would test their courage and resilience .

Joseph Howland was 28 years old in the spring of 1861 when, on May 15th, he enlisted to join this new regiment for a projected two year tour as adjutant. As a potential officer his qualifications were promising. In outlook and temperament he embodied that nineteenth-century ideal of masculinity defined as the "Christian Gentleman"—a composite which stressed "love, kindness and compassion as not only worthy *attitudes* for a man but also the basis for right *actions* on his part."[24] Joseph had, in fact, considered studying for the ministry as a youth, and although this plan had been abandoned in a period of ill health, he retained much of his early faith and idealism, with a determination to lead his life on the highest moral plane. But though Christian gentlemen like Joseph might strive for perfection in the mildest of terms, there was nothing pious or effete in their attitudes toward military service or the conflict in which they now engaged. The conscientious middle- and upper-class men who took up arms in the Civil War proved, more often than not, brave and resourceful officers, committed in their responsibilities, often heroic. For them, a sense of religious duty quite naturally conformed with, and was translated into, a devotion for shared Cause. Joe Howland, though young, was a firm disciplinarian who tempered his own youthful impetuosity with good sense and his personal bravery with a deep regard for the men in his command. Fortunately he seems also to have been blessed with patience and a high degree of humor—qualities which would prove essential as he adjusted his own views to accommodate the personally liberating ambitions of a determined wife and strong-willed sister-in-law who would share his wartime mission during the months ahead.

Eliza Woolsey Howland, Joseph's wife, was fifth of the seven sisters, next in age to Georgeanna, and closest to her emotionally. Although it is not known whether Joe shared the abolitionist convictions of her family, it is certain that he supported Abraham Lincoln's determination in the face of secession and that, with Eliza, he expressed familiar sentiments of reverence for "country and flag" typical of patriotic volunteers. Married in 1855, the young Howlands had been fond friends since childhood and were, in fact, cousins. Their union typified the multiple, long standing ties which bound old English and Dutch families of New York in a tight, mutually reinforcing milieu where intermarriage occurred frequently, and in which business and social relationships rested on an interlocking foundation of kinship. A second Woolsey sister had also married a Howland, and a third would make an "in-clan" marriage soon after the war.[25] Since their marriage Joseph and Eliza had lived almost constantly abroad, traveling for long periods through Europe and

Eliza Woolsey Howland

Joseph Howland

the Near East, often with Georgy as their companion. The three were devoted to one another—more often together than apart—and a wartime separation from Joe presaged almost as much pain for Georgy as for Eliza. In the spring of 1861 the thought of this severance became a spur to both women as they embarked upon their journey.

But parting from one another was not the only discontinuity the young Howlands would soon be forced to bear. They would also face separation from a most tangible symbol of their happiness: a home only just established after years abroad, already cherished as a quiet sanctuary and setting for useful work. Georgy wrote later of that spring, "Eliza and Joe were just taking possession of their beautiful new home, 'Tioronda,' at Fishkill, and all the little details of Eliza's letters have a pathos of their own in view of the speedy closing of the house and the sudden change from peaceful loveliness to the grimness of civil war."[26] For the Howlands, as for their extended family, Tioronda was a dreamlike refuge and destination; a farm estate sixty miles above Manhattan on the east bank of the Hudson, facing west across Newburgh Bay to the Catskills which stretched beyond the river and disappeared in the blue distance. To leave this haven was perhaps the most wrenching departure of all.[27]

In the early days of his enlistment, removed from Tioronda by only a few miles, Joe's alienation from its tranquil atmosphere was nonetheless complete. The accelerating realities of his first days as a Union officer are suggested in a history of the Sixteenth Volunteers whose author, Major-General Newton Martin Curtis, served with the regiment throughout its service and became Joe's lifelong friend. Curtis remembered that, "on June 1st, 1861, we, [under the command of Colonel Thomas A. Davies] in company with the Twenty-eighth New York under Colonel Donnelly, moved into camp at Normand's Kiln, Bethlehem, [near Albany] and commenced life under canvas. On the 15th, uniforms were received, and this acquisition did much to improve the health and spirits of the men. Nothing is more depressing to a respectable man than to be placed in a position where he is made uncomfortable and unpresentable by reason of deficient or worn out clothing."[28] Several weeks earlier one hundred and fifty 1840 model Springfield muskets had been issued to the new regiment for use in guard duty and in practicing the manual of arms, and so, thus clothed and equipped, the Sixteenth began military life in earnest.

As the days of their training lengthened, it became clear that these men were apt pupils at soldiering. At Bethlehem, as country boys put on new clothes and rehearsed the deadly sport they would play together from First Manassas to the Seven Days, from Antietam to the bloody forests at Chancellorsville, they also bonded into a cohesive and ultimately effective fighting unit. On June 24 young Captain Curtis recalled proudly that the Sixteenth was reviewed by Governor Morgan of New York, and remembered that "the soldiers entertained the Governor with a sham battle, the final charge of which was made with vociferous cheers and might properly have been called a 'howling success.'" The next day, with the mock skirmish behind them, they were issued five hundred more vintage Springfield muskets and marched to Albany, where they paraded smartly through town to board a steamer for their voyage down the Hudson to New York. For them, the serious business of war would now begin.[29]

In those early, idealistic months of 1861, when both North and South entertained hopes of a swift and relatively painless victory, there were few sights more stirring for patriotic citizens than the departure of each regiment as it marched through city streets to its point of embarkation. Before crowds of cheering well-wishers, suffused with optimism, recruits marched with uniforms pristine as bands played, horses pranced, and regimental colors were presented, unfurled, and displayed for the first time to be borne resolutely through whatever trials might lie ahead. These banners, symbols of a regiment's faithfulness, trust and courage, were tendered and accepted with appropriate ceremony. Newton Curtis remembered the presentation of his regiment's colors years later, writing that, "the

The Seventh New York Volunteers, recruited some weeks earlier than their brother regiment, the Sixteenth, march down Broadway in April, 1861. Watercolor by George Hayward in the Boston Museum of Fine Arts.

Sixteenth marched down Broadway to 8th Street, and thence to Washington Square, where it was presented with a national flag and a stand of state colors by Mr. Robert S. Hone on behalf of Mrs. Joseph Howland, the wife of our adjutant." Hone, as he made this presentation to Col. Davies, expressed sentiments which would become sadly familiar during the ensuing years. As he paid tribute to Eliza, he noted gravely that "Mrs. Howland's heart is, as you know, full of the tenderest emotions at this moment of departure of the Sixteenth Regiment for the seat of war. I can vouch for it that she, as fully as any of you, is doing her duty, making her sacrifice at the altar of her country." In turn, Col Davies expressed his own gratitude to Eliza for her attentiveness to his men, and for her contributions of necessary supplies to them during the initial weeks in training. Then, asking that the colors be raised before the regiment, he asked for assurance that the flag and banners just received would be defended and protected—a request which brought forth a roar of assent as all hands returned the promise. Curtis recalled much later, with great pride, that this pledge was confirmed many times and in many places. During the Sixteenth Regiment's two year term of enlistment more than twenty color guards were killed or wounded in the performance of their duty. Seeing their charge as an honor which exceeded mere symbolism, these men prevailed against fierce odds to protect their emblems from loss or dishonor. In this resolve they conformed with a high, indeed a chivalric, standard of conduct shared by their counterparts on both sides of the conflict.[30]

For the Woolsey women, standing by quietly to watch the presentation tableau, this was inevitably an emotional parting. They had, from its first muster, considered the Sixteenth "their" regiment, and they would continue to do so throughout its active service. The family's efforts, supportive of the Union Army in its largest sense, would nevertheless focus most fondly upon these New York men for whose welfare they cared so deeply. Soon, each soldier's name would be familiar to the Woolseys, each man's family recognized by them, their needs supplied by Woolsey and Howland generosity. On this summer afternoon, as they contemplated what lay ahead, listening to speeches of inspiration and portent, the women presented an appropriately modest, retiring mien: supportive of their men through open-heartedness and good works; remaining discreetly in the background. Yet this gentle conception of duty would soon be exchanged for a more assertive role. If Georgeanna had begun to press forward and outward through the medium of nursing, she was only the first of this family to envision a widened sphere of wartime engagement. Within days Eliza would follow her.

As the Sixteenth and other newly-formed regiments marched away to their uncertain futures, and as nursing graduates struggled through the initial phases of their unorthodox careers, a serious problem was developing which would absorb Louisa Schuyler's New York volunteers and would test their recently-acquired managerial skills. Families from all parts of the North were now appealing to the WCAR in deep concern, urging Schuyler to resolve an accelerat-

ing situation which had become acute as military recruitment gathered momentum. Mothers and wives, who had sent their loved ones
off to war on a high note of patriotism, learned now that conditions
in the army were not as they or their men had imagined them to be.
They discovered that most military camps were filthy, that officers
could be dissolute and intemperate, and that rations of fresh food
were often scarce or nonexistent. To counter these circumstances
women prepared and packed their own supplies and mailed them
to recruits at camp. But these haphazard shipments, however well
intended, frequently languished on railroad sidings or were deliberately withheld from designated recipients. Incensed civilians
throughout the North witnessed appalling scenes of waste at depots like this one described by Sanitary Commission worker Mary
Ashton Livermore:[31]

> Women rifled their store-rooms and preserve-closets
> of canned fruits and pots of jam and marmalade, which
> they packed with clothing and blankets, books and statio-
> nery, photographs and "comfort bags." Baggage cars were
> soon flooded with fermenting sweetmeats . . . Decaying fruit
> and vegetables, pastry and cakes in a demoralized condi-
> tion, badly canned soups and meats were thrown away en
> route. And with them went the clothing and stationery satu-
> rated with the effervescing and putrefying compounds
> which they enfolded. . . .[32]

Here was a miscarriage of generosity which now fell to the
WCAR for resolution. Each mail brought similar tales of waste to
Schuyler's office, and, though at first overwhelmed by the the sheer
volume of complaints, she and her volunteers soon rallied to confront the problem as best they could.[33] These were the very circumstances their organization had been designed to address, and although Schuyler had not as yet been given official authority to act,
she was determined to *initiate* action—and in so doing communi-
cated her concern to Henry Bellows, who agreed to formulate a plan
of his own which would secure formal recognition for the WCAR

and thus empower Schuyler to effectively deal with the crisis at hand.[34]

Accordingly, on May 15, Bellows left New York by rail for Washington accompanied by a delegation determined to press for an audience with government officials. With him went Dr. Elisha Harris, Dr. W. H. Van Buren of the "Physicians and Surgeons of New York Hospitals," and Dr. Jacob Harsen of the Lint and Bandage Association. As they traveled south the gentlemen consulted together, and by the time they reached their destination they had developed the rudiments of a strategy. As Bellows later wrote, "we improved the time during our journey to 'Wash' debating the plans we should adopt. Dr. Harris says that the first idea of the Sanitary Commission, which certainly had not entered my head when we left New York, was started between us in the cars twixt Philadelphia and Baltimore in a long and earnest conversation in which the British & French experiences in the Crimea formed the text."[35]

On May 16, comfortably settled at Willard's Hotel at the heart of official Washington just two blocks from the White House, this group drew up its first concrete plans for the U. S. Sanitary Commission, and over the next week presented them at meetings with President Lincoln, his cabinet, and ranking officers of the army Medical Bureau. They conferred also with Dorothea Dix, whose confirmation as Army Superintendent of Nurses was currently enmeshed in bureaucratic red tape, and discovered with her that government acceptance of *any* new concepts could be discouragingly slow. Recalling those first weeks in Washington, Bellows reflected that "the [War] Department regarded us as weak enthusiasts representing well-meaning but silly women."[36]

Yet although this period of waiting was tedious, it was nonetheless a valuable interlude for the Commission's Founders. On June 9, when Secretary of War Simon Cameron at last approved their appointment, Bellows and his colleagues had not only achieved patience, but had tentatively created their own board comprising some of the most distinguished men of their time. Bellows himself was named as president, with Alexander Dallas Bache, a grandson of

Louisa Lee Schuyler

Dorothea Dix

Benjamin Franklin and Superintendent of the U. S. Coast Survey, as vice president. Serving as treasurer would be George Templeton Strong, a successful and public-spirited New York lawyer. Others of the original Commission included Dr. Cornelius Rea Agnew, Professor Oliver Wolcott Gibbs, Dr. Elisha Harris, Dr. William Holme Van Buren and Dr. Samuel Gridley Howe of Harvard.[37] Given the eminence of these Directors, the women working with them in New York hoped now to be taken with corresponding seriousness in Washington—and to a large extent this hope would be fulfilled.

Although the overt goals articulated by the Sanitary Commission in its statement of purpose in 1861 came in response to a national emergency, it is important to recognize that there may have been other, less obvious themes embodied in its mission which can be seen as strictly its own. The Commission's philosophy would reflect the traditionalist perspective of a specific class and community of thinkers who shared a vision of ordered institutionalism in church, state and society. Historian George Fredrickson, in an incisive critique of the Sanitary Commission, has named such individuals "conservatives in a radical age," and characterized them as "men with an allegiance to well-established organizations or coherent social groups [who] had a stake in the preservation of traditional forms of social control."[38] Thinking in terms of class, they envisioned their leadership as a secular entity which should ideally resemble the clerical hierarchies of the past.

By 1860 the gentlemen of substance who would form the Sanitary Commission's leadership had already begun to see themselves as a beleaguered minority at the mercy of Democratic majoritarians. As believers in an ordered, "natural" hierarchy of privilege, Fredrickson has suggested that Bellows and his associates espoused a notion of America *not* as a promise of freedom, but as a "specific set of inherited institutions," a position linked with the arguments of Francis Lieber, the German-born political theorist who also viewed

America "not as a utopia in the making; [but as] a particular system of government which had received the blessing of history and experience."[39]

The Founders' determination to construct their Sanitary Commission as an ordered, even rigid, organization which would effect sanitary reform and regularize the exuberance of wartime benevolence, corresponded with their underlying conviction that *much was seriously wrong* with American society. Fredrickson identified the malaise that disturbed Bellows and his associates as a ground-swell of independent thinking, a questioning of established institutions, assumptions of class, and a confrontation of authority across a broad spectrum of American thought. He contended that, for many, the religious and social corollaries of this confrontation were evidenced in the passionate revivalism of the recent decades, the transcendentalism of Ralph Waldo Emerson, and the radical abolitionism of William Lloyd Garrison—movements which celebrated man's individual worth and the potential of the self rather than submission to a tradition of established institutions.[40]

And for many Americans, anti-institutionalism came coupled with grave disillusionment in the political process. In 1860 Whigs saw their party virtually dissolved, while Democrats found themselves sectionally fragmented over the divisive issue of slavery. At the same time "Conscience Whigs," Free Soilers, and Liberty Party abolitionists coalesced to realize new strength as Republicans and succeeded in electing Abraham Lincoln as president. Yet Republicans found that, even in victory, there remained divisions within the ranks of their new party; and if Northern intellectuals converged in their opposition to the South, they were nonetheless often divided among themselves along the fault line of individualism versus institutionalism. Within this mix, Northern Conservatives like Bellows and his associates could be seen as essentially anti-democratic, for although they generally approved Lincoln's firmness in confronting the crisis of secession, they found radical abolitionists distasteful and shared the opinion that they, as a privileged and self-appointed consortium, could, if given the opportunity, conduct national affairs more efficiently than any elected politician.[41] Fredrickson has conjectured that in this sense some Sanitarians not only accepted the necessity of war, but welcomed it.[42] They saw their goal not simply in terms of ministering to the injuries and illnesses of men in a humanitarian sense, but more importantly they saw it in practical terms: the retention and rehabilitation of men *to be fighters in a disciplined army*. They imagined their Commission as a worthy endeavor which would promote their own conservative ends and at the same time prove compatible with patriotism in crisis.

But however distinguished the Founders' reputations, and however altruistically they defined their motives in 1861, the impressive roster of their combined names did not guarantee that their proposal would be taken seriously. On June 13, even as Lincoln signed the document which would confirm the Commission's status as an official body, the President disparaged the new organization as "a fifth wheel to the coach."[43] His words indicated a deep reluctance on the part of government to acknowledge a need for sanitary reform, and although the Sanitarians had cleared a number of major hurdles, much remained to be done before they could proceed effectively. Critically important to them was the appointment to one post which still remained vacant, a position which, if brilliantly filled, could enhance their dynamic as a credible body and strengthen their tenuous official sanction. Much would depend on the individual selected to serve as Executive Secretary to the Commission - and the Founders recognized this. As Bellows wrote, "if only we get a first rate Secretary—not yet agreed upon—everything will go smoothly. All depends on that."[44]

Happily, such a man was close at hand, and with his confirmation the real work of the Commission would commence. The Board's choice was Frederick Law Olmsted, who, more than any other save Bellows himself, would come to characterize the Sanitary Commission and define its goals. Olmsted seemed ideal for the job: a gifted administrator who had gained public acclaim as architect and superintendent of New York's recently developed Central Park. In its construction he had transformed 4,000 laborers, many of them immigrants, into a smoothly running workforce, an experience which had provided him with an exceptional administrative background. Katharine Prescott Wormeley, who would become Olmsted's lifelong friend as a result of their shared experience of service on the Peninsula, defined his direct, charismatic style of management: "I think he is a man of the most resolute self will—generally a very wise will . . . born an autocrat, and as such very satisfactory to serve under. His reticence is one of his strong points: he directs everything in the fewest possible words; there is a deep, calm thoughtfulness about him which is always attractive and sometimes—provoking. . . . he is a great administrator, because he comprehends details, but trusts his subordinates: if they are good he relies on them; if they are weak, there's an end to them."[45]

Besides his executive abilities, Olmsted was widely acknowledged as an astute social commentator whose opinions coincided well with the professed goals of the newly-born Sanitary Commission. During the 1850s he had written a series of works describing his travels through the South which offered sharp critical analyses of the antebellum cotton culture sustained by slavery. But although he decried the paternalism of the slave states and favored abolition, Olmsted's criticism was perhaps more persuasive in terms of basic economics than in its appeal to Garrisonian humanitarianism. As Fredrickson noted, "his famous travel writings about the South had little in common with abolitionist attempts to portray the suffering of the slave. The hardheaded Olmsted concerned himself less with the *inhumanity of slavery than with its apparent unprofitability.*"[46] Whether or not Fredrickson may have been too harsh in this evaluation, indeed the views expressed by Olmsted in *The Cotton Kingdom* were predominantly practical rather than emotional, and they encouraged many Northern thinkers to regard the culture and society of the South from a new perspective.

Olmsted, as he came to see Southern secession as inevitable, had considered several wartime occupations for himself and had

initially been attracted to a quite different role than the one which
the Sanitary Commission would offer. In May 1861 Secretary
Stanton had approved a plan, originally proposed by General Benjamin Butler, to appropriate all runaway slaves of Confederate
masters who attached themselves to Union troops. These former
slaves would be retained by the North and designated as "contraband of war" to be used in construction or other labor by the Union
army. Olmsted had long considered the practical problems which
would accompany the transition of blacks from slavery to freedom,
and in Butler's solution he saw an opportunity for himself in the
role of Superintendent of Contraband Labor.[47] Prudently realizing
that he would need a powerful sponsor before applying for any government post, Olmsted turned for support to Bellows—a natural
move on his part, for the minister had lately written with admiration of the Central Park project in the *Atlantic* and had praised its
design and its creator's administrative abilities. But instead of com-
plying with Olmsted's request for sponsorship, Bellows considered
the applicant in quite a different context, seeing him as a natural
adjunct to a Board now crying out for a hand experienced in management. So with the unanimous support of his Executive Committee, Bellows invited Olmsted to become secretary of the Sanitary
Commission. This invitation was promptly accepted, and on June
22 Bellows noted with relief that "F. L. Olmsted of the Central Park
has accepted the post of Resident Sec'ty of our Commission & will
take a large part of the immediate responsibility off my aching shoulders."[48] The final piece was now in place.

With Olmsted's coming the Commission at last became truly
functional—an organization with a curious agenda of benevolence
wedded to control which would seek to impose upon free-thinking
Union soldiers its own conservative standards of conformity, even
as it "sanitized" their camps and hospitals. Theirs was an initiative
that would brook no halfway measures. They were absolutists with

vision. Men and women alike, Sanitarian leaders revered a structured society and the institutionalism which defined it. How their rationale would evolve, and how they themselves might develop and survive, as a group and as individuals, was still in doubt. How their message would play out in the pressured environment of war remained to be seen.

Chapter III

WASHINGTON: 1861

The Sixteenth New York Volunteers reached Washington on June 29th, 1861, one of many regiments pressing daily into the capitol and its environs. Their journey south had been an anxious one, especially so as they negotiated their way through Baltimore, an embattled city of divided loyalties in a period of intense unrest.[1] Regiments passing through the city from the north were obliged to march directly across town from one railroad station to another, and in the process a number of ugly confrontations had already occurred in which Union soldiers had been injured and killed. Writing to Eliza soon after their arrival in Washington, Joseph noted with relief that,

> our passage through Baltimore was unmolested, but was one of the most impressive scenes imaginable. We marched through at eight o'clock without music and with colors furled, in perfect silence, marching in quick time, only pausing once.

The streets were full of people, but we did not get a word of welcome or a single smile - except from two little girls in an upper window and half a dozen old darkies standing in a doorway. At the head of the column . . . the colonel walked with his sword sheathed and a hickory stick in his hand. Once a rough fellow in the crowd (a city official) asked tauntingly, "where's your music?' and Colonel Davies replied, "in our cartridge boxes!" . . . . The crowd looked cold and bitter at us, and we looked stern and ready at them. All the road from Harrisburg to Washington is guarded by strong bodies of Federal troops. They are needed.[2]

For Georgeanna, the departure of the Sixteenth served as a clarion call. Chafing to be at the center of war-driven activity, and hoping to utilize her recently-acquired nursing skills, she urged Eliza to join her husband in Washington so that a journey for both women might be justified. The plan was not a new thought, for the sisters —especially Georgy—had determined from the very first that Joe should not leave them behind as he embarked on his adventure of war. On May 15, even as the new adjutant was assuming his duties, Georgy had begun her campaign, writing to Eliza at Tioronda and urging her to action:

> I supposed you would go to Albany. I am sure *I* should have, and I hope you will take into serious consideration the small plan I suggested to you about being a nurse—at any rate about fitting yourself as far as you can for looking after the sick, if you go, as I suppose you will want to, to Washington. . . . We all mean to be very brave about Joe, and I'm sure you will be;—it's a way you have; especially as you and I will be near him in Washington at one of the hotels or hospitals. I shall not be satisfied at all to stay at home while Joe is down there. . . . So, my dear, be keeping the little plan in view in making your arrangements, and don't say a word to anybody. . .[3]

Eliza needed little persuasion, and soon set about making arrangements at Tioronda, planning not only for her husband's indefinite absence, but for her own as well. The estate was well-staffed, and its farm self-sustaining under the eye of a resident overseer. Only the house would need closing until its owners returned. On July 2 the two sisters left New York, accompanied by their younger brother Charley. It was an adventurous move for well-bred ladies, yet one which would soon become increasingly sanctioned by the preternatural environment of war. Energetic, upper-class women—"ladies"—like the Woolseys, managed to take advantage of the unusual circumstances and turn them to their own purposes. As they did so, they adroitly sidestepped the gendered conventions of their time to work and travel with new freedom. An innate quality of being "above reproach" became their passport, and the fact of their gentility gave them the power to transcend the constraints of their accustomed domestic sphere. For the ingenious sisters, although Joseph's assigned maneuvers would provide the spurs to drive their adventure, in a sense even he would become incidental. The women would soon require no pretext. For Georgeanna, if not always for Eliza, the momentum of a vocation would become self-propelling, needing no further incentive. Throughout the war she would stand close to the fire, seeming always to gather strength as pressure and necessity escalated.[4] An initiator, an instigator, an implementor—Georgeanna was essentially active. More easily than Eliza, whose obligation would be, by choice and necessity, to her husband, Georgy would break free from all demands save those of her own choosing. Long before the Peninsula Campaign she had begun to devise a fluid "professional" persona, and in the creation of this role she would recreate herself. The summer of 1861 was the first taste of many freedoms, and for both Woolsey sisters all concerns for safety—or propriety—were now reconciled.

Washingtonians who remained in the city during that first wartime summer endured fierce heat, trying conditions and debilitating suspense. As raw regiments straggled into their camps along the Potomac, the river ran warm and dirty, with water snakes so numerous that exhausted soldiers were discouraged from bathing. Dust devils swirled in the hot wind along city streets, and mosquitoes rose from the malarial "foggy bottom" west of the half-completed Capitol.[5] Green recruits and distinguished visitors sweltered equally. George Templeton Strong remembered that "of all the detestable places, Washington is the first. . . Crowd, heat, bad quarters, bad fare, bad smells, mosquitoes, and a plague of flies transcending everything in my experience. They absolutely blackened the tablecloths and flew into one's mouth at dinner . . ."[6]

For the officers and men of the Sixteenth New York, conditions became more tolerable than most. On their arrival in Washington they had immediately moved into quarters northeast of the Capitol on damp, muddy ground that was subject to frequent flooding and which more than confirmed Strong's assessment of insect infestation. But within two weeks they were fortunate enough to be sent across the Potomac to a spot near Mount Vernon where, by sheer coincidence, they were ordered to make their camp on land once owned by Mrs. Woolsey's Virginia forebears. Eliza later described this felicitous location: "Our regiment pitched its tents on Cameron Run, a little west of Alexandria, in fields that were once the property of our great-great aunt, whose plantation was famous for its flour, ground by the mill on the run. . . . It was a pretty spot—the hillside, covered with white tents, sloping to a green meadow and a bright, clear little river." Meditating on the irony of circumstance, Eliza wrote of the peaceful scene, "Now we, two generations after [our aunt's] time, have come back to pitch our tents in the old wheat field and make ready for war."[7]

On July 13th the Sixteenth was, in company with the New York Eighteenth, Thirty-first and Thirty-second regiments, brought together under the command of their own Colonel Davies and issued new Enfield rifles which replaced the outdated muskets. Thus equipped and strengthened, they now would form the Second Brigade of the Fifth Division of Brigadier General Irvin McDowell's Army of Northeastern Virginia. As part of this new configuration Joseph Howland was appointed acting assistant adjutant-general and placed on Davies' staff.

With these new responsibilities, Joe found little time to look after his wife and sister-in-law, but the prospect of being on their own apparently did not phase the sisters in the least. Well prepared and eager for independence, they immediately settled into Washington's Ebbitt House, "a rambling, untidy hotel on F Street, which was fast becoming a sort of army headquarters." Woolsey biographer Anne

Austin noted that Georgy and Eliza were given a large parlor on the second floor where cots were set up for them. There they began a "sort of half-army life," with bundles of accumulated hospital supplies stacked in all corners of their room and hastily-improvised amenities arranged for their comfort. The Ebbitt was close to Willard's Hotel, at the hub of all that was happening, and so it soon became a meeting place for Woolsey friends and family members visiting in Washington. The temporary headquarters of the Sanitary Commission were located just across the street in the Treasury building—an ideal location from which the women could launch their careers as nurses and enhance their connections and opportunities generally.[8]

In Washington the sisters' wartime service began in earnest. Even before they were assigned to hospital duties on a regular basis, they visited the camp on Cameron Run each day to try their hands at nursing when the need arose. In this they were, perhaps, over-eager in their willingness; for, as it happened, they soon found a number of sick recruits housed in a little shanty behind headquarters to whom they felt they should minister. Filled with zeal, "they set to work cleaning the house, putting up shelves, filling up sacks with straw for beds, preparing diets and feeding the men."[9] But unfortunately these unsolicited services created something of a stir, for in their eagerness the would-be nurses had committed a serious breach of propriety as trespassers in a male preserve. Although their *gaffe* was diplomatically smoothed away, and the "patients" removed to a more sanitary facility, the incident was nonetheless indicative of a pervasive resistance to the improvements of "meddlesome civilians"—especially women— by the military. In this sense it proved prophetic.

The sisters' awkward misstep barely slowed their momentum, however. Woolseys were as well-connected in Washington as they were in New York, and this access to powerful friends brought the women many new opportunities. They were soon accepted as members of an aid network of highly skilled volunteers which moved them into new areas of responsibility, and, as their commitment to hospital work deepened, their efforts were valued in settings defined solely by their own initiative. For a time they worked in wards set up in the building which now houses the National Portrait Gallery and were also called upon to fulfill a variety of administrative tasks. Austin noted that "Dr. Blackwell requested Georgy to evaluate the management of hospitals where Sanitary Commission nurses were to be stationed, and to secure guarantees that they would be furnished with the proper certificates of appointment."[10] *All* nurses were required to take an oath of allegiance and to secure passes for government ambulances to take them to their destinations—a tedious process which became increasingly frustrating.

In July, not wishing to be so restricted, the sisters solved their own transportation problems with characteristic resourcefulness, sending for Moritz, Eliza's man-servant, who soon arrived from Tioronda with the Howland carriage, horses, and George, a coachman or groom. With their mobility and manpower thus expanded, the sisters were flexible enough to transport large loads of supplies each day as they crossed the bridges from Washington to the hospitals in Alexandria.[11] But with these freedoms came frustrations. Georgeanna's letters, filled with candor and biting humor, reveal strength as well as irritation in a variety of discouraging situations. Expressing disgust at inconsistency and high-handedness, she recounted a typical confrontation in a Washington hospital on a sweltering July day as she sat at the bedside of a seriously ill soldier fanning him and reading to him as he lay near death:

> I could have fanned him all day for the pleasure it was to help him, but the Bogie [army surgeon] came in, and gave me a look of icy inquiry [bringing] all the weight of professional indignation to bear upon me. I must "leave immediately," [he declared.] Who was I, that I should bring myself and my presumptuous fan, without direct commission from the Surgeon General into the hospital? Not only must I leave at once, but I must *never return. . .*
>
> I reviewed my position, notified myself that I was the Benevolent Public, and decided that the sick soldiers were, in some sense, the property of the B. P. . . I informed the Bogie (how well it rhymes with Fogie) that I had ordered my carriage to return at such-and-such an hour, that the sun was hot, that I had no intention of walking out in it, and that, in short, I had decided to remain.[12]

As the Woolsey sisters and other privileged women fashioned their own care networks, Sanitary Commission officials also began to implement programs of camp and hospital improvement—hectoring the army, petitioning the government, and insisting on reformed standards of hygiene. Frederick Olmsted grappled daily with the mounting demands of his office, working at the Commission's Washington headquarters and at Willard's Hotel, where the pulse of impending events throbbed about him. Never a strong man physically, Olmsted slept little and exerted his always-frail body to the limit. Yet he managed to surmount each day's challenge with gusto and a high, nervous energy. Jane Turner Censer, editor of Olmsted's wartime papers, noted that "weak eyes and poor health had limited his formal education"— but never his determination.[13] In 1862 Katharine Wormeley would also describe Olmsted as "small and lame from a terrible accident; but although the lameness is decided, it is scarcely observable, for he gives the sense that he triumphs over it by doing as if it did not exist."[14] During 1861 and 1862 Olmsted drove himself unmercifully, often falling asleep in his clothes in the Commission's offices and breakfasting there without returning to his room at the Willard—yet steadily, through frustration and exhilaration, he crafted the methodology which would establish the Sanitary Commission as a miracle of efficiency.[15]

In this summer of '61 Olmsted, Bellows, Harris and Strong met daily with military and government representatives, urging them to petition Congress and the War Department to implement an array of systems which would ease the stress of mass recruitment. Among these innovations were the proposed construction of new general hospitals, the establishment of way stations to temporarily house and feed recruits passing through the city, and the creation of a banking plan which would allow soldiers to forward military pay directly to their families.[16]

Yet despite these efforts the Sanitarians were often mired in frustration by labyrinthine bureaucracy and difficult personalities. Cooperation from the army medical department was virtually nonexistent, and even with its presidential sanction, the Commission was viewed with some suspicion. At that time Lincoln's steady, unassum-

George Templeton Strong

Frederick Law Olmsted

ing management style had not yet impressed the Sanitarians, and their respect for him as president was minimal. Olmsted described him as having "no element of dignity; no tact; not a spark of genius. . . .He is an honest, good fellow. His cabinet is not that. There is the greatest possible dearth of administrative talent." At the same time Olmsted's exasperation with lesser bureaucrats became chronic: "They do nothing but discourage & obstruct, & so of all officials. The official machinery is absurdly inadequate for the emergency & there is no time to think of enlarging it. I feel that the whole business is exceedingly uncertain & should not be much surprised to find Jeff Davis in the White House."[17]

The Sanitarians saw their most important task as an evaluation of the physical and disciplinary conditions in the expanding Union army as it attempted to coalesce into an effective fighting force. Olmsted had already noted the difficulties inherent in this transition as he traveled from New York through New Jersey, Delaware and Maryland in late June, witnessing casual squalor in military camps along the way. "Approaching Havre de Grace, the first war sign is seen in a shantee with a charcoal sign. 'Bloody 11th Camp C.' and a dozen or more fellows in shirt sleeves and dirty havelocks with muskets . . . [others in] shirt sleeves and motley, hospital tents close to the road with sun-struck fat men being fanned [and] more lounging fellows in shirt sleeves."[18]

The wartime environment of the capital was equally slack. As massive waves of Union volunteers swarmed into the city, swelling the ranks of army regulars already lying in cantonments across the Potomac, they were received in over-crowded, poorly drained sites. One of Olmsted's first actions, with Elisha Harris as his partner, was to initiate an ambitious program of camp inspection which soon revealed alarming conditions that were already threatening the health of thousands. Medical historian Paul Steiner noted of these early Civil War camps that "army life in wartime greatly enhanced the pathogenic potential of microorganisms over civilian conditions in a number of ways. Most of the amenities of civil life were lacking, including many which unknowingly protected against disease. The military brought together large numbers of disease-susceptibles under conditions of overcrowding and bad ventilation."[19] Dysentery, diarrhea and typhoid were already spreading through the hastily erected camps. Soldiers' diets, though ample in quantity, depended heavily on salt pork and dried beans and were largely devoid of fruits, vegetables and other fresh components.[20] A disproportionate number of recruits were sick. Because there was no standardized procedure for army physical examinations, many enlistees arrived in camp with hernias, consumption and other infirmities rendering them useless as fighters or workers.[21] Raw country boys fresh from isolated farms were exposed for the first time to childhood diseases. Inevitably they sickened and required hospitalization. Many of them died in camp.[22]

These were conditions that the Sanitarians proposed to eliminate—along with the common soldier's distressing lack of personal hygiene, a failure of discipline that Olmsted blamed on ill-trained, intemperate officers.[23] Censer noted that "to Olmsted, the need for discipline and for officers and soldiers to know their duties and fulfill them, went hand in hand with sanitary reform. He saw the demoralized soldiers as frightened savages [and he] found disheartening the attitude of many officers—physicians among them—that anything more than crude living conditions and bare necessities pampered the soldier and spoiled him as a fighting man." Men who enlisted out of patriotism, moral rage—even religious zeal—found themselves sidetracked. Olmsted wrote, "[The soldier's] original excitement had all been exhausted. He came fully expecting immediate battle with the traitors. He had no experience of anything so simply tiresome as this war."[24]

Sanitarians rightly believed that many of these faults stemmed from one fundamental problem: the enlistment and outfitting of troops by individual states rather than the federal government. William Quentin Maxwell has noted that "state rights made discipline hard to achieve, especially with three-month enlistments. Training was almost impossible; federal supervision began when regiments had filled their quota and were on the way to camp or firing line. . . too many officers were self-seekers, their epaulettes covering ignorance and carelessness."[25] Early in the summer, in an attempt to confront these problems, Olmsted issued a comprehensive *Circular Addressed to the Colo-*

nels of the Army, insisting that camp illnesses, sanitation, and lax disciplinary standards were directly linked with, and caused by, the failure of regimental officers.

Yet in all fairness it should be acknowledged that at least some members of the military were attempting to rectify a deteriorating situation. Olmsted was not without cooperation from a number of enlightened officers, among them Joseph Howland and his colleagues of the Sixteenth New York, who supported sanitary reform at the regimental level. George Worthington Adams, who, like Steiner, documented camp conditions of the time, has suggested the frustrations of Commission personnel and army officers alike as they "ran headlong into the incorrigible 'rugged individualism' of the American people" who, on reaching camp, "frequently let themselves go. . . giving little attention to the Sanitary Commission's ideas of camp cleanliness or to the advice of medical officers." Confronting this ingrained recalcitrance—considered by some soldiers as an "inalienable right"—became the task of conscientious officers and Sanitarians as each went about their separate duties of training and leadership.[26]

In the hot summer of 1861 military hospitals presented as severe a state of disarray as camps. The same resistance to interference encountered by the Woolsey sisters in their small program of sanitary reform was, in fact, a microcosm of the blindness and neglect that affected hospitals in Washington and beyond. When Olmsted's inspectors made their rounds they found crowded, poorly ventilated "storehouses of morbid emanations."[27] They discovered bathing and toilet facilities that were either filthy or nonexistent and kitchen-food storage areas that were verminous. Although the "germ theory" of disease was yet to be acknowledged, and both doctors and lay people believed that "emanations," "miasmas," and "effluvia" were the causes of infectious epidemics, American army hospitals in 1861 willfully ignored even those rules of sanitation that *were* understood and had been demonstrated in the Crimea. In its obdurate resistance to reforms, the military hierarchy perpetuated sinkholes of the very dampness and decay that contributed to infection.[28] General hospitals, to which patients were sent from camp or field hospitals, were a heterogeneous collection of buildings hastily appropriated and ill-suited to their new role.[29] Some had been hotels, others schools, churches, warehouses or factories. One had been a jail. Often these facilities were without beds, medicines, blankets, or bandages.[30]

Yet despite discouraging odds, and even as they struggled to overcome the ambiguity of their status, Sanitarians managed gradually to improve the quality of hospital life for many Union soldiers. In July Olmsted wrote of spending a day visiting the hospitals in Alexandria. "The wounded are all doing very well," he noted. "We have provided them with shirts, sheets &c, have a barber going round, provide ice, ad libitum, face covers, bed tables, backgammon boards, paper & pens &c. &c. . . . I have . . . on hand a stock of hospital stores more than sufficient for the present. More than 200 tons of ice. Several casks of spirit and wine. . ."[31] Olmsted also listed the donated supplies that had already become a flood, arriving daily in systematic deliveries and channeled through the expanded organizational network of the Commission's auxiliaries. By 1862 these networks would increase, both in number and efficiency, and Olmsted's small inventory of items and services would expand to include every available medical and physical necessity.

In 1861 the immediate challenge for the Sanitary Commission was unquestionably the control of epidemic contagion in military camps and hospitals. Yet underlying its overt mission there very likely remained a shadowy and controversial agenda: the conservative vision which had absorbed Bellows from the first. Fredrickson has noted that "an examination of commission literature reveals from the outset that the organization was not concerned with the relief of suffering as an end in itself."[32] As articulated by Olmsted, the Sanitarians believed that a broad segment of lower-class Americans could be educated to "genteel standards of domestic tidiness and taste."[33] They also believed that orderliness of thought and behavior could be imposed. In 1863 Katharine Wormeley would characterize the Commission as "a great teacher . . . guiding the national instincts; showing the value of order, and the dignity of work, [with] the means for a national education of ideas."[34] Her male colleagues reasoned that a discipline of obedience would not only preserve men's usefulness as fighters, but would lead them, through a learned respect for themselves, to a corresponding respect for their "betters" and compliance with authority - the concept of a coercive public conformity. This, if true, presents an interesting perspective on the Sanitarians' acknowledged statement of purpose.[35]

But although Bellows and his associates sought to transform the individual soldier, they sought also to preserve the *army itself* as an institution. The Sanitarians perceived their mission to the military as one of influencing, not restructuring. Despite their difficulties with the medical department, they avoided an iconoclastic role, seeking instead to support established chains of command. Indeed, the Commission's founders valued the army as a solid body standing firm against the anti-establishment sentiments that had so disturbed them during the antebellum years. It was fundamental that they should preserve such a system even as they reformed it. Interestingly, their convictions in this respect would become conflicted during the Peninsula Campaign and would create problems for the women volunteers— an ideology of control at odds with a mission of service.

These controversial goals are troubling when viewed in retrospect, and they may justifiably lessen the Commission's luster to some extent. Yet it is undeniable that their practical achievements of sanitary reform and their professionalization of random benevolence were, and should be acknowledged as, the Sanitarians' principal legacy. Whatever degree of altruism may or may not have been involved in their program, the fact remains that its results were impressive.

The Commission's ongoing problems with army rigidity would soon precipitate sweeping reforms on a number of levels. Foremost among these would be improved standards of appointment for surgeons within the medical department—an issue which the Medical Reform Bill of April, 1862 would further address and correct. Throughout 1861 Sanitary Commission directors lobbied tirelessly for this bill's passage, using all the political influence at their disposal. Allan Nevins, in Strong's diaries wrote that although "it was not all that Strong and his associates desired, [the Reform Bill] marked a tremendous advance. It provided that the Surgeon General and higher officers of the [Medical] Bureau staff were to be chosen from the most competent officers of the whole corps, and were no longer to be selected by the silly rule of seniority."[36] Passage of this bill would mark a significant turning point for the Sanitary Commission, and the subsequent appointment of William A. Hammond as Surgeon General would further reinforce many of the Sanitarians' goals.[37]

By late fall in 1861 much of Olmsted's organizational network would be functioning smoothly, but on July 21, before his goals could be fully realized, an event occurred that dramatically enhanced the Sanitarians' message and coincidentally brought their program of reform to the public's attention. The First Battle of Bull Run, or Manassas, was therapeutic in that it forced the Union army to confront its own inadequacies of medical preparedness in a catalytic moment of truth—though it came close to being an unmitigated disaster for the North.

The ill-fated military engagement itself was undertaken with some foreboding by its commanding officer, General Irvin McDowell, at the behest of Washington bureaucrats who urged a preemptive strike. Pundits and politicians alike craved action. Voices of quasi-officials joined with the editorial badgerings of an ambitious Northern press to demand a military offensive. Three months had passed since Fort Sumter, and impatience was the mood in Washington and New York. Subduing a rebel force at Manassas would, these "strategists" reasoned, soon lead the Union army into Richmond, and with the conquest of the Southern capitol, the defeat of the Confederacy itself would follow presently.[38]

McDowell was well aware that the plan to invade Virginia was problematic. Although his force of 35,000 men outnumbered the Confederate opponent's, his men were as yet unprepared for the complex maneuverings of a stylized form of warfare which was, as Bruce Catton noted, "as intricate as its weapons themselves were simple," and although Confederate General Pierre G. T. Beauregard's raw young Southerners were no better trained than their Yankee counterparts, their orders demanded only that they defend their position, a somewhat easier task for inexperienced troops than the mounting of an offensive attack. Reinforcing their natural strategic advantage on high ground with a commanding view, the Confederates were also supported by a railroad which ran through Manassas Junction, a way station lying conveniently behind their lines.[39]

But on July 16, as ordered, McDowell moved his troops from Arlington Heights outside Washington and proceeded towards Manassas, concentrating his forces approximately six miles from the area where Beauregard's Confederates waited. Adjutant Joseph Howland and the Sixteenth New York Volunteers took part in this Union advance. Eliza remembered, "our regiment had only been encamped a short while on Cameron's Run when the move against the enemy at Manassas was ordered, and we two women watched the brigade break camp and march down the peaceful country road, carrying Joe away from us. We stood alone, and looked after them as long as they were in sight, and then made our way back to Washington."[40]

The sisters' angst at this exclusion strengthened their already-firm determination *never* to be left behind again, and their later writings bear this out.[41] Unlike a majority of women who waited patiently at home for word of their loved ones, Eliza's and Georgy's concern for husband and brother-in-law was matched by their yearning to be at the center of activity—and these motivations, when combined with their powerful connections and well-developed ability to place themselves strategically, enabled the Woolseys to participate in the dangerous adventure of war. The separation at Cameron Run would not be repeated.

On the morning of July 21, when the opposing armies engaged at Manassas, they seemed at first to be quite evenly matched: two novice legions facing each other across a gently modulated terrain. However, George Worthington Adams noted one significant difference: "The [Union] troops had had no breakfast and were exhausted from hurried marching under the sun of an exceptionally hot day. Some had eaten no supper the night before, and had little or no sleep. Reports that they were heavily outnumbered by the enemy made them nervous."[42] Nevertheless, McDowell's force seemed to be winning until the afternoon, when the tide of battle turned. It was then that

General Joseph E. Johnston, commander of all Confederate forces to the west, arrived to save the day for the Confederates.

Johnston had been camped with his men only sixty miles from Manassas. He had noted McDowell's advance, and had made himself ready to come to Beauregard's assistance if the need arose. This he soon did, bringing his troops straight to the scene of battle and arriving by train at Manassas Junction in the afternoon to drive the Union troops back in disorderly retreat. Union defeat came at five o'clock in the afternoon. Fleeing soldiers, horses and vehicles jammed the road as they commenced the infamous and well-documented flight to Washington, with panic-stricken soldiers and civilians swirling together past overturned wagons and their spilled contents. Demoralization ensued as vigorous officers fled on horseback, leaving most of the wounded on the field. In a discouraging opening round the Union Army had lost almost 2,000 killed and disabled. But happily there were honorable exceptions to this disappointing scene. Late on the evening of July 21st Eliza Howland received a hand-delivered note, scribbled on soiled paper and brought to her at the Ebbitt House by an exhausted soldier. Joseph, whose men had stood firm and acquitted themselves commendably, wrote, "Evening, half past seven. A complete rout. The Sixteenth safe. We are making a final stand. J. H."[43]

The disaster of Bull Run confirmed the Sanitary Commission's contention that the army must restructure its medical organization. Adams noted that "the battle tested all medical arrangements of the army and proved them wanting. There was no articulated organization, and chaos piled horror upon horror. . . . Each regimental surgeon assumed responsibility for the men of his own unit only, while soldiers shot at a distance from their regimental surgeon might be left untended."[44]   Maxwell concurred: "Bull Run proved that an armed mob did not make an army; it showed that the individual exertions of doctors could not make a medical corps."[45]

For Olmsted the period immediately following Bull Run was one of despondency and anger: at the federal government's lack of leadership and administrative ability, and at the Army Medical Bureau's failure to fulfill its commitment to a volunteer army whose welfare

should have been its most basic concern.[46] Nevertheless, a direct result of the debacle at Manassas, and a highly positive one from the
standpoint of the Sanitarians, was the appointment of George Brinton
McClellan as commander in chief of the Army of the Potomac, a move
which presaged a new phase in the conduct of the war. Eager to believe that this change would prove a turning point for the Union, most
Northern citizens hailed McClellan unreservedly. Allan Nevins has
summarized the young general's qualifications, while at the same time
suggesting the Napoleonic ego which would eventually prove problematic. "[McClellan] had served with distinction in Mexico, had been
an official observer in the Crimean War, and combined a West Point
education with managerial experience in business. . . [His] handsome,
soldierly presence, kind, modest manners, and evident care for his
troops, made a happy impression. The obverse of the medal was his
readiness to lay claim to credit belonging to others, to deprecate and
rebuke subordinates publicly, and to exaggerate enemy strength [to
his own credit]."[47]

For Eliza and Georgy, McClellan's appointment came as the well-
deserved recognition of a gifted acquaintance. In the fall and winter of
1861, as McClellan's star rose, the sisters were already well established in a diverse circle which included high-level military officers
and members of Lincoln's administration. The new commander was
naturally a part of this group, for he was an affable guest, and, with
his young wife, in some demand among Washington hostesses. A letter from Eliza to Joe in camp describes the typical social excitements
of that winter, and identifies some of the powerful friends the Woolseys
saw often and enjoyed.

> The only thing of interest I have to tell you is of a very
> nice call we had last evening from General Williams (your
> friend Seth). He got Miss Wilkes to bring him round and in-
> troduce him, and told us he had long wanted to call on us and
> offer his services. . . . Miss Wilkes, who came with him, asked
> us all to spend Friday evening with them to meet a small
> party of Washington people and a few strangers. "Mrs.
> McClellan would be there and they hoped to see the General

too," and I suppose the Franklins and Porters, and our friend
General Williams and "other officers of note." Don't you want
to come in? We shall go, as it will be a nice chance for Mother
and [sister] Carry to see the notabilities and will be pleasant
for all. . . . How dismal the weather is again and how wretched
the camp must be![48]

These military friendships, begun in the winter of 1861, would
be continued some months later in far more perilous circumstances—
for the Woolseys' new friends were the officers who would command
the divisions and corps of McClellan's Grand Army in its assault upon
Richmond. All of these generals anticipated the moment when
McClellan would disclose his plan of action, but if they harbored any
doubts about their commander's history as a tactician, they, like the
civilians around them, preferred to dwell upon his successes and hope
for the best. The majority of Washingtonians held high aspirations for
McClellan and were confident in his abilities. They ignored, or were
unaware of, his unhappy inclination to postpone military action and
had not yet observed the obsessive perfectionism which would prove
his fatal flaw. Indeed, the General's paralyzing insistence on over-
preparedness was not yet apparent, or, if so, came disguised as a vir-
tue of prudence and orderliness. These inherent weaknesses would,
within the year, precipitate McClellan's decline; yet in the aftermath
of Bull Run few Northerners, even those close to him, sensed danger
in their eagerness for an heroic leader. The general's dedication to
strict discipline, meticulous drill, and above all to the morale of his
troops were hailed by all and, in fact, they wrought stunning changes.
    During the fall and winter of 1861-'62 McClellan transformed
the "armed mob" of Manassas into an army of trained specialists, much
as the Sanitary commissioners sought to transform military camps
and hospitals into efficient, hygienic environments. The general's
methods were thoroughly consistent with those of the Commission,
and its directors were outspoken in their praise for him. Olmsted described the new commander admiringly, and even George Templeton
Strong, though characteristically less effusive, wrote in a generally

favorable tone. "We think very well of McClellan. His activity and industry and attention to details may not be equivalent to military genius, but are of great practical value nonetheless."[49] The general's troops affectionately christened him "Little Mac" and adored him.

And so McClellan, with the Army of the Potomac at his command, and political leaders temporarily in the palm of his hand, moved to a serious regime of winter training. His overall goal for the coming campaign would be a concentrated offensive against Richmond with the confident hope that this strategy would insure its rapid surrender and effectively end the war. Yet as he weighed his alternatives, the general kept his own counsel, and by late 1861 his tactical plan was yet to be announced—even to Lincoln, his Commander in Chief.

In the offices of the Sanitary Commission, Bellows and his supporters now saw many of their ambitious plans become reality. Olmsted, who would lead the relief mission to Virginia, labored to consolidate his gains in camp inspection and organizational structuring. Like McClellan, he now conceived and gradually implemented specific plans for the coming campaign.

Similarly motivated and working within the Sanitary Commission's framework, a small but significant cohort of newly "professional" women intensified their work of efficient benevolence and were noticed for their steadiness and ability. It was, for them, a time of preparation and reflection. The aspiring nurses, the idealistic Olmsted, and the newly-appointed general shared youth, determination and an ambition to achieve substantive goals; of humanitarian service, military glory or reform. For each, the Peninsula Campaign would prove the high water mark of her or his wartime experience.

Chapter IV

TO THE PENINSULA: 1862

Tidewater Virginia, from the mouth of the Potomac south to Norfolk, is deeply fringed by rivers running southeast into Chesapeake Bay. Upstream, as these rivers wander and diverge, they create a network of creeks and swamps which water the flat, often thickly wooded landscape. Any consideration of McClellan's Peninsula Campaign must be predicated upon an understanding of the crucial role these waterways played in its tactical design and eventual outcome.

"The Peninsula," as designated in Civil War histories and military records, refers specifically to that tongue of land bounded by the York River on its north, and by the James River to the south. The York divides some thirty miles upstream from Yorktown at the town of West Point, at which juncture its south fork becomes the Pamunkey. In the 1860s this winding waterway was navigable by large vessels at least as far upriver as White House Landing. A third river, much smaller than the others, bisects the Peninsula diagonally. Called the Chicka-hominy, it twists and meanders from Mechanicsville northeast of Rich-mond to empty into the James several miles west of Williamsburg. Although of no use to either army in the transport of supplies, the Chickahominy presented a significant obstacle, and as such would play a crucial role in the Peninsula Campaign.

Mark Nesbitt has noted that "the importance of navigable wa-ters to nineteenth-century warfare cannot be overestimated. Ships traveling upon them were able to haul more ammunition, weapons, medical supplies and foodstuffs than any wagon train, and were less vulnerable to mounted raiders, the most pervasive destroyers of sup-plies traveling overland."[1] It was essential, then, that McClellan, as he formulated his campaign to conquer Richmond, secure a direct water transport and supply line for Union troops that he supposed would be advancing steadily upon the Confederate capital. Similarly, the Sani-tary Commission, as it planned its own role of care and evacuation, would be obliged to provide hospital transports capable of accommo-dating large numbers of casualties.

As the major offensive strike against Richmond was discussed during the winter of 1861-'62, several plans came under consideration. An early choice favored by Lincoln and his Secretary of War involved an advance overland from Centreville across the old Bull Run terrain. A second—proposed and supported by McClellan—involved a water approach via the Rappahannock River which would subsequently pro-ceed westward by land from Urbanna, Virginia. Throughout the win-ter months, discussions produced little or no consensus, the general frequently uncommunicative, even obdurate. In December, compli-cating matters still further, he fell seriously ill with typhoid fever, remaining secluded for a number of weeks.

On March 7, in desperation, Lincoln met face to face with his recalcitrant general and attempted to force from him some disclosure of decisive action. With that, McClellan called his command staff to-gether in a council of war, and despite some disagreement among his generals, devised a plan of attack which would, with various permu-tations, emerge as the design now remembered as the Peninsula Cam-paign. In essence the plan was relatively simple. The army would first proceed by river transport down the Potomac and south through the Chesapeake to Fort Monroe. It would then disembark, advance upon Yorktown, and subdue the occupying Confederate force, by siege if necessary. The Union navy would seize control of the York and James Rivers, and McClellan's troops would advance up the peninsula to Richmond.[2]

Lincoln was concerned that a sufficient federal force be available to him in Washington to defend against possible incursions by entrenched Confederates remaining in the countryside west of the capital. He also needed this assurance as a guard against the considerable, and highly mobile, force under Stonewall Jackson which controlled the Shenandoah Valley and, he feared, might sweep down upon Washington while the Army of the Potomac was concentrated on the Virginia peninsula. This stipulation on the President's part necessarily curtailed the size of McClellan's army, and it would create acrimony throughout the summer. The general became obsessed by the notion that his forces were outnumbered by their Confederate opponents, and begged repeatedly that his President send him further reinforcements. Although mistaken in his estimations of the enemy's strength, McClellan would not be dissuaded from them, and Lincoln's resistance produced frustration for both leaders. The general's intelligence operation was also sadly inadequate, and this, too, would plague him in the months ahead. Its chief agent, Detective Allen Pinkerton—who operated under disguise as a Major E. J. Allen—was personally at fault in attempting to exaggerate the size of Confederate troop concentrations and in discouraging McClellan from taking decisive action on several occasions. Through Pinkerton's reliance on inaccurate maps and careless researching of road conditions, this department was responsible for repeated crises of misinformation as the campaign progressed.[3]

In March, however, these problems had not yet become tangible, and when, after months of indecision and conflict, a tactical plan for the Peninsula Campaign was agreed upon, an armada of record proportions began gradually to assemble. Soon after March 13, 1862, the

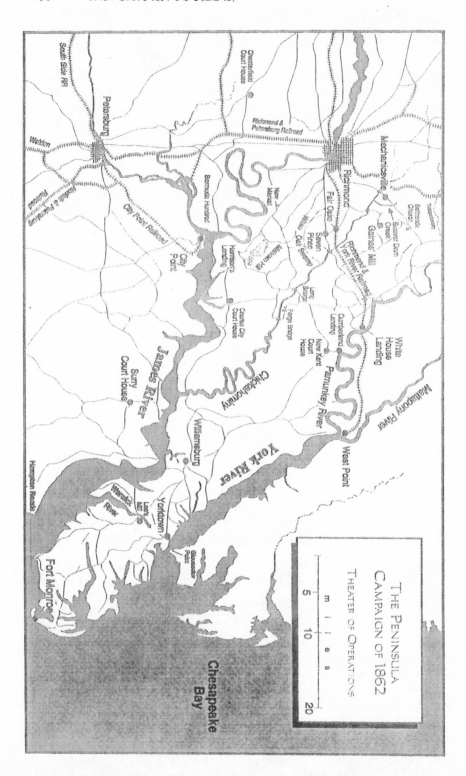

THE PENINSULA
CAMPAIGN OF 1862
THEATER OF OPERATIONS

first vessels embarked at Alexandria to begin their journey down the Potomac. Allan Nevins has described the scene vividly.

> A singularly impressive movement it was. The flotilla, scurrying to and fro in the waters about Washington, filled the air with smoke, fluttering flags, and deep bass whistles. For three weeks the dingy streets of Alexandria were clangorous with military bands and the tread of marching boots. . . nearly 15,000 horses and mules, more than 1,100 wagons, and 44 batteries were loaded aboard. With them went rolls of telegraph wire, timbers for pontoons, forges for repairs, medicines for field hospitals, and an endless variety of stores. Down the Potomac fell the craft, down the Chesapeake, past the mouths of the Rappahannock and York and on to Fort Monroe and Hampton Roads.[4]

On March 7 Joseph Howland was appointed Colonel of his regiment on the promotion of Col. Davies to a brigade-level post. As Joe prepared the Sixteenth for imminent departure, and as the general exodus from Washington accelerated, his wife and sister-in-law became increasingly restive. Ambitious to carry their now-professional skills into a more charged arena, and longing to participate in the campaign at its epicenter, the women once again improvised a plan of their own. Eliza, knowing that Joe would shortly join the advance on the Peninsula, urged in an April letter that she and Georgy be allowed to follow him, bringing along their carriage and servants, synchronizing their own travels with the movements of his regiment—an idea which, if not entirely unexpected, still elicited considerable resistance on his part. "I feel that it is my *right* and privilege to follow you," wrote Eliza, "not only for my own satisfaction in being near you, but because we know that we can be of great use among the troops. I trust you, dear," she added persuasively, "to do all you can to forward our plan, and I am sure you will not leave us in doubt and indecision *longer than you can help.*"

Georgy also initiated an exchange of letters with her brother-in-law, and, true to form, urged even more insistently than her sister that she be on hand for whatever action might ensue: "We want to be within an hour's ride, at the most, of the battlefield, and to be there ready," she wrote. "There will always be some roof of a barn that would give us shelter. . . . When I try to talk to you, you laugh —and so I must write. It was bad enough to go through Bull Run in Washington. *Nothing* can be more miserable than a second such experience."[5]

It is difficult not to feel sympathy for Joseph Howland who, preoccupied with his new command, and reflecting on his responsibility for the women's safety, was caught in a trying dilemma. As he resisted their plan, he tried to convince them to remain in Washington until *after* any military action had taken place on the Peninsula—but here he clearly underestimated the sisters' determination. Georgeanna reacted to his moderate suggestion with barely-concealed scorn. "What *possible* use would there be of our coming when it is all over," she wrote—as she continued to press for some new initiative that might achieve the desired results.[6]

In mid-April Joseph moved the regiment to its point of embarkation and made his good-byes. His letters to Eliza during that week as he joined the armada south describe graphically the difficulties of transporting a large company of men by water, and tell of one officer's endeavors to implement his own measures of sanitary reform:

> *Steamer Daniel Webster II, April 18*
> I have a chance to send a boat ashore to get mail, and so can say good morning to you. All the steamers are lying in the stream two or three miles below Alexandria, receiving their "tows." There are about a hundred schooners to take down. We tow four. All's well, the boat is crowded but the men are more comfortable than I imagined they could be, and are behaving admirably. . . . I have 820 officers and men on this boat and four schooners . . .

Moored in the Chesapeake two days later, crowding and inactivity were beginning to cause concern.

> *Near Fortress Monroe, April 20*
> No orders. The boat is becoming very dirty and cannot

be cleaned as she is so crowded that there is no place to put any number of men while the cleaning is done. The regiment is behaving well. I have had to punish only one man since we left Alexandria, but have made an example of him for smuggling and selling liquor. . . . The men are very attentive. The more I see of the regiment the more highly I think of it. I am sure the Sixteenth will behave creditably.

Successive letters continue the story of the regiment's deployment:

York River, April 22
Here we still are, awaiting orders, without a word of news and nothing to do. The boat is so crowded and dirty that life is becoming intensely disgusting, yet there appears to be no prospect of getting away. Last night there was heavy firing towards Yorktown, and we could see the flashing of guns; but we do not know what it was.

April 24
Yesterday, at last, I landed the regiment, having asked permission to do so, and have the boat thoroughly cleaned. Having picked out a piece of level ground at the head of a little bay where there were plenty of oysters, I got a stern-wheeler and sent the regiment ashore by companies, and got all fairly into camp by sunset.[7]

Meanwhile, waiting impatiently in Washington, luck seemed at last to be on the sisters' side; and, not surprisingly, it was the Sanitary Commission which provided their longed-for opportunity. During March, as McClellan's army moved steadily southward, the Sanitarians commenced preparations of their own. They realized that a move from Washington's temperate spring weather to the summer wetlands of the Peninsula would inevitably result in an increased incidence of fever, and further complicate the projected casualties of battle. Knowing that time was short, and reflecting upon the inadequacies of the army's medical preparedness, Commission leaders set to work preparing for any exigency. They approached the Medical Bureau with

an offer to supplement its provisions with stores of their own, and
Olmsted applied to the quartermaster corps for permission to appropriate any large steamships not currently in use to outfit and recom-
mission them as hospital transports. At last, after a series of now-
familiar bureaucratic delays, he received authorization for these vessels, and the *Daniel Webster* was assigned to his use on April 25.[8] This
vessel, along with her sister ship, the *Daniel Webster II*, upon which
Joseph Howland had transported his regiment, would now become
the nucleus of the Sanitary Commission fleet.

As Olmsted assembled the workers who would staff these new
transports—large passenger steamers capable of navigating both rivers and ocean—he turned to the Woolsey sisters with an offer to join
the company. Eliza described the circumstances triumphantly in a
letter to her husband: "Saturday afternoon . . . Mr. Olmsted and Mr.
Knapp came over to see us, and to our great surprise and pleasure
proposed to us to come down with them in the ship as 'nurses at large,'
or matrons, or what not—to do all we can for the sick and wounded
men in the approaching battle. . . we only had one night's notice, as
they were to leave Sunday morning, but we accepted the offer at once,
and here we are!"[9] Saying a hasty good-bye to their mother, who was
once again visiting from New York, and leaving their little dog in the
care of General Franklin's wife, Georgy and Eliza boarded the *Webster*
at Alexandria early on the morning of April 27 and slipped down the
Potomac, joining the stream of vessels headed south.

Although Olmsted's company was called together hastily, its elements had been planned and composed with his characteristic concern for efficiency. As well as the Woolsey sisters, the group of workers
included two other soon-to-be nurse-superintendents, Mrs. Christine
Griffin and Mrs. Caroline Lane. Olmsted, as head of the mission, traveled with his assistant, Frederick Knapp. Supervising the medical
contingent were Drs. Cornelius Agnew and James M. Grymes, accompanied by twenty male nurses and six young doctors and medical students—several of them friends of Georgy's from her hospital training
days. George Templeton Strong represented the Commission's executive board, and a complement of painters and contrabands completed
the group.[10] Young Charles Woolsey remained temporarily in Wash-

ington to complete arrangements for his sisters' possessions at the Ebbitt, but he, too, would soon follow the Sanitarians, and would serve as Olmsted's purser, hospital orderly and general helper throughout the campaign. Moritz, the Howlands' servant, would also become a member of the support crew, assisting Eliza in the wards, preparing meals for the ladies, and working energetically wherever his services were needed.[11]

While recognizing the gravity of their mission, the band of travelers was nonetheless in an anticipatory, even holiday mood. As the *Webster* gathered speed downriver on that April Sunday morning, her decks and interior were virtually transformed: wards were constructed, bunks built, floors scrubbed and sanded, walls whitewashed. The gentlemen unpacked quantities of stores, while the ladies sewed a large yellow flag which would identify the vessel as a hospital ship. Ward diet books were prepared amid hymn-singing, laughter, and the reciting of psalms.

Olmsted had designed the Peninsula mission to be somewhat flexible. Sanitary Commission ships would stand ready to "ferry the wounded and ill from railhead to Northern general hospitals, to act as supply bases for tent hospitals on shore, and, if small enough, to fetch wounded directly from the battlefield. Each transport was to carry a surgeon-in-charge, eight medical students, twenty male wardmasters and nurses, and four lady nurse-superintendents." Woolsey, Howland and their female colleagues, as superintendents, would be responsible for creating and stocking kitchens, setting up stoves, and arranging shelves. They would make "hundreds of patient beds, devise locked storage areas for wines, spirits and other expensive items, and make themselves generally available for whatever tasks might arise." These duties seemed simple enough, yet as the ladies steamed southward, the full import of their new responsibilities remained obscure, and the implications of the life they now entered could barely be imagined. They knew only that their elation at being part of this expedition was reward enough, and they thought themselves well prepared for whatever might lie ahead.[12]

On the following morning Eliza reported their progress to Joe once more: "We are now on the way down to Cheeseman's Creek, near

Ship Point, [Virginia] and when you receive this we shall be lying just there. . . .There is a P. O. station at Cheeseman's Creek to which please direct your letters to me, care of Fred. Law Olmsted, Hospital Ship of Sanitary Commission."[13] The sisters' private Peninsula campaign was proceeding nicely. It was not yet a week since Joe had arrived at the York River.

When, later that evening, the Sanitarians reached their journey's end, they would come face-to-face with the Army of the Potomac once again—but now in a new guise and venue. Basing her own description on contemporary accounts, Laura Roper imagined the scene as the *Webster* steamed cautiously into the congested anchorage at Cheesesman's Creek and secured her temporary mooring: "On either shore the woods were studded with tents and alive with masses of men, and the stream was dense with hundreds of transports—steamers and sailing vessels, big and little—some of them packed with men who had been waiting days for the order to debark." As the Sanitary Commission ship threaded her way through the throng, and as night fell, Georgy and Eliza "watched the ships about them light up, until the fleet sparkled in the harbor like a floating city. Campfires glowed from either shore, and huge bonfires, set to get rid of brush and small timber useless for road building, reddened the night sky. The sound of singing, drums, and bugles arose from camp and fleet and floated across the water."[14]

One day earlier, on the same April Sunday that Olmsted and his party left Alexandria, a woman in Rhode Island was preparing herself for a similar journey. Writing to her sister in Boston on that morning, Katharine Wormeley of Newport proposed a plan of action no less determined than the Woolseys'. "I am thinking of going to Yorktown," she announced, "how should you view it? The Sanitary Commission has today sent off from Washington a large steamship to be fitted up as a hospital transport. Mrs. Griffin has gone down in her with Mr.

Katharine Prescott Wormeley

Olmsted at his request. I have great confidence in her. She is a lady, whose presence is guarantee enough that I, or any other woman, may go there with propriety." Cautiously, Wormeley had considered this project for some time, and the possibility of a nurse-superintendent post had become increasingly attractive to her. Now, with Mrs. Griffin's presence assured, her plan could be set in motion.[15]

Katharine Wormeley and the Woolsey sisters shared much in common. Like them, she was the daughter of a conservative, aristocratic family; and like Georgy, she had been born in England. The third child of Ralph Randolph Wormeley and his wife, the former Caroline Preble of Boston, Katharine was, on her mother's side, the descendent of prosperous East India merchants; on her father's, of six generations of Virginia Randolphs whose extensive lands had been deeded them by Royal Charter during the reign of Charles II. Katharine's mother was remembered as "a lady in every motion, thought, and instinct," and her three daughters were carefully raised to emulate her virtues. Their father, Ralph Randolph Wormeley, had emigrated from Virginia to England as a child and remained to establish himself successfully as an adult. He became a British citizen, entered enthusiastically into political dialogue as a Liberal, and rose to the rank of rear admiral in the British navy. Wormeley was a man who perceived and lived his moral duty faithfully, and his children were trained to a high sense of social responsibility. Until she was eighteen Katharine had lived in England and traveled widely with her family through Europe, members of an urbane circle of well-bred intellectuals which included many celebrated literary figures of the day.[16]

In 1852, while visiting Newport during an extended trip to America, the graceful routine of Katharine's life had been saddened and disrupted by the death of her father and, several years later, the death of her only brother. Making the decision to remain in Newport, Caroline Wormeley and her daughters continued to live quietly there, and, as the other sisters married, Katharine remained with her mother alone.[17] Now, at thirty-two, she was still single, energetic, an articulate leader of cultural and benevolent causes and, like other women who became active in the Sanitary Commission, was possessed of unusual business acumen and managerial talent. Laura Wood Roper has described Katharine in the spring of 1862 as "high-minded, humorless and homely, as well as clever and cultivated," and noted the qualities which would suit her well for the service she now undertook. "Her executive capacity made her an outstanding lieutenant for Olmsted, as her literary skill made her an effective propagandist for the Sanitary Commission."[18]

But Katharine was never as humorless as she appeared. In Virginia she would find time to record her adventure with deep feeling, simplicity and subtle wit—a wit quite possibly enhanced by her close friendship with Georgy Woolsey, a woman whose notable lightness of spirit affected Katharine from the first. Wormeley's letters from the Peninsula are unsurpassed as perceptive journalism, their candor and sense of immediacy making them classics of the genre. Reflected in them are the pain and pathos inherent in her duties, and also hints of the fraught relationship of "platonic intimacy" formed with Olmsted during the weeks on board the transports. Roper has described Wormeley's attachment to her leader as veneration "with a dash of something very like ardor." The friendship shared by these two would lead to an intense exchange of letters lasting many years, and would ultimately bring satisfaction, solace, and some pain to both.[19]

Katharine's preparation for wartime service was unlike Georgy Woolsey's in that it included no nursing experience. Instead, she had prepared through the administrative route as secretary and co-founder of the Newport Woman's Union Aid Society, an affiliate of the WCAR. Early in 1862 she had earned high praise for devising an innovative and successful plan for providing uniforms to the Union Army which not only saved the government money, but also helped support needy families of recruits. Working with similarly affluent friends who helped guarantee her costs, Wormeley had contracted with government sources for garments destined for army use, and had then apportioned out piece work to impoverished wives of Newport volunteers.[20] The potential for bureaucratic red-tape in this scheme may have been daunting, but in her dealings with the army Wormeley deliberately exerted ladylike persuasiveness, never allowing the project to become side-tracked—a prodigious feat. In this she earned the lasting respect of Col. Vinton, the Quartermaster General in New York. Now the final phase was nearing completion and the time seemed right to announce her decision and make a life-changing transition. To her sister she wrote,"My work here is closing. I have drained the community dry as to hospital supplies, and the churches have lately sent in $1,800. A drawing together of circumstances seems to point to this thing, and I enter upon it as if it were obviously the next thing to be done."[21]

As Sanitary Commission personnel completed their arrangements in the North and arrived at the York River, military action on the Peninsula took an unexpected turn. After a month of siege, while McClellan made elaborate preparations and moved up his heaviest siege guns for a crushing barrage of the enemy at Yorktown, it became plain to Joseph E. Johnston, his Confederate opponent, that whenever this artillery contest might begin, his Southern forces must inevitably be the losers. With that certainty came his decision to evacuate his position secretly during the night of May 3. Describing Johnston's task, historian Stephen Sears noted that "evacuating an army of twenty-six brigades of infantry and cavalry and thirty-six batteries of field artillery—56,000 men all told—and their equipment, and carrying out the evacuation secretly in the face of the enemy, was a challenging task. It was also a complicated task, and Johnston had to endure delays caused by every imaginable complication."[22]

On the appointed night, under cover of a tremendous bombardment and fiery display over Yorktown, Johnston quietly withdrew his troops, and on May 4 chagrined Union officers realized, too late, that they had been hoodwinked. This was only the first of many elusive surprises which Southern commanders would employ with great effect throughout the Peninsula campaign—but in this instance the advantage would be short-lived. On May 5, unable to maintain his fighting retreat, and with the Yankees in close pursuit, Johnston was overtaken and engaged by a portion of McClellan's force at Williamsburg. It was a battle which has been described as "a savage, confused combat, waged in heavy rain driven by an icy wind and ending inconclusively"—a disappointment to both contenders.[23]

This was the news as Katharine Wormeley began her journey. On May 9 she boarded the *Daniel Webster* in New York as it concluded its first trip north carrying casualties from the Peninsula. Like Georgy's and Eliza's Potomac voyage, her passage south was a deceptively tranquil introduction to transport life, lying on deck, sewing the yellow hospital flag, dreaming under a blue sky; a transitional interlude between known and unknown lives, bringing her closer to a war which would now assume tangible form. On May 11, moored off Yorktown, she wrote "last evening, as we entered the Chesapeake, we saw the crimson glow of a great fire in the direction of Fortress Monroe or Norfolk; and this morning we heard the dull, heavy sound of explosion or brief cannonading . . . Good-bye! *This is life.*" With these thoughts and sights her adventure had begun.[24]

The horizontal glow, so clearly visible to Katharine as she watched from the *Webster's* deck, was fueled by departing Confederates as they fired the docks at Yorktown behind them. The explosion she heard was the sound of the *Merrimac* being destroyed by their guns in an effort to prevent the famous ironclad from falling intact to the Union navy. These things she learned much later. Next day, lying just offshore at Gloucester Point, she reported that "the press of work here is tremendous. I am writing with everyone about me. Surgeons are coming off to us in tugs and row-boats, clamorous for brandy, beef-stock, lemons, and all stimulating and supporting things . . . as far as I can judge, our duty is to be very much that of a housekeeper. We attend to the beds, the linen, the clothing of the patients; we have a pantry and store-room, and are required to do all the cooking for the sick.[25]

On her first day, in a new role, Katharine met her companions-in-arms, describing them concisely and with admiration. Of the doctor who would be both mentor and friend she wrote, "I am inclined to like the surgeon-in-charge, Dr. Grymes, very much. He commands here. [He suffers] from consumption, and today is hanging about, languid and nerveless; they tell me that tomorrow he will be taut, tireless, hawk-eyed, and the spirit of the emergency."[26] Throughout her tour of duty Katharine would write of Grymes and Dr. Robert

Dr. Robert Ware

Ware with great affection and would regard them highly—despite her Anglican distrust of their "Boston Unitarianism." Grymes' infirmities would be borne with great fortitude throughout the campaign and he would persevere to the end. He and Ware represented the cream of Sanitarian medical personnel, standing in marked contrast to those doctors of whom Georgeanna Woolsey had written in scorn and anger.

Addressing the first of many letters to an anonymous correspondent identified simply as "dear friend," on May 11 Katharine described her first morning of transport duty, a novice in a strange new environment. "Up at five o'clock to give the finishing touches to the wards. How you would laugh to see me, without a hoop, mounted on the ledge of the second tier of berths, making beds for the third tier. At seven we were called to breakfast, and found Mr. Olmsted and Mr. Knapp on board; McClellan is nine miles beyond West Point. We are to get sick men on board this afternoon, and sail tomorrow—unless Mr. Olmsted wants us to go elsewhere; Mrs. Griffin and I have volunteered to do so."[27]

From the first, Wormeley accepted Olmsted's authority with deep respect if not downright awe; and as it happened, she did not sail that night. Instead, she and Christine Griffin were transferred to the *Wilson Small,* the ship which would serve as their base throughout the campaign. Olmsted was already assembling his core staff, those men and women whom he trusted above all and with whom he worked most smoothly. Katharine, the Woolsey sisters and Griffin would remain members of this inner circle to the end. Although other nurses would shuttle back and forth between Yorktown, New York and Washington, assisting the evacuation of patients to hospitals in the North, Olmsted decreed that these four women would remain on the Peninsula as a permanent nucleus to provide continuity on board the Commission flag ship *Wilson Small.* They would become his most valued lieutenants, and would repay his respect with untiring willingness and a near-fanatic commitment to him and to his undertaking.

The Sanitarians' fleet now numbered eight vessels. As well as the original *Daniel Webster* and *Daniel Webster II*, these included the *Samuel S. Spaulding*, the *Elm City*, the *Wilson Small*, the *Ocean Queen*,

the *Elizabeth*, the *Knickerbocker* and the *Wissahickon*, a small supply
tender. Although the four core nurses lived on board Olmsted's command ship *Wilson Small*, all of the women were routinely pressed into
service where needed, and served alternately on all these ships, rotat-
ing whenever casualties were received. On one May evening, watching for the first time as ill and wounded men were transferred from
one boat to another, Katharine described a scene that would be repeated almost daily during the campaign—an exercise in which calm
and coordination were essential. "On board the *Webster* we have just
received, stowed, and fed two hundred men, most of them very ill with
typhoid fever," she wrote. "The *Webster* could not get up to the wharf,
so the sick men were brought off to us in tug boats. As each man came
on board (raised from one vessel and lowered to the second deck of
ours on cradles) he was registered and "bunked." In my ward, as each
man was laid in his berth, I gave him brandy and water, and, after all
were placed, tea and bread and butter, if they could take it, or more
brandy or beef tea if they were sinking. Of course it was painful; but
there was so much to be done, and done quietly and quickly, that there
was no time to be conscious of pain. One little drummer boy thought
he was going to die instantly. 'Pooh,' I said, 'you'll walk off the ship at
New York. Take your tea.'" On that night Wormeley and Griffin could
not settle their patients until after 1:00 A. M. when they packed and
transferred to the *Wilson Small*. Such midnight moves would soon
become routine, but of this first one Wormeley remembered only that
"if I had it to do over again, I'd have an organized carpet-bag, with
compartments for everything. As it was, [all my possessions] were
poked in and stamped upon."[28]

Katharine described the *Wilson Small*, her new home, as "a little
boat, headquarters of the Sanitary Commission," and noted that, "Mr.
Olmsted, the General Secretary, in charge of the whole transport service, and Mr. Knapp, his second in command, live on board." She also
listed her nurse-superintendent companions as "Mrs. Joseph Howland, wife of the colonel of a regiment in the advance, Mrs. George T.
Strong, wife of the Treasurer of the Sanitary Commission, and a tall,
symmetrical Miss Whetton." With some diffidence she wrote that "they
all seem easy and at home in their work, as if they had been at it all

their lives. I use my eyes and learn, and have taken a hand here and there as the occasion offers."[29] And Katharine also noted that "there is a general cry throughout the female department for 'Georgy.' 'Where is Georgy?' 'Oh, if Georgy were here!' 'Georgy' is on a hospital boat called the 'Knickerbocker,' which appears to be missing. As I have little to do just now, I speculate a good deal as to who or what 'Georgy' may be."[30]

With many Williamsburg casualties now being evacuated to the North, the women's nursing duties centered on the care of fever patients. Yet reminders of that first battle persisted nonetheless, and Katharine's indoctrination to the care of wounds began almost immediately. On May 13 she wrote, "terrible things happened yesterday. Many of the wounded of the Williamsburg battle were found lying in the woods with their wounds not dressed, and starving. Mrs. Strong saw them, and says it was like going over a battlefield."[31] As these patients were brought on board, Katharine, though still unsure of her abilities, was pressed into service—and next day she was able to write of her own ability with increased confidence. "I took my first watch last night; and this morning I feel the same ease about the work which yesterday I was surprised to see in others." She described a progression of duties which the nurses would perfect during the summer and which would become the basis of their care routine. "We begin the day by getting them all washed, and breakfasted. Then the surgeons and dressers make their rounds, open the wounds, apply the remedies, and replace the bandages. This is an awful hour; I sat with my fingers in my ears this morning. When it is over, we go back to the men and put the ward in order once more; giving them clean handkerchiefs with a little cologne or bay-water on them—so prized in the sickening atmosphere of wounds. We sponge the bandages over the wounds constantly—we talk with some, read to others, write letters for them; and occasionally give medicine or brandy."[32]

On board the *Small*, on the morning after Katharine's first all-night watch, a minor mystery was solved and an important friendship begun. To her mother Katharine reported that "the *Elm City*, filled with wounded men, sailed this morning [and] 'Georgy' has re-

The Daniel Webster, above,
and The Samuel S. Spaulding, below,
on the Pamunkey River, summer 1862.
Photographs by Mathew Brady

turned with another vessel, the *Knickerbocker*, in perfect order. It seems that the Quartermaster's department ran away with the boat for some purpose of its own, carrying the ladies in her—for Georgy is a *lady*, sister of Mrs. Howland! Miss Rosalie Butler accompanied her. They made the most of their time, and have brought her back in perfect order. They have had her cleansed from top to toe—from hold to hurricane deck, that is. Then they prepared the cots, mattresses and bunks, and made the beds; arranged every ward with the necessary appliances; filled the linen closets with proper quantities of bed-linen, hospital-clothing, socks, bandages, lint, rags, etc. They got ready the hospital kitchen, stole a stove for it, as far as I can make out, and had all the necessary stores unpacked and moved into place. These girls are splendidly efficient. It is not the *doing* of it, but the knowing how it should be done, and handling the whole affair with as much ease as if they were arranging a doll's house, that delights me."[33]

Here were the duties of housekeeping elevated to a high art. Wormeley had been presented a demonstration of female Sanitarian *modus operandi* at its best, the startling, no-nonsense efficiency with which women like Georgeanna Woolsey undertook work and initiated whatever action they saw fit—including the appropriation of kitchen equipment. Katharine would write later that Georgy was forthright in her determination to "steal" whatever appliances, food or comforts were needed—if it would benefit her patients. The medical department, the quartermaster corps, or anyone else who stood in her way were helpless before her resolve. When it came to special delicacies for their patients, or small, handy gadgets for their own use, the women were cheerfully light-fingered. In June Katharine would note that, "kleptomania is the prevailing disease among us. To us the arrival of all our various steamers, the consequent visits, inquiries, and *thefts*, are of great importance. We think nothing of watching the proprietor of some nicety out of the way, and then pocketing the article. After such a visit, Georgy's unfathomable pockets are a mine of wealth as to nutmeg graters, corkscrews, forks and spoons, and the like. I, being less nimble at pilfering, content myself by carrying off tin pails with an abstracted air. For us who remain here [away from the Commission's supply base] such articles are as precious as pure gold."[34]

It was soon after Georgy's return with the hijacked *Knickerbocker* that she and Katharine began to share a cabin on the *Small*, an arrangement which would continue throughout the campaign. The friendship thus begun became very important to both women, and for Wormeley especially beneficial as she absorbed much of Woolsey's expertise and initiative, if not always her insouciance.

Having now experienced some of the rigors that lay ahead of her, Katharine's novitiate actually decelerated and continued rather gently for several days. As fever patients and remaining casualties from Williamsburg were evacuated to the North, partially-filled transports awaited orders that would send them up the York River in the wake of McClellan's advance. In this short interlude the women found time for writing and reflection—even organizing an excursion for an afternoon of sightseeing on shore to view the hastily-abandoned Confederate works. "Yesterday we went all over Yorktown," Katharine wrote. "It is amazing that it was so soon evacuated. Its strength seems very great, not only its defenses, but from the lay of the land. [There are] range after range of hills and ravines, every hill commanding the plain over which our army had to creep up, and which was also covered by [Confederate] water batteries at Gloucester, until our gunboats silenced them. We went round the fortifications and saw everything— the siege guns, eighty of them; the fine log-houses of the [rebels]; the ten thousand abandoned tents. Our guards were placed about the magazines; and at various points in the paths we came upon placards marked 'Dangerous' as a warning of torpedoes. I saw the fragments of a flour barrel in which one torpedo had been buried, killing the man who dipped into it; also a walnut tree under which the earth was torn up, and where yesterday six men were blown to fragments by someone stepping on the fuse. . . . We paid a visit to General Van Alen, commanding the post, and called upon Miss Dix at the hospital— Lord Cornwallis's headquarters; the best house in the place."[35]

Katharine remarked that Lafayette's headquarters at Yorktown was now a prison where Confederate soldiers "seemed very little guarded or regarded," and, perhaps conscious of her own role in an epochal event, she reflected that "in the midst of our excitements these historical places impressed us. It was hard to believe that the filth, destruction and confusion about us were making a new history." She brought home a trophy from the day's sightseeing for her nephew, Ralph, in Boston: "an iron pulley from the celebrated gun which McClellan telegraphed had 'been impertinent this morning' and which had afterwards burst, to the great relief of our men."[36]

During these initial days Wormeley found time also to evaluate her female colleagues and remarked once again on the peculiarities of nursing dress. Lacking the hospital training received by Georgy and her fellow nursing students, Katharine had had no forewarning that she must abandon that essential element of mid-century fashion, the crinoline. "We shuffle about without hoops," she wrote, "Mrs. Griffin says it is *de rigueur* that they shall not be worn in hospital service. I like it very well on board ship: it is becoming to Miss Whetton, who is symmetry itself; but it must be owed that some of us look rather mediaeval."[37]

Accustomed to the exaggerated, bell-shaped silhouette of the 1860s, these well-bred women may have felt that without their cage-like underpinnings they compromised not only femininity but modesty. The hoops were, for all their cumbersome weight, flattering and concealing accessories, for as they extended the full skirts of the '60s to enormous widths, they also minimized figure imperfections. A woman who possessed a neat waist and shapely ankles (laced up tightly in the corsets and high shoes of the period) could always present a fashionable outline. Whatever disparities might lie between waist and ankles remained a mystery. The "medieval" look, apparently so becoming to well-proportioned women like Harriet Whetton and Christine Griffin, suggested the angularity of gothic statuary and presented a drastically altered configuration to which the nurses acquiesced from necessity—but generally with some reservation. Even Georgeanna Woolsey, far more concerned with efficiency than with fashion, included in her nursing wardrobe two voluminous "stick out" petticoats that could be starched to achieve the desired effect.[38] Yet once accustomed to going without hoops, it seems clear from the nurses' letters that they not only enjoyed the new freedom of movement, but may ultimately have chosen to see their changed appearance as somehow symbolic of an inwardly liberated state.

During the two weeks following the battle at Williamsburg, the Army of the Potomac advanced steadily toward White House, a plantation landing on the Pamunkey River. This destination lay at the point where the Richmond and York railroad crossed the river, connecting it to both Richmond and West Point. It had been the spot selected by McClellan in his initial plans, during the winter of '61-'62 when the Urbanna route to Richmond via the Rappahannock was still considered feasible. While that earlier strategy had since been altered, White House Landing remained the chosen base from which the general planned to direct and support his assault upon the Confederate capitol. Here he would situate his command headquarters, and here Army medical personnel would arrange hospital facilities, the quartermaster corps would erect warehouses, and the wide river would accommodate a fleet of supply barges. White House thus became the destination of the Sanitary Commission flagship *Wilson Small* as well, along with any others of their transports deemed necessary as skirmishing produced casualties along the army's line of march.

As the Sanitarians proceeded upriver, their journey coincided with the advance of the Sixteenth New York Volunteers, moving nearly abreast of them by land and water. Eliza and Georgy, now keeping pace with Joe's regiment "within one hour's ride of him and at the heels of the army" were fulfilling their ambition more exactly than even they had hoped. The Sixteenth had left its encampment near Yorktown on the evening of May 4th, re-embarked, and on the morning of May 6th, with other units of General William B. Franklin's First Division, had been transported up the York River. The general planned to put his force ashore at Eltham's Landing, a wide, flat plantation situated opposite and slightly above West Point on the South bank of the Pamunkey, and, working through the night by torchlight, he had completed this operation by dawn on May 7th and dispatched the transports back downriver to ferry up more divisions, while he remained with his troops to await further orders.

At nine o'clock that morning, quite unexpectedly, Newton's brigade of Franklin's division was attacked by a sizable Confederate force, and Slocum's brigade—of which the Sixteenth New York made up a part—was promptly ordered to support them. The engagement, to be known thereafter as the Battle of West Point, was actually little more than a skirmish, described by Alexander Webb as "a smart action continuing until three o'clock, when the enemy withdrew."[39] But small as it was, the sharp little clash took a considerable toll. The wounded, which included several from Joseph's regiment, were soon removed to the *Wilson Small* and an accompanying transport. These were the first casualties suffered by the Sixteenth—and it was in this action that Newton Curtis, later to become the regiment's historian, was himself seriously wounded. Slocum's Brigade remained near the battlefield at West Point for four days more, then marched the short distance to Eltham where it made camp on May 11th.

It was at Eltham that McClellan paid one of his signature visits to the Sixteenth, speaking informally with rank and file and demonstrating the charismatic leadership style for which he was already famous. As he toured the regimental encampment, praising the soldiers' conduct in the recent action and making encouraging suggestions, he endeared himself to Joe Howland's men as he had to so many others. Although Curtis was himself absent for this surprise visit—nursed tenderly by the ladies on board the *Wilson Small* —he recounted later that "this call upon the regiment furnished an illustration of General McClellan's strong interest in the welfare of his soldiers; he first instructed them, then watched their progress, and commended their well-doing. This element of his character affords one of the reasons why the General possessed that enthusiastic affection of the soldiers of the Army of the Potomac which was held by no other commander under which it marched and fought."[40] Because of McClellan's caring demeanor and intense personal appeal, Howland and his men would, throughout the campaign, defend him from all detractors; and if, in years to come the general's reputation was diminished, his flaws would be mitigated in the minds of many veterans by such memories as these.

Regaining the momentum of their advance, on May 13th the Sixteenth, with other units of Franklin's division, left Eltham on a ten mile march to Cumberland Landing "beginning at three o'clock in the morning and ending in the broiling sun." Here they were joined by the larger body of McClellan's army which had fought at Williamsburg, and at last, wrote Curtis, "on May 15th we formed line at daylight and marched the final eight miles in a heavy rain storm, to White House, our destination."[41] The New York regiment reached the Commander's riverside base only two days before the *Wilson Small* arrived from Cumberland Landing, navigating carefully among the tangle of vessels in the anchorage to take her place just off shore near Franklin's headquarters.

Throughout this upstream progress, frequent skirmishing and a high incidence of fever among the troops had significantly swelled the transports' patient load. As the Sanitary Commission boats kept pace with the army, off-loading wounded men from makeshift riverside docks and ferrying between Yorktown, West Point and Cumberland Landing, the nurses were able to acclimate themselves still further to surroundings of stress, illness and death. Wormeley's daily letters traced her journey and detailed its stern realities. On board the *Wilson Small* she wrote, "this boat has run up the York as far as West Point (where a battle was fought last Thursday) [coming] in obedience to a telegram from the Medical Director of the Army, requesting the Commission take off two hundred wounded men immediately. . . . We carry thirty very bad cases—four or five amputations. One poor fellow, a lieutenant shot through the knee, and enduring more than mortal agony; a fair-haired boy of seventeen, shot through the lungs, every breath he draws hissing through the wound; another man, a poet, with seven holes in him, but irrepressibly poetic. He dictated to me last night a foolscap sheet full of poetry composed for the occasion. There is also a captain of the Sixteenth New York Volunteers, mortally wounded while leading his company against a regiment. He is said to measure six feet seven inches."[42]

Changing their position daily, sometimes hourly, in response to the army's call, Wormeley reported some days later that all her "poor fellows" with the exception of the "extensive hero," Captain Curtis of the Sixteenth New York, had been removed to the *Elm City* which would presently depart for Washington via the Potomac. "It is an immense piece of work to get the patients (many of them very low, or in great agony) on board and into their beds, stimulated, fed and made comfortable. We are now making ready to run up the Pamunkey again as far as the advance of the army at Cumberland."[43] Thus the days were spent as the approach to White House shortened.

In mid-May, as the Sanitarians went about their mission of support, proud of their mobility to respond instantly wherever the need arose, the campaign itself reached an interesting, and for McClellan, a frustrating plateau. Imagining, as he often did, that his army was seriously outnumbered, the general pressed for reinforcement by McDowell, currently being retained by Lincoln at Fredericksburg. The fact that this support was not to be forthcoming soon became a major irritant to McClellan, but although a threat to Washington from Stonewall Jackson in the Valley seemed, for the moment, a remote possibility, Lincoln was nonetheless unwilling to relinquish McDowell. Moreover, he stipulated that when McDowell *was* indeed sent, it would be overland rather than by the faster water route. In an effort to placate McClellan, and at the same time build strength for McDowell, Lincoln compromised by ordering reinforcements for McDowell, and promised that he would be dispatched from Fredericksburg to White House by May 17. Reluctantly, McClellan would be forced to accept this schedule.

Second- and third-hand accounts of these machinations reached the Sanitarians as they made their way upriver, and it is relevant here to note that virtually all on board the transports were as passionate in their support of McClellan and defensive of his strategy as were his troops in the field. Like the men of Joe Howland's regiment, most transport workers would remain loyal to their commander for the duration of the Peninsula campaign, and for some this loyalty would continue beyond 1865. Others would, in retrospect, come to criticize the general's judgment and acknowledge his weaknesses, though this was a hard and difficult disillusionment. Katharine

Transports glide upriver between the wooded banks of the Pamunkey, above, and dock at the newly-costructed piers at White House Landing, below. These would be the scenes of the women's new home when the "Wilson Small" arrived to pick up her mooring in the river near McClellan's command headquarters.

Wormeley would be one of these reluctant followers, eventually realizing the hero's flaws and coming to admit them.

But in May and June of 1862 Wormeley, like her colleagues, defended all the general's initiatives, and it is important to recognize the context in which her letters were composed—a climate of optimism and faith, and heroic valorization. Wormeley was still resentful that McClellan had been denied reinforcements when he had called for them before Williamsburg, and she expressed this to her correspondents. "Great regret is felt that General McDowell was not allowed to cooperate at Gloucester," she wrote on May 15. "The spirit of our men, their confidence in their leaders, their pride in belonging to McClellan and the Army of the Potomac, is splendid, so far as I can see it." Later in the summer she would grow even more adamant on this subject. Late in June, at the height of the bloody Seven Days fighting, she would again write, "it is all very well for political idiots and men at ease to talk about 'cutting our way into Richmond.' If they want it done, why don't they give McClellan strength enough to do it? Col. Howland says we must trust him; that whatever he does, be it *act* or *wait*, will be well done. When will the nation learn that it is in the hands of its greatest man, and wait for *his results*, only taking care in the meantime to strengthen his hands?"[44]

On May 17 the *Wilson Small's* journey to White House neared its end and as the vessel penetrated farther upstream, vistas of serene beauty revealed themselves at every turn. "The passage has been enchanting," Katharine wrote. "We ran so close to the shore that I could almost have thrown my glove upon it. The verdure is in its freshest spring beauty; the lovely shores are belted with trees and shrubs of every brilliant and tender shade of green, broken now and then by creeks, running up little valleys till they are lost in the blue distance." For her, the peaceful scene held deep associations which reached back beyond memory. These meadows and woodlands flanking the York and Pamunkey rivers were, in fact, a part of her own patrimony; thirteen thousand acres bequeathed through Royal favor to Ralph Wormeley 2d., first of her family to settle in America. Although Katharine's own father had left Virginia while still a boy, and her letters make no mention of Wormeleys who might still manage these plantations, the possibility of such relatives cannot be discounted. Like Eliza Howland at Cameron Run, Katharine reflected upon the irony of war in this pastoral setting of her ancestors, and as the transport moved quietly upriver she mused at the ambiguity of her own presence, the Yankee daughter of Virginia slave-owners, on these homeland plantations which now became the skirmishing ground of opposing armies.[45]

The day ended in silent glory. "The sun set as we rounded the last bend in the Pamunkey; the sky and the water gleamed golden alike, and the trees suddenly grew black as the glow dazzled our eyes," wrote Katharine. "We anchored there off Cumberland, and I went to sleep in the still lingering twilight, listening to the whippoorwill." At dawn she discovered that the journey to White House had been completed during the early hours, and as she emerged from her cabin she found her chief already on deck. "Mr. Olmsted called me forward into the bows: and what a sight was there to greet us! . . . We had reached [our destination] and ran up to the head of the fleet, in sight of army headquarters, to the burned railroad bridge beyond which no one could go."[46]

"After breakfast we went ashore, where General Franklin met us and took us through part of his command—through trains of armywagons drawn by four mules; through a ploughed field across which mounted officers and their staffs were galloping at full speed; through suttlers' tents and commissary stores, and batteries and caissons. It was like a vast fairground!"[47]

The riverfront at White House was an impressive scene, but no more striking than the personalities who ordered it into being and now inhabited it. On that morning Katharine met the high-ranking officers who would orchestrate the deadly serious events of the weeks ahead; Eliza's and Georgy's military friends from Washington, now relocated to their natural environment of war. The generals' easy friendships with the Woolsey sisters were now expanding to include Katharine, and impressions of these new associations dominate her first letters from White House. Re-envisioning the officers for her mother's benefit, she described General Fitz-John Porter as "a man of fine spirit [who] probably has less power than General Franklin, [but] is more excitable and sympathetic . . . with an expression of devotion about him which inspires great confidence." General [George W.] Morrell [who would command Porter's First Division] was "an interesting man who received the command of a division yesterday." General Seth Williams "gave us all great pleasure . . . I am told that if any man possesses in an equal degree the respect and attachment of others, he does; yet his quiet, modest manner and plain appearance would hardly instruct a stranger as to his position . . . these gentlemen are accompanied by many young officers, all spurs and swords and clanking. They were all very guarded, of course, in what they said of the future; but two hours' talk with such men in such places teaches much."[48]

In their ready access to officers like Franklin, Porter, Williams and Morell, the Sanitary Commission nurses were exceptionally fortunate, for these friendships allowed them to come away from the Peninsula experience with an expanded perception of what occurred beyond the immediate environment of their transports. For although the generals were invariably discreet as to specifics, the overall strategy of McClellan's campaign emerged for the women as they talked casually with members of his command staff. In a class-conscious era, and in a milieu governed by strict military etiquette, the Sanitarian ladies were accepted unconditionally in the orbit of high-ranking officers—a privilege not generally accorded nurses who served concurrently under different auspices.[49] When time permitted, as it occasionally did during the fortnight before Fair Oaks, a cordial late afternoon or evening hour provided respite for hard-pressed men who knew they neared the volcano's brink, yet preserved what sociability they might until the sparks flew; and it would appear from the nurses' letters that both groups benefited from this very civil exchange.

Of that first morning at McClellan's command headquarters, Katharine wrote, "General Franklin took us to the White House—a house and estate just quitted by the son of General Lee, whose wife was a Custis. It is a small cottage, by no means a white house." She noticed that there still remained sufficient furnishings throughout the abandoned rooms to show that once the small plantation had been "adorned with modern elegance."[50] And both she and Eliza Howland remembered a notice within, written in a lady's hand on a half sheet of note-paper, and nailed to the wall of the entrance:

> "'Northern soldiers! who profess to reverence the memory of Washington, forebear to desecrate the home of his first married life, the property of his wife, and now owned by her descendants.' and signed,
> A Granddaughter of Mrs. Washington.'"

Describing the posted sign to her mother, Katharine noted that, "underneath was written (in the handwriting, as I was told, of General Williams, Adjutant-General of the army): 'Lady—A northern soldier has protected this property within sight of the enemy, and at the request of your overseer.'"

"And so it was," wrote Katharine. "General McClellan would not even make his headquarters within the grounds. Guards were stationed at the gates and fences, on the lawns and piazzas. Within, all was beautiful, untrodden and fresh, while without was the tumult and trampling of war . . . already a barren and dusty plain."

Here, as at Cameron Run, and across the acres of the Wormeley Royal Grant, peace and war were curiously juxtaposed. Below the women as they walked with the general, in the gently sloping fields surrounding the farm, the Sixteenth New York was already encamped, only one of Franklin's regiments pausing here before moving on towards Richmond. Wandering through the plantation which had until recently dominated the waterfront falling away before them, Katharine gazed across "peaceful lawns looking down upon the river now crowded with transports and ammunition barges. . . . The glow of the morning mist, the black gunboats, the shining river, the gleam of white sails and the tents along the shore, made a picture to be painted only by Turner."[51]

This deceptively quiet landscape would, in little more than a fortnight, become a maelstrom of activity and suffering; energy and death. Within six weeks White House plantation would itself be abandoned and sacrificed, its lawns rutted and its buildings destroyed in the crossfire of onslaught and retreat. The anchorage and riverside would be transformed violently to become a setting for the women's most severe testing. What had gone before was merely preparation.

Chapter V

WHITE HOUSE

Wormeley's poetic evocation of White House as a Turner-esque plantation riverscape peopled with men and horses is echoed and expanded by Stephen Sears in his description of a massive and progressive installation.

> The shallows between riverbank and deep water were bridged by floating docks constructed of planked-over barges and canal boats. Acres of boxes and barrels and crates holding rations and ammunition and supplies and equipment of every sort covered the landing. There were wagon parks and artillery parks and great piles of baled forage. Vessels freighted with locomotives, boxcars, and flatcars soon arrived from Baltimore, and in a matter of days as much of the railroad as the Yankees controlled was in operation. Except for burning a few bridges, the retreating Confederates had left the line intact, much to the disgust of Jefferson Davis.[1]

The Anchorage At White House Landing

Mathew Brady photographed docks lined with cargo transports, schooners and tugs, above; and captured a moment of repose as contrabands and Union soldiers rested on shore, below.

Access to White House Landing by both land and water was eased here because the steep banks of the Pamunkey fell gently away at the river's edge.[2] Moored just offshore of McClellan's headquarters, the transports of the Sanitary Commission were within easy reach of the government medical facilities which they hoped to supplement and, further down river, a cache of their own supplies. But they were also closer to a swampy, malarial terrain that stretched for miles on either side of the Chickahominy which lay inland from the new base. These swamps extended in many places toward the Pamunkey, causing most soldiers who came on board to present specific medical problems which reflected their peculiarly unhealthy surroundings. A New Hampshire regimental historian remembered this environment in vivid terms:

> The Chickahominy is a narrow, sluggish stream flow-
> ing through swamp land . . . covered with a rank, dense,
> tangled growth of trees, reeds, grasses and water plants.
> Vines climb and mosses festoon the trees . . . its stagnant
> water is poisonous; moccasins and malaria abound; flies and
> mosquitoes swarm; turtles and lizards bask; buzzards and
> polecats stink . . . here was to be [our] home . . . Here [we]
> were to dwell in the midst of [war's] alarms for two months in
> this horrible place, during the very hottest months of the
> Southern year.[3]

Diseases associated with the Chickahominy's jungle-like atmosphere were notoriously virulent, and as McClellan's soldiers worked and fought through the summer they developed an array of ills. Ailments presented to the transport nurses daily were cholera, malaria, acute diarrhea and dysentery, epidemic bronchitis, typhoid and typhus, purulent eye disorders, boils, and scarlet fever. Such illnesses were directly related to the men's environment but were often complicated by existing conditions of pneumonia, jaundice, measles, mumps, syphilis, gonorrhea, tuberculosis, erysipelas, smallpox and diphtheria. Transport personnel were at high risk, and were required to "prophylac" daily with quinine and other reputedly preventive substances. Not surprisingly many of them sickened and had to be sent home.[4] In letters to her family, Katharine Wormeley attempted to make light of this hazard by meeting it head-on: "You are not to be alarmed by the word 'typhoid,'" she wrote. "I foresee that it will occur on every page of my letters, nearly all of our sick cases being that or [complicated by] that. [But] the idea of infection is simply absurd. The ventilation of these ships is excellent; besides, people employed in such a variety of work and in high health and spirits are not liable to infection. Nobody here ever thinks of such a thing, and I only mention it to check your imagination." Several days later she insisted, "I am perfectly well. To please others, I 'prophylac' with the rest. I drink coffee in excess, and whiskey (with quinine) occasionally, and eat alarming dinners."[5]

In her abiding belief in "excellent ventilation" and an optimistic outlook, Wormeley affirmed the rationale of Florence Nightingale who drew upon a combination of theories and moral beliefs to arrive at the "Nightingale model" of nursing care. As a sanitarian she placed great emphasis on physical, philosophical, and environmental order within the hospital setting. Clean drains, fresh air and appropriate diets, she believed, created "hospital morale" which, in turn, induced healing. Nightingale never accepted the germ theory, and felt that medical and surgical innovations were secondary to a strictly practiced set of nursing procedures which would produce patient well-being and, not incidentally, enhance optimism and enthusiasm among medical caregivers. A sense of women's "special" duties and obligations were central to Nightingale's theory, and with this belief the elite nurses of the transports concurred.

Although the role of each nurse-superintendent had originally been envisioned as something like a head housekeeper, by the time the transports established their base at White House it had become clear that indeed their job was far more complex; emotionally draining, often dangerous. On an evening in late May, not long before the battle of Fair Oaks, as a severe storm swept across the Peninsula, Katharine was dispatched on an errand which demonstrated just how far the demands of her job had now been stretched. "Two steamers

Chickahominy Fever Country

This photograph by James Gibson of White Oak Swamp, a portion of the ubiquitous swampland surrounding the Chickahominy, presents a more park-like view than was generally the case. Even today, undrained portions of these swamps can be tangled with dense undergrowth and festooned with vines, re-sembling the New Hampshire historian's memory. Happily, the threat of indigenous disease has long been removed.

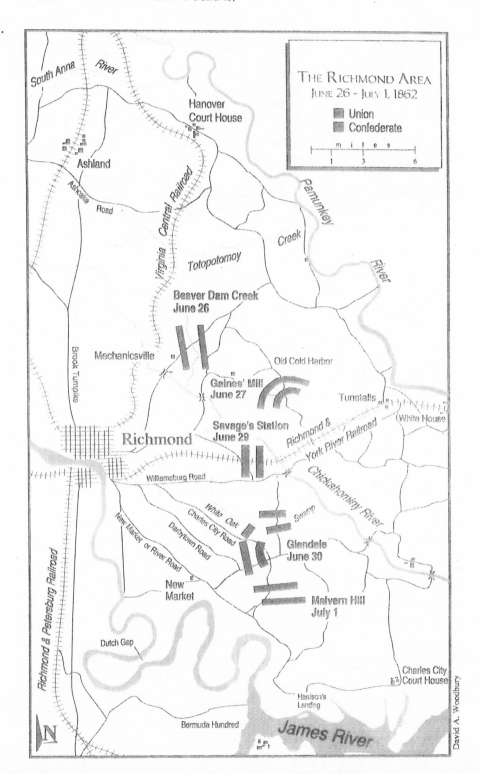

THE RICHMOND AREA
JUNE 26 – JULY 1, 1862

Union
Confederate

miles
1   3   6

came alongside," she wrote, "each with a hundred sick on board, bringing word that another vessel was aground with two hundred more,
having no one in charge and nothing to eat. So amid the wildest and
most beautiful storm of lightning and thunder, Georgy, Dr.Ware, Mrs.
Reading and I pulled off to her in a little boat with tea, brandy, and
beef essence. (No one can tell how it tries my nerves to go toppling
around at night in little boats, and clambering up ships' sides on little
ladders!) You will see that we women do more than is set down for us
in the programme; for, in fact, we do a little of everything."[6]

At White House, even in the relative quiet before Fair Oaks, the
nurses' days remained long and physically arduous. Although they
were assigned to perform their duties in shifts, in fact these schedules
were frequently broken when incoming casualties arrived. Often government authorities moved, with no prior notice, to appropriate the
Commission's transports, generally returning them dirty and
unsupplied. The theme of government irresponsibility in this respect
dominates Wormeley's letters from the new headquarters. On these
occasions all of the Sanitarians worked around the clock without a
break, moving patients, rescuing precious supplies and personal
effects.[7] The women would catch moments of sleep wherever they could
find a vacant corner, though often they were too tired—or too over-
wrought—to rest. Katharine noted that,"I have learned to sleep on
my arm, and it is very 'comfy.' As for Georgy, she curls herself up anywhere, like a little gray kitten, and is asleep in a minute."[8]

In addition to familiar nursing duties, the provision of nutritious
meals for their patients was *the* overriding concern of nurse-superintendents. On "normal" days, as well as during major crises, it was
their duty to arrange for the "sick food"—special diets ordered by doctors for patients suffering from a variety of ills and injuries. Such
food, prepared in huge quantities, included milk punch, beef tea, milk
toast, soups, gruels, tea, coffee, whisky toddies and punches.   It also
included whatever fresh and homelike treats the nurses might impro-
vise or extract from their own packages from home—jams, preserves,
pickles, crackers and chocolate—or in the event of a successful local
scavenging mission, perhaps chicken, scrambled eggs or apple sauce.
The women's ingenuity in procurement and preparation was a crucial
asset—one greatly valued by their charges.

"Sick food" was personally prepared several times each day by the nurses for their patients at the doctors' request. On some few transports the women had their own kitchen for this purpose—more often they had to cajole their way into the ship's galley. This was seldom an easy negotiation. General catering on board these vessels was carried out by galley crews who were not under the supervision of the Sanitary Commission and who, more often than not, declined to cooperate with the lady-nurses' requests or suggestions. The kitchen staff was often composed of contrabands who had difficulty understanding what the women wanted.Other workers were simply defiant of the nurses' authority and refused their requests outright."House diets"—meals for staff and patients who did not require special invalid food—were seldom served on any discernible schedule to the intense frustration of the ladies. Often these meals were poorly cooked or inadequate. In their battle to achieve timely and orderly servings the women used whatever tact or force or intimidation they could. It was a constant test of wills and perseverance.[9]

Nina Bennett Smith has noted that the Civil War nurse was "generally the workhorse of the hospital," and this proved true on board the river transports as well. Nurses did everything that no one else could or would do, including psychological and religious counseling. This was especially true of elite, well-educated women to whom men turned for a special sort of wisdom and solace."These ladies served functions that now are considered essential to health care; they listened, they tried to soothe loneliness, homesickness, doubt and dread."[10] They also suffered from a sense of personal helplessness in the face of massive carnage. On the transports they dealt with men crazed with fever. They observed piles of severed limbs collected around operating tables and when they went on shore they witnessed lines of hopelessly wounded men laid out on the ground to save beds for those with some hope of recovery.[11]

As the women mustered strength to deal with these shifting realities, certain other aspects of their position came to light. Soon after the Sanitarians arrived at White House they realized that their work had taken on a new sense of urgency. Although originally sent upriver to the army's general headquarters on a movable or temporary basis for "medicines and to pick up information," the crew of the *Wilson Small* had had no firm plan to transfer their own base away from Yorktown. This situation was now changed. As they encountered the near-disastrous conditions existing in government-run hospital facilities at the new command center they decided to remain. Even Olmsted, in his enthusiasm, had not anticipated how timely their arrival would be, nor how badly their assistance was needed. In the event of a major battle, now predicted to occur within days, the preparations made by the Army Medical Department proved to be woefully inadequate. In a letter to her mother Wormeley noted that "Mr. Olmsted finds such a state of disorganization and sixes-and-seven's in the medical arrangements that he has determined to make his headquarters here for the present. Mr. Knapp has [left] orders for our hospital-fleet to follow us up the river as they arrive from the North. The 'Webster' came up in perfect order, ready to ship her men as soon as cargo was discharged. She is now loading, and sails for Boston this afternoon. Dr. Grymes is still in charge of her, and Mrs. Trotter reigns over the women's department with great success. We remain here. Mr. Olmsted is anxious to keep his own "staff" at the heels of the army. I like this much better myself. It is more interesting, and the work, though harder, is more satisfactory in every way."[12]

Explaining the relationship that now developed between Sanitarians and military doctors, Wormeley wrote, "the state of affairs here is somewhat this: when the march from Yorktown began, and the men dropped by thousands, exhausted, sick, and wounded, The Medical Department, unprepared and harassed, flung itself upon the Sanitary Commission. When it became known that our transports were lying in the river, the brigade-surgeons sent their sick on board [and] the Medical Director sanctioned the practice. The hospitals at Yorktown, Fortress Monroe, and Newport News are full."[13]

The army's habit of alternately exploiting and ignoring the Sanitary Commission was distressing to Olmsted and infuriating to the loyal workers who were devoted to him. Wormeley was convinced that through taking advantage of the Commission's willingness, the army itself would suffer. "Every man who falls exhausted in the ranks is sent to us," she wrote. "The men will come to think that illness, real or shammed, is the way to get home. Already suspicious 'rheumatic' cases have appeared. This will prove in the end actually demoralizing for the army if not checked. Mr. Olmsted remonstrates against the system, but of course he has to act under the medical authority."[14]

On May 25 steady rains began which would last until the battle of Fair Oaks. Olmsted, concerned for the casualties already on board, and fearing the influx soon to descend, complained of government negligence and praised his female volunteers both as care-givers and in their original role as housekeepers. "[Today] we have a stormy day and are loading the *Spaulding* from the *Elm City*," he wrote. "Shall send her to New York tomorrow. Mrs. Strong goes home with her. Her tact and energy have saved many souls on the *Elm City* from the narrow incompetence of the [army] surgeons—not as surgeons, but as hotel keepers. Mrs. Strong can keep a hotel. So can Mrs. Griffin and Miss Woolsy [sic] and Miss Wormly [sic] and perhaps some of the others. They beat the doctors all to pieces. I should have sunk the ships in despair before this if it hadn't been for their handiness and good nature."[15]

At this point in his campaign, with an elaborate base of operations established at White House and a major battle in the offing, McClellan decreed that his chain of command be reorganized in a manner which he believed would improve the army's effectiveness as it approached the offensive thrust which he supposed would conquer Richmond. These changes touched many brigades, realigning certain units across all six Army Corps. Those modifications directly affecting the Sixteenth New York Volunteers are of particular interest, and should be noted here, for they would directly affect Joe's life, as well as Eliza's and Georgy's, in the weeks just ahead.

Gen. William B. Franklin was now designated commander of the Sixth Corps, with his First Division going to the former Second Brigade commander, Gen. Henry W. Slocum. Col. Joseph Bartlett would command the Second Brigade that had been Slocum's, and thus would be the senior officer to whom Joe Howland would report. Bartlett's Brigade also included the 5th Maine, the 27th New York and the 96th

Pennsylvania. It was in this configuration, and with these comrades, that the Sixteenth would support the action at Fair Oaks and would go into battle during the desperate Seven Days.

As he approached these major engagements before Richmond, McClellan commanded the waters of the York and Pamunkey. But his domination of the James River was much less assured. On May 15 five Union vessels, including the famous ironclad *Monitor,* had attempted to penetrate the upper James only to be repulsed at Drewry's Bluff eight miles below Richmond. The successful defense mounted here by a Confederate battery placed on the heights above the river had so far discouraged further naval penetration, and would continue to deter Union shelling of the Confederate capital throughout the summer of 1862.

On his northern flank McClellan's prospects were also less perfect than he had originally thought them. Although his installation at White House was supported by the Richmond & York River Railroad and supplied by a fleet of vessels on the Pamunkey, he had, in fact, established a defective base for his operations. Allan Nevins identified a fatal discrepancy in McClellan's plan when he noted that,

> The Pamunkey was too small to afford proper naval protection.Much more importantly, any army advancing on Richmond from the White House would have to push part of its force across the Chickahominy while keeping another part on the near side. That is, one section would have to remain on the north bank to hold the communications with White House Landing while the other crossed to the south bank to attack the Southern capital. Such a division of the army would be safe if the weather proved dry . . . it would be highly unsafe if storms raised the river, flooded the lowlands, and swept away jerry-built crossings.[16]

And unsafe it proved to be. The Chickahominy was a disastrous stumbling block as McClellan prepared for one of the pivotal encounters of his campaign, and he had not advanced far before it became evident that the river, rapidly rising within its dense surrounding swampland, presented a serious obstacle. Realizing the army's pre-

The village at Mechanicsville

Stationed at this small hamlet five miles from Richmond, Joe Howland and his men were critically positioned on McClellan's right flank. Although this placed them at some distance from the action at Fair Oaks and Seven Pines, it would become a prime target within a month as the first of the Seven Days battles began.

dicament, and well aware that a major engagement was fast approaching, the transport nurses prepared for an onslaught of wounded—and, on a personal level, Eliza Howland grew restive, longing for some word of her husband. It had been some time since any letters had come through to her from the front, and she was unsure exactly where the Sixteenth was positioned. Writing to Joe on May 27, four days before the battle, she barely masked her apprehension as she wondered at his silence. "Still not a word from you for a fortnight," she wrote. "I am beginning to be very hungry—not anxious, only *hungry*, for your letters. I only hear in indirect ways that our division was near the Chickahominy a day or two ago and was ordered to march into Richmond next morning . . . I dream about it all, and wonder, but know nothing. . ."[17]

In fact, Eliza's rumored information had been quite accurate. The Sixteenth, in company with other elements of Bartlett's Brigade, *was* just outside Richmond at the far right of McClellan's extended line. On May 22nd, with the Twenty-seventh New York and a squadron of the First New York Cavalry, Joe Howland's men had been ordered on reconnaissance toward Mechanicsville, "a small hamlet with a guide-board reading, 'Five miles to Richmond.'" The detachment of New York-ers succeeded in driving back Confederate pickets near the village and advanced close enough to fix their position positively. Armed with this information and a force of cavalry, General Stoneman moved to secure the ground on the following day. Newton Curtis remembered that, "our occupation of Mechanicsville deprived the people of Rich-mond of a pleasure they had long enjoyed: driving there on summer evenings and dining on the banks of the Chickahominy." This posi-tion, north of the river on McClellan's far-extended right, had been selected as the designated point of rendezvous for the anticipated com-ing of McDowell when at last that event should take place. As such it was deemed too important to leave, and therefor, in the end, would preclude the Sixteenth from taking part in the battles of Fair Oaks and Seven Pines.[18]

For the moment, stationed so close to Richmond at the end of a line stretched thin, the regiment was uncomfortably—even danger-ously—situated. Well prepared, and in a condition of readiness, they had as yet received no definitive orders, and so remained in a state of some tension. But as Eliza learned of their position, and contemplated the risks involved in it, she could at least take comfort knowing that Joe's men were enjoying some relief from the destructive heat and had, coincidentally, acquired a distinctive token which would see them through hard times ahead. As they settled into their steamy post in the swamps near Mechanicsville, men of the Sixteenth now put on the white straw hats which would become their signature throughout the campaign. This unusual accessory had been Joe's inspiration, for he had realized early that the dark, virtually brimless standard issue forage caps worn by all personnel were very poorly suited to extended wear in hot weather. Designed in a cool climate, the caps absorbed heat and afforded little shade, often becoming more dangerous than no hats at all. Acting on impulse, and using Eliza's name, he had req-uisitioned a full complement of wide-brimmed summer straws from a New York haberdasher and had them shipped down to him on a re-turning transport. Now, as Yankee soldiers sweltered through the

Federal Lines Facing Richmond

James Gibson photographed McClellan's extensive works before Richmond in
mid-June 1862. Above is Redoubt Number 5 near Fair Oaks Station. Other
emplacements, below, were situated at regular intervals along the line.

hottest months of a Virginia summer, Joe's men were well and dis-
tinctively equipped, cooler than less fortunate comrades-in-arms, and
recognized by all as the "Straw Hat Regiment." For this, the men gave
full credit to Eliza, for although they realized that their Colonel had
devised the plan, they chose to believe that it was she who brought
this gift to them.

     As Union troops maneuvered into place along both sides of the
Chickahominy, Confederate General Joseph E. Johnston wasted no
time in seizing the unique opportunity being offered him. Observing
the division of McClellan's strength, and wishing to take full advantage of this split, Johnston massed his own troops against the two
Union corps *south* of the river, and, as he did so, the forces of nature
converged in his favor. The extreme weather during the days and hours
preceding the battle of Fair Oaks proved as effective a weapon to the
Confederate commander as thousands of fighting men; for it virtually
immobilized McClellan's army astride the Chickahominy.
     But the Union general was not alone in his disquietude at this
developing situation. Preparedness and positioning were also issues
for the Sanitarians to consider strategically. Although they had begun
to think of themselves as seasoned professionals, the sharp double
encounter at Fair Oaks and Seven Pines, coming barely a month after
their arrival from the North, challenged the nurses to a final testing
for which they could only hope they were sufficiently prepared. It also
stretched the capacities of the transports.
     On May 30, the eve of Fair Oaks, severe thunderstorms began
early and continued all night. When, on the morning of May 31, under
still-lowering skies, Johnston attacked, it was with a fury which threatened to decimate the Union forces arrayed against him. Fighting
continued for hours unabated, each side advancing and being repulsed
with heavy losses to both. Saving the day, at least partially, for
McClellan was Edwin V. Sumner, the veteran general, who advanced
south across the Chickahominy late in the afternoon arriving in time
to reinforce Generals Keyes and Heintzelman whose divisions were

now dangerously reduced. Though the Chickahominy was in full flood, and only one broken bridge still stood—precariously tied and with all of its approaches afloat—a solid column of Sumner's infantry passed over it safely, upon which the bridge collapsed, its wreckage swept away downstream as the last men reached the far bank. Alexander Webb, who observed the battle, remembered the daring feat and the experienced elder officer's words: "The enemy may win a victory, but we must make it a victory that will ruin him."[19]

Ultimately, on the second day of battle, Federal forces managed to hold their lines intact—but only barely. Losses for both armies were heavy—and Fair Oaks/Seven Pines would never be considered a clear cut victory for either side. The tide had shifted many times, and when at last both armies retired, the double engagement could be seen only as a putative advantage for the Union general, its significance largely in the perception. Nevins noted that "both sides were so severely shaken that they were immobilized; and worst shaken was McClellan's reputation as a strategist. He had committed a terrible error in throwing his army astraddle a dangerous river and leaving a corps standing isolated for several days within reach of a crushing blow from Johnston."[20]

But perhaps the most significant result of this engagement was an abrupt realignment of the Confederate command. At the height of battle Joe Johnston was himself incapacitated—severely wounded on the afternoon of the first day, thus changing the equation of leadership permanently. His injury would affect his army far beyond the immediate trauma, for it would precipitate his replacement by Robert E. Lee and would initiate a strategic reordering of style for Confederate forces on the Peninsula.

In the days immediately preceding Fair Oaks, as Sanitary Commission workers had gone about their preparations, the dissonance existing between their organization and government medical authorities had remained at a simmer. Yet despite all obstacles thrown up in his way, Olmsted managed to augment the army's efforts through a number of his own strategies, and in the aftermath of battle Georgeanna Woolsey was able to praise his improvement of existing

shore facilities even as she damned the army's medical unpreparedness. Describing the role played by her chief, she wrote, "Mr. Olmsted
has had a new Hospital tent pitched on shore, near the railroad landing, for a kitchen and store-house, and we women take charge of it,
feeding nearly all of the three to four thousand men who are brought
down from the battle-field."[21] On June 3, two days after the engagement, she noted that, "the trains of wounded and sick arrive at all
hours of the night, the last one just before daybreak. As soon as the
whistle is heard Dr. Ware is on hand and we are ready in the tent,
blazing trench fires and kettles all in a row, bright lights and piles of
fresh bread and pots of coffee. The tent door is opened wide, the road
leading to it from the train dotted all along with little fires or lighted
candles. First comes the procession of slightly wounded, these followed
by the slow-moving line of bearers and stretchers. The poor fellows on
the stretches have brandy, or wine, or iced lemonade. It takes but a
minute's delay to pour something down their throats and put oranges
in their hands, and it saves them from exhaustion. For these men no
provision has been made by the Government, and they are left on our
hands, sometimes for days. They would fare badly but for the sleep-
less devotion of Dr. Ware who works with them night after night until
two and three o'clock in the morning. The government boats so far
have been inadequately provisioned, wretchedly officered and in a
general state of confusion. Dr. Agnew calls it 'damnable.'" Later, deeply
angered, Woolsey remembered that "one poor man was without nour-
ishment all day until an hour before his shoulder was taken off. Then
the surgeon hurried over and asked us to take him beef tea and egg-
nog. I crossed the coal barges and fed him myself—and this after the
doctor had told me they needed no help."[22]

During those days and nights Sanitary Commission doctors
passed constantly through the arriving trains of wounded, lanterns
in hand, giving emergency care and selecting the worst surgical cases
while the ladies followed close behind them to distribute cool drinks
or administer stimulants. Wounded men were tightly packed into
freight cars, often piled on top of one another. On June 3, in a letter to
Henry Bellows, Olmsted described the transportation of casualties in
the days following Fair Oaks. "The wounded were arriving by every

After the Battle

Above, Alfred Waud sketched officers as they supervised burial details and burned dead horses after the battles at Fair Oaks and Seven Pines. Below, Arthur Lumley's drawing, with notes, shows ambulances, litters and sedan chairs arriving at the Seven Pines railroad station bearing the wounded for transport to White House. Some cars were open to the heat and rain, as this one; others were sealed in, with bodies piled on top of one another.

train, entirely unattended, or at most with a detail of two soldiers to a train of two hundred. They were without beds, without straw, . . . they arrived dead and alive together, in the same close box, many with awful wounds festering and alive with maggots. The stench was such as to produce vomiting with some of our strong men, habituated to the duty of attending to sick and wounded."

"Shall I tell you that our noble women . . . were always ready and eager, and almost always the first, to press into these places of horror, going to them in torrents of rain, groping their way by dim, lantern light, at all hours of the night, carrying spirits, ice and water, calling back to life those who were in the despair of utter exhaustion, or catching for mother or wife the last, priceless whispers of the dying."[23]

The nurses were similarly awed by the conduct of male colleagues, recognizing in them qualities of tenderness and compassion that reached beyond strength and endurance. In a letter to a close friend Wormeley wrote, "remember that I have told you only about ourselves,—the women. What the gentlemen have been . . . is beyond my power to relate. Some of them fainted from time to time. Never did men work as ours have worked. No description can give you a full idea of the pressure upon them. . . Dr. Robert Ware is all that is gentle, sensible, energetic, and *successful*."[24] Even a detail of Zouave orderlies were described as "kind, nimble and gentle, having none of the dull, obstinate ways" of their sex. Georgeanna Woolsey wrote of Olmsted, "Late at night I would look around and find him sitting by [a patient] with his arm around his pillow as nearly around his neck as possible talking tenderly to him, and slipping away again quietly, only [coming] when the ward was quiet and no one round to look at him."[25] Here, where men and women labored side by side to alleviate suffering, conventional gendered behaviors blurred. Female volunteers found their initiatives valued equally, without question, without remark. Taking confidence from their own proven bravery and self-control, they now celebrated qualities of gentleness in their male colleagues— a balancing of masculine and feminine strengths in comrades who worked together; a complementary reversal strangely at odds with nineteenth-century role perceptions.

But not even the Sanitary Commission, with its vast stores of donated supplies and willing volunteers, could stem the tide of suffering in the wake of a major two-day engagement in alternating conditions of torrential rain and tropical heat. As bridges washed away, roads became sloughs of mud. Horses, mules and vehicles were irretrievably mired. Ambulances were often immobilized en route to hospital or simply abandoned. Scores of wounded men were left to die in the rain, and many who reached the inadequate government facilities received only minimal relief. Nightmarish scenes followed the battles of Fair Oaks and Seven Pines. Wormeley wrote in anguish of her work during that week, "no one, it is believed, can tell the story, *as it occurred*, of the next three days;—no one can tell distinctly what boats they were on [or where] they lived and worked through those days and nights. They remember scenes and sounds, but they remember nothing as a whole; and, to this day, if they are feverish and weary, comes back the sight of men in every condition of horror shattered and shrieking."[26]

Even in the heat of this emergency the uneasy relationship of Government and Sanitary Commission persisted. In an indignant letter Wormeley noted that "the trouble the medical authorities give Mr. Olmsted is terrible. They send the most conflicting orders, and there is no United States medical officer here, at this most important point, to refer to . . . Mr. Olmsted and Mr. Knapp are working their brains and their physical strength to the utmost. Conceive of the Medical Director sending down four thousand five hundred wounded men without—yes literally without—anything for them: without surgeons; no one authorized to take charge of them; nothing but empty boats to receive them. You *can't conceive* what it is to stem the torrent of this disorder and utter want of organization. We can only thank God that we are here, with health, strength, and *head*. To think or speak of the things we see would be fatal."

Recounting the events of a twenty-four-hour ordeal when one emergency succeeded another without respite, Wormeley wrote, "that night Mrs. Griffin and I begged Mr. Olmsted not to refrain from sending us [on board a government boat to help] merely because we had been up all night. He said he wouldn't *send* us, but if we chose to offer our services to the [army] surgeon, it would be merciful. Our offer was seized. We went on board; and such a scene as we entered and lived in for two days I trust never to see again. The men had been without food for three days, but there was nothing on board either boat for them. We got through at 1 A.M., Mrs. Howland and Georgy having come off duty to reinforce us. We were sitting for a few moments, resting and talking it over, and bitterly asking why the Government— so lavish in its other arrangements, should leave its wounded almost literally to take care of themselves—when a message was brought saying that one hundred and fifty men were just arriving in the cars. It was raining in torrents, and both boats were full. We went on shore again, and [yesterday's] scene was repeated. . . . I must not, I ought not, tell you the horrors of that morning. When shall I forget the sunrise as it looked in through the little window beside me! When can I cease to remember the feelings with which I saw it!"[27]

Wormeley, a high-strung woman whose letters hint at a fierce inner battle to control her own emotions, was sorely tried by the sounds, sights and smells that surrounded her. The wounds she was called upon to confront were horrifying—and the remedies and methods used in their treatment were perhaps even more difficult to behold. Although it is true that approximately three times as many soldiers died from illness as from wounds during the Civil War, it is the care of wounded men that stands out as the most distressing task nurses were called upon to face.[28] The wounds they treated in the course of each day were unique in their destructiveness and quite unlike those of modern warfare. The methods used to care for these injuries were also vastly different. Nina Bennett Smith has described them graphically, noting that,

> The typical battle wound came from the Minie-ball, a
> conical lead bullet weighing an ounce or more. It traveled
> slowly and was not sterilized in flight by its own speed as a
> modern steel-jacketed bullet would be. It flattened on impact,

causing large, ragged flesh wounds and generally shattering bones and joints. It could carry bits of cloth and foreign matter deep into the wound, making infection inevitable.

Head or abdominal wounds inflicted by these bullets were almost invariably fatal, and if a Minie-ball shattered an arm or a leg, amputation was generally required. All flesh wounds were treated with water dressings: old, soft muslin cloths or lint satu-rated with cold water and bound around arm or a leg, amputa-tion was usually inevitable. Wounds were treated with water dressings: old, soft muslin cloths or lint saturated with cold water and bound around the infected area.[29]

Wormeley remembered soldiers' wounds being probed and opened by doctors, and dressings that required changing daily, with intense pain. Meanwhile, a perpetual round continued as nurses soaked the bandages to prevent their drying. Smith described as a universal treat-ment an ointment called simple cerate "consisting of two parts of fresh lard to one of white wax," and noted that "in warm weather the wounds often became full of maggots."[30]

This was the season of the women's severest testing. Their duties as comforters of anguished men and the impressions and emotions that accompanied their working days and nights would never be forgotten. As she struggled to preserve detachment Wormeley wrote, "I find I can bear anything with calmness and, in a sense, indifference, so long as I am beside it and engaged in it, but no tongue can tell what I suffer when I am obliged to stay [off duty] to rest, and listen to the groans of men undergoing operations on the "Louisiana" [a government boat] to which we are moored. Oh! the cries of men."[31] Another nurse recalled that her first patient "had had his lower jaw and tongue shot away," and that after her initial hospital shift she had paced about her room all night, agitated and unable to sleep, questioning the dignity of such horrendous sacrifice and the ultimate morality of war itself.[32]

In an era and culture imbued with heroic—even chivalric—notions of courage, men sought combat as a test of manhood. Young men and boys enlisted eagerly, anticipating glory. Pain and crippling wounds were rarely a prior consideration. Long casualty lists confirmed a unit with distinction. "Courage had for the Civil War soldiers a narrow, rigid, and powerful meaning: heroic action undertaken without fear."[33] This image confronted its own dark reflection in hospital wards and transports, where men were "unmanned" in despair and insupportable pain. The women who nursed them were raised with an equally insistent vision of man's and woman's behavior which associated weakness only with women and demanded an immovable fortitude in men. For these volunteer nurses, it was not only horrifying to witness strong men reduced in agony, it became a role reversal that challenged their conceptions of gender, faith and cultural values. Katharine Wormeley, feeling the anguish of others engulf her as she went about her duties, wrote wearily to her mother, "I beg you to offer the Prayer for the Sick, and that for the Afflicted, every Sunday in the Chapel." And though scarcely more than a conventionally devout Anglican herself, she asked, "can you not change and add something to them, to fill out and express all that we feel?" As she closed this letter, written in exhaustion during the waking nightmare of Fair Oaks, she added, "Good bye! I hope you may be happy this summer,—it would be something to be able to think of happiness as existing somewhere."[34]

Chapter VI

"LET NO ONE PITY OR PRAISE US"

Against this background of taxing physical drudgery, violence and high emotion, how could the "new life" sought—and apparently found—by these women be defined? It was a life of mixed extremes, of reward and sacrifice, of growth and expenditure. The nurses who served on board the transports discovered profound reserves of strength within themselves as they touched the depths and breadths of human suffering, dealt with the frustrations of plans made and broken, and contended daily with engulfing disorder and chaos.

As weeks passed, they developed a grace under pressure which became their defense against emotional disintegration. They learned the satisfactions of fellowship that arise from shared adversity, and learned to muster humor in the face of horror. Of this humor Wormeley wrote with some surprise, "the moment the pressure is off, we all turn-to to 'be as funny as we can.' I am astonished at the cheerful devotion of the surgeon and medical students. [They] toil all day at the severest work . . . then turn in wherever a mattress is handy . . .

and come out of it full of fun—in which we all join until the next work comes, and we are fresh to work in cheerful concert together. This seems the best way to do the work; nothing morbid comes of it,—which is the danger."[1]

Contrasting with periods of bitter crisis were more routine days which gradually assumed their own patterns and small rituals. As weeks passed, life on board the transports became increasingly catch-as-catch-can for all participants, and the informality of this was fascinating to Katharine. She remembered the core staff, Olmsted's "elect", eating their meals without plates, picnic fashion, dining from a jury-rigged table constructed by the young doctors. "Dinner we serve out ourselves," she wrote, "our dinner table being the top of an old stove, with slices of bread for plates, fingers for knives and forks, and carpet bags for chairs,—all this because everything available is being used for our poor fellows."[2] During one lull between shipments of patients, when a bit more space was available, she reported, "Our dinner-table, the stove, is now being removed, and Dr. Ware is improvising a better, with a plank across the railing of the stairs."[3] Enjoying a rare, and still more lavish version of dining, she described a scene of relative luxury when staff-members were, for the moment, unoccupied with alarms or emergencies:

> Captain Curtis is still on board doing well . . . . Now that our wounded men have gone, we have a dinner-table set, and the Captain lies on his cot on one side of the cabin, laughing at the fun and nonsense which go on at meals. . . . Mrs. Howland has her man-servant, Maurice, (sic) on board. He is capital. He struggles to keep us proper in manners and appearance, and still dreams of *les convenances*. At dinner time he rushes through the various ships and wards: "My ladies, *j'ai un petit plat; je ne vous dirai pas ce que c'est*. I beg of you to be *ponctuelle*; I gif you half-hour's notis." The half-hour having expired, he sets out again on a voyage of entreaty and remonstrance. He won't let us help ourselves, and if we take a seat not close enough to the person above, he says: "No, no, move up; we must have order." His *petit plat* proved to be baked potatoes, which were received with acclamation, while

he stood bowing and smiling with a towel (or it may have been a rag) for a napkin. But I must tell you that Maurice is the tenderest of nurses, and gives every moment he can spare to the sick. He serves his mistress, but he is attentive, and, like a true Frenchman, he so identifies with the moment and its interests that he is, to all hospital intents and purposes, "one of us."[4]

In their new environment the women found, temporarily at least, that class distinctions could be malleable; that the server became the served, and that—in addition to stamina—sensitivity, civility, and compassion were indispensable in the face of crisis. To her mother Katharine Wormeley wrote, "Mrs.—'s mother writes dismal letters, which try her very much,—saying, for instance, that a lady must put away all delicacy and refinement for this work. Nothing could be more false. It is not too much to say that delicacy and refinement and the fact of being a gentlewoman could never *tell* more than they do here."[5] This "delicacy," with its implications of restraint and sensitivity for the needs of others, was the defining quality which these elite women believed gave them special suitability for the work they did. It also justified their presence in a setting where women seldom ventured. Refinement and gentility were, to them, synonymous with orderliness, and their sense of "how things should be done" proved invaluable in an environment of chaos.

Refinement never precluded lively improvisation. In their strange and specialized environment the women soon began to express their changing perspectives in practical and symbolic ways, including their manner of dress. Primarily dictated by the demands of work, the nurses' attire, as it altered, incidentally became a statement of liberation. Limited to two dresses apiece—all that a carpetbag could readily accommodate—their wardrobes became a problem after days and nights of heat, rain, mud and blood. Georgeanna proved especially creative in surmounting this obstacle, as Katharine recounted:

"Georgy,' I said the other day, "what am I to do? I *can't* put on that dress again, and the other one is a great deal worse."

"I know what *I* shall do,' says Georgy, (who is never at a
loss, and suggests the wildest things in the calmest way) 'Dr.
Agnew has some flannel shirts; he is going back to New York,
and can't want them. I shall get him to give me one."

Accordingly Santa Georgeanna has appeared in an easy
and graceful costume. I took the hint, and have followed suit
in a flannel shirt from the hospital stores; and now, having
tasted the sweets of that easy garment, we shall dread civili-
zation if we have to part with our "Agnews."[6]

As the ladies discarded hoops, curls and tightly laced corsets,
some, at least, managed to achieve an astonishing degree of athleticism.
Recalling the stamina with which her cabin-mate faced the desperate
succession of battle trains and their anguished cargoes in the days
after Fair Oaks, Katharine wrote, "Georgy's activity is a never-ending
marvel to me. I saw her today spring from the ground to the floor of a
freight car, with a can of beef tea in one hand, her flask in the other,
and a row of tin cups tied round her waist. Our precious flasks! They
do us good service at every turn. We wear them slung round our shoulders by a bit of ribbon or an end of rope . . ."[7]

Happily for Katharine and the Woolsey sisters, they soon came
to realize that they were especially fortunate in the full support they
enjoyed from families at home. Unlike some of their female colleagues,
their mothers had, after some initial misgivings, become reconciled,
even enthusiastically supportive, of their daughters' great adventure.
Fiercely patriotic themselves, they realized that the transport nurses
were performing a unique and important humanitarian service. Mothers and sisters in both families worked effectively with the WCAR or
aid societies connected with the Sanitary Commission, and their letters indicate that this work had taken over their wartime lives as
surely as it had the nurses'. Perhaps coincidentally, neither family
was headed by a husband or father, and it is possible that the absence
of a patriarchal figure standing by to dictate the women's behavior, or
disparage their seriousness of purpose, may have positively affected
their ability to act independently.

There were, nonetheless, some misgivings, and these seemed to
focus on the nurses' perceived womanly sensitivity and the "harden-

ing" of their sympathies through prolonged medical exposure. Early in the nurses' stay at White House, Georgy and Eliza received a letter from their elder sister, Jane —who would herself soon become a nurse— which expresses these fears: "I envy you from the bottom of my heart," she wrote, "but it is my opinion . . . that you are killing yourselves. It is not only the positive fatigue, but the awful drain on your sympathies, and the excitement, etc.—you will be wrung out and dried— yellow and grey, if you ever get home at all. All your softening of your labors for family consumption does not take us in in the least. However, as I said, I envy you, and I respond to the little song you are no doubt singing out of *Maud*,

> 'What matter if I go mad,
> I shall have had my day.'"[8]

Another letter, this one from their eldest sister, Abby, was addressed to Eliza, but is obviously intended for other ears: "Georgy's letter, we presume, was prepared for home consumption," wrote Abby. "She always tries to 'draw it mild' for our benefit; is always having a lazy, lovely good time, perfectly well and in the best of spirits, and as to the scenes of suffering around her, not caring a bit; has to pinch herself, I dare say, to see that she isn't stone—thinks she 'hasn't any heart,' etc., etc. Tell her of course she hasn't—or won't have soon—it's ossifying, that, or something kindred, is what all surgeons die of— suppressed emotion."[9]

Both letters indicate that there was at least some ambivalence about the transport nurses' work, and more than a little apprehensiveness that the sisters might be losing a requisite womanly softness to their own detriment. But the threat of this loss seems not to have bothered Georgy or Eliza. With confining attire eased, and ladylike sensitivities temporarily submerged, the nurses' definitions of acceptable "feminine" attitudes began to expand correspondingly. Imbued with a new sense of purposeful pragmatism, the women mocked insincerity and affectations of refinement. Georgy noted that her stay in the transports "'toughened' her; no more the genteel lady of culture, she could amuse herself by noting how many euphemisms doctors used to simply enquire if a patient had diarrhea."[10]

Interestingly, this "toughness," or realism, acquired through days and nights in the presence of *real* pain, freed the women from previously-imposed assumptions that wisdom and stoicism were characteristics inherently male. A conditioned respectfulness for the "strong sex" faded as they watched healthy men acquit themselves shamefully, even as they nursed others who bore their sufferings with equanimity. At such times the women's letters assumed a scathing tone as they described pomposity or callousness in men for whom they held little sympathy, and it seemed often to follow that those of elevated status proved the most offensive and were the more bitterly targeted. With scorn, Georgy described a group of visiting politicians and their female companions in silks and perfumes as "Sabbath-breaking picnickers on a battlefield." Katharine was similarly caustic and wrote at some length about the same unwelcome delegation who, as luck would have it, boarded the *Wilson Small* on a sweltering day already made difficult by an earlier influx of unwanted visitors.

"Painfulness was greatly increased by a visit from a Sunday picnic of Congressmen and ladies. One of the former went to Mr. Olmsted and complained to him of [the conditions] he saw on our boat. He said the men were in 'an awful state' —insisting that 'I saw with my own eyes flies settling on them and biting them!' This 'gentleman' came into the ward with a rose held to his nose; and when told they were all typhoid-fever cases ('That one close by you is the worst case I ever saw,' Georgy said maliciously), he went abruptly away. Had he stopped to examine the true condition of things, he would have seen that every man who could not brush the flies away for himself had mosquito netting suspended over him, and all the others had fans. The thermometer is at 90°, and the flies are an Egyptian plague; but all is done that can be done to alleviate it. I could see that this affair pained Mr. Olmsted exceedingly."[11]

Katharine wrote in disgust at the conclusion of this episode, "Colonel B.,—who was on the 'Elm City,' very ill with typhoid fever, was madly anxious to get home. He knew he was near death, and he craved to see his wife. The [congressmen] of the excursion party were asked to take the Colonel back in their boat. They refused; alleging that they were 'a select party,' and 'not prepared to incur infection:' they made the ladies the ground of their excuse. So Mrs. Griffin went at midnight to the ladies and begged them to consent to take him; *and of course they said yes.* I could enlarge on this, but the subject is hateful."[12]

Katharine described yet another group of men that had become especially odious to her, noting that "squads of civilian doctors are here, waiting about for 'surgical cases'. . . dozens of them doing nothing, and their boats doing nothing,—waiting for a battle. They would not look at a sick man; he's not their game! It is *'cases'* they want; and they palm off the sick upon the Commission so that they themselves may, when a battle occurs, get a harvest of wounded."[13]

Acknowledging Katharine's anger and affirming it was Newton Curtis, who quoted a medical friend currently serving at a shore hospital in the same sector: "Don't let more surgeons come here, if you can help it," he wrote. "We try to treat them civilly, but all, ashore or afloat, feel anything but civil to a man who graciously proposes to be entertained because, you understand, he is not one of your 'physicians' but a 'surgeon,' . . . if there is anything the regimental surgeons hate, it is to let these magnanimous surgical pretenders get hold of their own patients."[14] Curtis, in expressing his anger at such crassness, also addressed the universal inclination to assign a higher degree of honor to those who died "gloriously" in battle than to those who lay recuperating in hospital. Recognizing the dignity and contribution of the sick and recovering wounded as equally deserving, he quoted the English cleric Sidney G. Osborn who reflected upon this inequity in 1855 after visiting wounded British soldiers in Nightingale's hospital at Scutari:

> The hospital is only, after all, a part of the battlefield; it is a crowd of those who have fought, and who, fighting, have, through wounds and weakness, had to fall back from active service to passive suffering. They are still, as it were, in the ranks; still on duty to recover, to return, to die, or to be invalided home. If death comes to them on their beds, it is still a soldier's death.[15]

Standing in marked contrast to self-important politicians and medical parasites were the genial officers of the Quartermaster Corps stationed at White House. Exceptionally cordial relations developed early between the Sanitary Commission nurses and these gentlemen. William J. Miller has documented the Herculean task performed by the Quartermasters during the Peninsula Campaign, noting that Brig. Gen. Stewart Van Vliet was chief quartermaster for the Army of the Potomac, traveling with McClellan's headquarters wherever it moved. He listed Lieutenant Colonel Rufus Ingalls as Van Vliet's chief lieutenant, and Capt. Charles Sawtelle as the junior officer who assisted him. Miller noted that all three of these officers were West Point graduates with years of experience in the quartermaster department, and credited their performance with McClellan's advantage wherever that might depend upon superior inventories of equipment, building materials, animal forage, uniforms, food rations, arms, and a myriad other such items. For an army on campaign, the prompt, dependable procurement and movement of these vital supplies were fundamental to success—and in the performance of this duty Van Vliet and his men were highly successful.[16]

The hard-pressed and perpetually gracious quartermasters appear frequently in Katharine's and Georgy's letters, for many of the women's most difficult tasks were made easier through the willing ingenuity of these officers. Sawtelle was credited with the arrangement of the women's "beloved" kitchen/hospital tent near the rail terminus from which they fed and refreshed the thousands sent down from the battlefields of Fair Oaks/Seven Pines. "As for us women," Wormeley wrote during that stressful week, "all we can do is to give drink, stimulants, and food to the poor fellows, and what other little ease we can. We take great comfort in the tent-kitchen provided for us by Captain Sawtelle, from whom we receive much thoughtful, kind attention."[17]

Although the Quartermasters at White House were highly regarded by the nurses as allies in their procurement of supplies for Commission transports, they were, perhaps, even more valued as courteous, supportive friends who, like the young doctors, provided moments of non-serious conversation and good humor in the midst of suffering which cheered the women as much as the bouquets of flowers they frequently brought with them to decorate the *Wilson Small.* General Stewart VanVliet, their senior, was invariably described by Wormeley as "jolly" and "grandfatherly"—a favorite visitor on board the *Small.* But perhaps more importantly, he and his officers were also a source of inside, if not privileged, information from time to time, helping the nurses to more accurately assess what was occurring at the front, or, more entertainingly, what gossip was currently being circulated at headquarters. But like most cherished commodities, such news was not without its price—though happily that price could be a pleasant one to share. In a letter to her sister, Wormeley reported that "Captain Sawtelle sent me a present of mint to-day (his orderly could not restrain a smile as he gave it to me), and the Captain came just now with an eye, I fear, to that improper thing called a 'mint-julep.' You may think it very vulgar, but let me tell you it is very good; and you would think so too if you had been up all night, with the thermometer at 90°." In the midst of exhaustion, the chance to "prophylac" occasionally with mint and a dram of whisky must have presented a welcome variant to more conventional methods of preventive medication.[18]

In mid-June, between the crisis of Fair Oaks and the looming events of the Seven Days Battles, when successive loads of patients had been evacuated and others not yet received, occasional intervals occurred when escape from routine became possible for the Sanitarians. These hours were rare and much cherished. Although Olmsted's core group of nurses never traveled north with patients, thereby removing themselves temporarily from the stresses of the Pamunkey, there *were* infrequent interludes of peace—and, for Eliza, even moments that offered a semblance of romance. On June 12 Katharine wrote, "last evening we made our first pleasure excursion. Mr. Olmsted begged us ('us' always means himself and the staff) to take a run in the 'Wheelbarrow,' 'Wissahickon' or 'Wicked Chicken,' as we indiscriminately call our tug-boat, up the river beyond the burned bridge. We generally have one or two pleasant outsiders not far off. Last night it was Colonel Howland, who had come from the front to spend a short time with his wife. Oh, how we enjoyed our little holiday! It was sweet to run suddenly out of the noisy bustle of the wharves and the camp, out of the breath of hospitals, into the still river, shining with the amber lights of sunset, where nothing broke the silence but the cranes flying—and we. We came home by moonlight, refreshed and happy."[19]

Eliza also remembered the cruise fondly—for it would be the last such happiness the Howlands would share together during their Peninsula sojourn. Writing several days later, she recalled its beginning,"sitting in our parlor-cabin Wednesday, trying to keep cool, when Joe ran up the stairs into the midst of us. Everything was quiet at the front and in the regiment, and General Franklin told him 'he would rather have him come than not.' He and Captain Woolsey Hopkins rode the twenty-five miles down together, over roads more frightful than there ever were near Washington. We took them on board for the night in spite of the new rules excluding outsiders. As there was little to do, we ran up the river in the evening, in the *Wissahickon*, past the broken bridge and Colonel Ingalls' encampment and the lily pads, far up into the moonlight . . ."[20]

Far more typically the women's days were spent in hard work; sad and unremitting labor that developed in them both humility and a justifiable pride in their own emotional survival. Humility, and the beginning of a new self control, had come early for Katharine, during her very first week in service. "Dr. Grymes taught me a valuable lesson the night I was at Yorktown on the 'Webster,'" she remembered. "A man with a ghastly wound—the first I ever saw—asked for something and I turned hastily to get it, with some sort of exclamation. Dr. Grymes stopped me and said: 'Never do that again; never be hurried or excited, or you are not fit to be here.' I've thanked him ever since."[21] As she became more confident, Wormeley expressed satisfaction at being able to master her emotions successfully, and in a moment of exhaustion suggested her own formula for sustained endurance. "Do all you can, and be a machine, —that's the way to act; the only way."[22]

Yet the nurses' efforts to subdue their emotions while preserving "womanly" sympathy could produce conflicting responses —both in themselves and in others. As they sought to be "like men" in their fortitude and endurance, they also perceived their greatest productiveness, strength and resourcefulness as arising from their identity as women. Nina Bennett Smith has noted that, "all the nurses took the path of proving themselves by deed rather than words, but they would have been startled to find their abilities and accomplishments belittled—celebrated for being, in effect, timid and unaggressive."[23] Most men, whether doctors or patients, chose to regard them as "essentially passive," self-effacing and submissive, surmounting their natural delicacy in a supreme act of self-sacrifice *in spite of* their femininity. "Men had their own concept of the role of a nurse as an extension of womanly duties; they saw it not as an expression of women's power, but as a confirmation of woman's special weakness."[24]

In the memoirs of soldiers, nurses were seldom remembered as efficient, assertive or independent. Instead they were more typically imagined as "gentle denizens of another world who had conquered 'the rebellious delicacy of their own more exquisite senses' in the pursuit of self-sacrifice, the duty appropriate to their passive natures."[25] This view seems borne out in a sentimental poem, written by a lieutenant of the Sixteenth in honor of Eliza, his colonel's wife, who nursed him for several weeks on board the transports. The verses he composed expressed reverence for her "other-worldliness" perhaps more than they did gratitude for her efficient care, and he chose to employ such terms as "Christlike," "blessed," "gentle," and "sweet saint" to describe a creature quite unlike the mortal, self-driven nurse who cared for him.

In fact, Eliza Howland *did* present an interesting combination of contemporary female virtues which were, perhaps, both more and less "typical" than those of her comrades. She had been made an object of worshipful respect—even adoration—from the very earliest days of the regiment's existence: presenting its ceremonial Colors; supplying cool straw hats to protect its members from the Pamunkey heat; arranging for fruit, eggs, vegetables and chickens to be sent down to them from Tioronda. She possessed the gentle Victorian mystique of "wife" and sacred domesticity—yet now she came to warriors in the midst of war, forcefully and independently, with them, yet elevated from them by her now-professional status; ministering to her husband and his men under horrific circumstances which were far from "other-worldly." Eliza had become a cherished figurehead, a talisman for these soldiers—but although she may indeed have personified all the symbolic and ephemeral qualities attributed to her by them, it is unlikely that she imagined herself a sanctified being—or that she considered veneration a useful incentive as she summoned strength and calm to go about her job in a stressful environment.

Such conflicting perceptions of the nurse's role often *did* affect the women, and despite their resolve to remain emotionally uninvolved, such conflict created a certain ambivalence in the way they saw themselves and their work. Women, like the men they cared for, saw nursing as an extension of their womanhood, although, unlike their charges, they preferred to recognize it as an affirmation of their strength. As they made their rounds, comforting, bathing, feeding, often staying at a soldier's bedside late into the night, inevitably the nurses came to be romanticized by weakened men. And although their patients expressions of adoration generally elicited rueful embarrassment, they also subtly undermined the women's self-imposed determination to rise above sentimentality. As Wormeley commented, "Somebody said the other day, (*à propos* of what, I forget), that he wished to kiss the hem of my garment. I thought of the condition of that article, and shuddered. From chin to belt [our dresses] are yellow with lemon-juice, sticky with sugar, greasy with beef tea, and pasted with milk porridge. Further down I dare not inquire into them."[26] Yet although her wry humor *seemed* to reject valorization, she clearly felt some justifiable pride, and was careful to repeat the story in just this way and to include it in her published letters.

The sentimental poem which celebrated Eliza, ("To one borne from the sullen battle's roar, / Dearer the greeting of thy gentle eyes, / When he aweary, torn and bleeding lies, / Than all the glory of the victor's prize," etc.) was also received with mixed emotions by its subject.[27] Though Howland herself professed "much entertainment" at the adoration she received from the men of the Sixteenth, and apparently discounted these particular verses as the outpouring of an invalid emotionally diminished by suffering, she, like Wormeley, did not fail to include the poem in the collection of family letters which

"Our Heroines"

This fanciful contemporary illustration, essentially an allegory, presents a popular conception of Sanitary Commission women as romanticized beings. Transport nurses deplored such imagery, often finding it difficult to separate the reality of their serious work from widely-accepted notions of themselves as saints in immaculate ruffled aprons.

The drawing includes a number of interesting inaccuracies, among them a representation of nuns serving in Commission settings, and the presence of Sanitarian nurses as ministering angels on the battlefield. Although Roman Catholic Sisters of Charity often worked productively and cooperatively with Sanitarians, they were not part of the Commission network; and it was the intrepid Clara Barton who went directly onto the field of battle to remove wounded men, preferring to avoid Sanitary Commission protocol to work independently with her own staff and resources.

Small lozenges at the bottom left and right show women preparing supplies for the WCAR in their homes, and affluent families attending a large "Sanitary Fair" where their purchases of donated gifts raised funds to support the work of the Sanitary Commission.

were privately published and given as presents to friends, relatives, and at least one historian. These seemingly contradictory images—and the women's ambivalent reactions to them—suggest that on board the transports the stern Sanitarian ethic of unsentimental benevolence was tempered by very human circumstance. Here, the determination to become a "machine" merged with, and remained somehow compatible with sentiment.

When viewed from a broader cultural perspective this is not surprising. These nurses lived in an era of heroic journalism, sentimental fiction and romantic illustration. While they strived constantly to maintain humor and a measure of detachment, they nonetheless would have found it difficult to escape the idealized expectations of their time. Conflicting perceptions of who and what a nurse was expected to be, how she conducted herself, and how her duties conformed to, or conflicted with, prevailing concepts of femininity, created puzzling ambiguities. Florence Nightingale herself stressed the interconnection of ideal nursing behavior with stereotypical feminine qualities: innate tenderness, morality and sacrifice. In a wry parody of Longfellow's "lady with a lamp," Wormeley attempted to capture the ambivalence of the volunteer nurse by stripping away sentimental illusions about the nursing life.

> A lady with a flask shall stand,
> Beef-tea and punch in either hand,—
> Heroic mass of mud
> And dirt and stains and blood![22]

Why *did* the elite women who worked as nurses in the Peninsula campaign choose this life? Given the more comfortable alternatives of wartime service on the home-front, what exactly were the compelling inner fires which led them to endure the emotional discipline and physical demands of the transport service above equally valued, yet less harrowing areas of benevolence?

Certainly most Northern women who went to the war longed to equal the dedication of their men and shared with them an abiding loyalty to the Union and reverence to the symbolism of their country's flag. These sentiments they shared with their Confederate counterparts. Women on both sides of the conflict were convinced that their cause represented the right, and that their men fought to preserve fundamental freedoms delineated by the Founding Fathers. Through their work they also discovered, often for the first time, how to "make active patriotism their own." Jane Woolsey, an elder sister of Georgeanna and Eliza, expressed a wholly new sense of patriotic appropriation as she wrote "it seems that we were never alive till now; never a country till now." As Nina Bennett Smith has noted, "the war introduced nationalism to American women, because in a total war the contributions which only women could offer, at home and on the battlefield, were sorely needed for victory."[29]

For many Northern women there were also deeply-felt convictions arising from religious belief and from the anti-slavery movement. Like the soldiers they cared for, female Sanitarians had absorbed, to whatever extent, the Christian fervor of the Second Great Awakening and the pervasive spirit of revivalism which accompanied it. Historian James McPherson has remarked that "the men in Civil War armies were, arguably, the most religious in American history."[30] This would likely have applied equally to the women who nursed them on the scene and supported them on the home-front. Abby Woolsey, who served throughout the war with the WCAR, was both strongly religious *and* a passionate abolitionist who frequently expressed her family's sentiments on the subject of slavery. In 1862, in a letter to her sisters on board the transports, she linked national apathy on the question of emancipation with Divine retribution. "*God's curse,* and not his blessing, is evidently on the whole country now," she wrote, "and will be while such burning sins as the Fugitive Slave Law are perpetrated on the very Capitol steps at Washington. . . . Mobs in Baltimore, panic everywhere, and we are just where we were more than a year ago . . ."[31]

These convictions might motivate women raised in the fiercely anti-slavery home environment of the Woolseys, yet not all of their colleagues shared such sentiments. Katharine Wormeley, the descendent of Virginia Randolphs who had owned slaves since the early years of the colony, "hated abolitionists and blamed extremists both in the South and New England for the Civil War."[32] Yet she expressed the feelings of many women when she described a strong attraction to nursing for its own sake and pleasure in the self-affirming rewards it brought to her as an individual. Early in her tour of duty, in a reassuring letter to her family, she wrote, "don't fret if you do not hear from me. . . you may not hear for a week. Let no one pity or praise us. I admit to painfulness; but no one can tell how sweet it is to be the drop of comfort to so much agony." Some weeks later she wrote in the same vein, "we all know in our hearts that it is thorough enjoyment to be here,—*it is life,* in short; and we wouldn't be anywhere else for anything in the world."[33]

And there was a further incentive which drove some women to volunteer, although they might not have cited it honestly if asked their motivation: they served simply to escape. These women were typically beyond the first blush of youth and unmarried—considered "spinsters" with no foreseeable prospects of matrimony. Living in a society which dictated marriage as woman's only appropriate goal, a sense of their own uselessness could well become overwhelming for women in such circumstances. Often their only outlets, if such they could be called, were the care of aged relatives or the questionable joys of minding a brother's or sister's children in return for room and board. Victorians were seldom as emotionally supportive of unmarried women as they might have been, and spinster aunts or sisters were often viewed as misfits; their lives barren and filled with ennui.

One spirited woman who found herself in this situation was Louisa May Alcott who, like the lady Sanitarians, volunteered to go to war as a nurse. Her journal for November 1862 begins with these words:

> Thirty years old. Decided to go to Washington as a nurse
> if I could find a place. I love nursing, and must let out my
> pent-up energy in some way . . . . I want new experiences, and

am sure to get 'em if I go. So I've sent in my name, and bide
my time writing tales, and mending up my old clothes,—for
nurses don't need nice things, thank Heaven![34]

It would seem that, like Alcott, some volunteer nurses were
frankly attracted to action and adventure, and for those who aspired
to the transport service, these predilections suited them especially
well. Georgeanna Woolsey loved the freedoms —as well as the obligations—that this new life provided and commented that "I shall never
be able to settle down into the conventionalities of society after the
wandering life I have led for these years. Once a vagabond always a
vagabond; I shall marry an army surgeon and go out to the frontier!"[35]
In an age when to be an "adventuress" implied doubtful connotations,
these women managed to combine high adventure with virtuous duty,
thereby reconciling what many conservatives might have seen as unbecoming boldness with an appearance of feminine passivity. In the
transport service women like Woolsey satisfied, even celebrated, a
craving for action with perfect propriety.

Interestingly, however, the candor with which Georgeanna expressed such longing in 1862 is tempered in her later writing, as it is
in Katharine's, suggesting once again how vulnerable women were to
cultural expectations of how they *should* feel. A comparison of letters
and journals with their more formal expressions—published or unpublished—often discloses a tension between actual memory and in-
terpretation.[36] In the complex interplay of ideology, reality and idealism, it was difficult to leave an unvarnished picture of the writer, her
motivations, or her lived experience. Unlike the published wartime
memoirs of Louisa May Alcott, in which the author candidly acknowledged her longing to "do something" for the war effort which involved
an element of adventure, many such women's later testimonies tended
to conceal motivations which might be perceived as self-serving.[37] Years
after the war, Georgeanna Woolsey sought to present her experience
in a light which emphasized sacrifice, loyalty and patriotism rather
than self-fulfilling exhilaration. Although such *post facto* emotions were
undoubtedly heartfelt, still they seem oddly conventional when com-
pared with earlier expressions of her determination to be in the fight

for its own sake. In an 1893 preface to the Woolsey sisters' collected letters, Georgeanna reminded her nieces and nephews that "your own land is made sacred by the death of half a million steadfast men, and by the thought of thousands and thousands of heartbroken women at home, who quietly acquiesced in this great sacrifice out of love and loyalty to their country's flag."[38]

It is relevant to note that such acquiescence, along with piety, purity and domesticity, was praised as one of the cardinal virtues of the nineteenth-century feminine composite idealized in the "Cult of True Womanhood"—a celebration of men's and women's "separate spheres" which defined each gender's occupations and specific roles. The "cult" itself was an ideological construct which flourished in America and Britain during the 1830s through 1860s, and it became the rule against which society measured feminine behavior—at least for the middle and upper classes. Cult lore envisioned man as the active, material provider, husband and patriarch, dominant in the public sphere of business, politics—and war. At the same time it enshrined woman, the gentle occupant of home and hearth, whose passive mission lay in the moral and physical well-being of her husband and children. It also urged discreet submissiveness as an essential feminine trait, seeing independence and adventurousness as unbecoming.

In these terms it would seem difficult to reconcile a love of adventure with feminine irreproachability unless adventurousness were presented as *acquiescence to duty.* And it is interesting to realize that both Wormeley and the Woolseys ultimately did present their Peninsula experience in just that way for posterity. Yet in their spontaneously written letters from the transports the women revealed undisguised enthusiasm for *work as work,* and joy in the autonomy it brought to them. While they welcomed the opportunity to serve their country, they also knew delight in the active life for its own sake, suggesting that they were *not* simply acquiescing to a perceived moral duty but realizing, instead, a personal ambition as its own reward.

Also motivating these elite nurses was a shared sense of purpose and *esprit de corps*, a conviction that they, because of their privileged background, superior education and organizational skills, were literally born to do this work. Wormeley and the Woolseys valued their administrative abilities highly, and acknowledged them as priceless assets. For women like this there was a powerful temptation to participate in what feminist scholar Kristie Ross has termed a "politically momentous event." Convinced that a "gentlewoman's special abilities" shone forth in the stressful setting of the transports, the nurses also believed themselves the *"moral superiors* of men, not their equals."[39]

The female Sanitarians went to war, in part, because they *knew* their contributions were sorely needed. They went, Nina Bennett Smith wrote, "to provide men with those things that only women could provide: understanding and housework. . . *but only ladies*, as opposed to both men and lower class women, had mastered the principles of cleanliness and order and possessed the inner strength to endure privation and danger and remain uncorrupted." Their aptitude was, therefore, determined by both womanhood and class; their elite background guaranteed them the requirements of courage and delicacy. Smith remarked of women like Wormeley that "they believed their sex, class and culture combined to make them a sort of moral aristocracy, the arbiters of health of the Republic in both mind and body."[40] In this they reinforced notions of a "Sanitary Elite" and gave notice that class identity could instill that unique self-control and grace in adversity which proved so remarkable.

In the month of June, 1862, on the Peninsula, the "passionate efficiency" of these displaced aristocrats was at last effecting change. Through the combined efforts of transport personnel and enlightened military doctors on shore who shared their views, the Sanitarians' influence began now to assume tangible form. Friction between shore and transports eased, and gradually the Commission's goal of teaching the military how to care for its own suddenly seemed closer at hand. Wormeley wrote with some excitement that "the Great Mogul, the Medical Inspector, Col. Vollum has arrived. He is staying on board the 'Small.' He ranks every other medical officer; therefore on him our hopes [for a more comprehensive system of patient-handling] depend. A run to Yorktown on 'special business' was made to give the Chief and the Inspector a chance of quietly discussing the whole matter. Mr. Olmsted has just come, full of brightness, to tell me that everything is arranged satisfactorily, and to read me the signed agreement."[41]

This document, so painfully slow in coming, included several key provisions crucial to the Sanitarians: All badly wounded men, all amputations and compound fractures of the lower extremities, and all other cases that should not be transported would now remain on Sanitary Commission transports in the river until they could be moved. The government would now agree to spend a sum not exceeding ten thousand dollars to accomplish this. It would also agree to receive and accommodate three thousand wounded men at its hospital at Fort Monroe *whenever* a battle occurred, and in addition to receive and transport forty-five hundred men to the North within twelve days of any such battle. The government would assume the costs of these operations also. "Thus, you see, the Commission gains the certainty that the worst cases and the greatest suffering shall be under its own eye and care," wrote Wormeley. "The rest—the slightly wounded, or those so wounded as to be able to help themselves—are the ones that are left to the Government." This agreement, co-signed by Olmsted and Col. Vollum, was received with elation by the Sanitarians. It defined the Commission's area of authority, and, as it affected relations between the army and the Commission, was a considerable step toward *deténte*.[42]

But the Peninsula was not the only venue which now saw progress for the Sanitarians' reforms. Elsewhere throughout the North the Commission's innovations became increasingly successful. Through political perseverance a new Surgeon General was appointed and a new Medical Director would soon be named. The goal of "returning soldiers as fighters" was being fulfilled, and the objective of reinvigorating an ideology of conservative American institutionalism, although not overtly emphasized, nonetheless remained constant. Bellows, Strong and others of the Executive Board still held the vision which had animated them from the first. But for Olmsted, new imperatives and new orientations had become a daily reality which, in a sense, distanced him from his associates in Washington. Through his service on the Peninsula he seemed to resolve for himself a tension between cool efficiency and hands-on humanitarianism. Yet despite this subtle and very personal transition, the dominant ideology of the Commission remained the same. Olmsted was, from first to last, an autocrat who upheld its rigid proscriptives, and the women's letters suggest that their leader's strict adherence to form may have become rather too onerous for them as their service lengthened.[43]

In early June, becoming impatient at Olmsted's unremitting control, Wormeley revealed an unexpected area of friction, noting that "a new Surgeon-in-charge has been appointed to the Shore hospital . . . [who] seems a kind man [and] is very cordial to us women. I often feel the pleasantness of our footing among all these persons,—official, military, naval, and medical. They clearly respect our work, and rightly appreciate it. Mr. Olmsted, however, frowns upon the idea [that we might work together] and remains impenetrably silent,—which is worse, because we can't rebel at it."[44]

Katharine had singled out an aspect of the women's experience that would distress and frustrate them as time went on. The Sanitary Commission's rules, designed to govern the professional behavior of its female personnel, denied them freedom to participate in other nursing activities, no matter how pressing the need. Olmsted, in his position as chief of the mission, was opposed to any infringement of these rules, and he alone retained control as long as the group remained intact. In all fairness, his prohibitions *did* serve a useful purpose, for, as previously noted, the experience of Sanitary Commission nurses placed in army settings had not always been a pleasant one. "Ladies" by birth, and "professionals" by training, many nurses had been subjected to demeaning indignities when first assigned to military hospitals. Scorned, and to an extent feared by army doctors, they were set to the most menial tasks and treated with disrespect. Nina Bennett Smith cited one army surgeon who, when reminded that his nurses were ladies, reacted with anger—and in so doing defined the unpleasant dilemma faced by many elite nurses. "'Ladies!' he sneered, 'we have no ladies here! A hospital is no place for a lady. We have some women here who are cooks.'"[45]

Such attitudes cooled the initial enthusiasm of the Sanitary Commission and had, by 1862, prompted it to discontinue its training of nurses for general military use. In April, when the first nurses arrived on the Peninsula, *only* Commission facilities were staffed by Commission-trained women, and, in theory, these nurses were exposed only to Commission doctors and support personnel. But although this dictum sought to protect the ladies from unpleasant situations, in practice it proved severely limiting to their nursing role as they perceived it. Katharine and Georgeanna cited instances where their services might well have been more efficiently utilized, for there were occasional periods on board the transports, between shipments of patients or demanding crises, when the women actually had to find ways to keep themselves busy, and might more usefully have been employed on shore. Not surprisingly they viewed this as wasteful, and, as their confidence increased, saw their prized identity as nurses betrayed when denied the freedom to volunteer *when* and *where* they saw the need. Olmsted's authoritarian behavior, even though well-intentioned, was a problem which would return to plague them.

Chapter VII

DEPARTURES

In the two weeks following the bloody and inconclusive battle at Fair Oaks, both armies lay, for the most part, quietly recuperating. Robert E. Lee replaced the disabled Joseph E. Johnston as commander of Confederate forces, and McClellan, wracked by indecision, and awaiting reinforcement from McDowell—which did not come—chafed at White House. Persistent spring rains had elevated the Chickahominy to its highest level in decades, rendering any concerted Union advance impossible. For the Army of the Potomac it was a time of waiting. But for Lee, such a passive hiatus would not do.

With characteristic inventiveness he broke the stalemate, grasped the moment as his own, and ordered a series of bold assault and reconnaissance raids by Brig. Gen. J. E. B. Stuart, one of his most able lieutenants. Between June 12 and 15 Stuart's hard-riding cavalrymen, with lightning speed and the element of surprise, completed a circuit of McClellan's army, attacking points along the Union line and disclosing valuable intelligence of Northern positions and conditions of readiness. Thus fore-armed, Lee took the initiative even as McClellan hesitated.

On June 13, as Stuart's riders swept across the countryside east of Richmond, burning supply depots and penetrating Union installations, their route brought them along the Richmond & York River railroad within striking distance of White House. This incursion, so close to transport patients and personnel, caused some considerable alarm and confusion—throughout which the women apparently remained calm. As Eliza described the episode,

> It was Friday night our stampede happened. We were all quietly at work in our tent on shore . . . preparing for the night when a soldier came by with the news that the train had been fired upon by rebel cavalry near Tunstall's Station, three and a half miles from White House. One man was killed, and six or eight wounded, but the train pushed on and gave the alarm. We felt no fear whatever for ourselves, but I was very anxious to hear of Joe's safe arrival in camp [following the overnight visit of June 11]. A peremptory order came from Quartermaster-General Ingalls to Mr. Olmsted: "Put your women behind the iron walls of the *Spaulding*, and drop down below the gunboats." So we reluctantly hurried on board the "Small" with all the staff. . . and skedaddled ignominiously. Two hundred wagons were burnt, forage destroyed, several teamsters killed . . .[1]

During this brief crisis, as wounded men were lifted from damaged railroad cars and doctors hurried to treat them, the women remained at work in their hospital-kitchen until ordered to leave—which they did at last, though only under some duress, "moving as slowly as possible and asking questions as we went along."[2] Wormeley regarded Ingall's directive—however well intended—and Olmsted's summary order sending the women back to the transport as demeaning affronts. She recalled that, "Georgy and I were highly indignant at being sent away; we thought it shirking our duty, and very inglorious." Irked by the submission being forced upon them, and still smarting from other restrictions recently endured, they reacted with predictable resentment. "At last our tongues got loose," wrote Katharine. "We said all we thought,—or at least I did. I said more than I *thought* because I was in a passion; and all I got for it was the sense of having hurt and wounded Mr. Olmsted." The accumulated stress of long hours and imposed silence had erupted in a torrent of frustration.

The Chief himself was seemingly unmoved as he deposited the women on board the *Wilson Small*, offering no words in the face of their outburst and rowing back to the shore alone, leaving Katharine to suffer pangs of guilt at having "injured" her friend and superior. "Though I dare say I can tell it now as a joke," she wrote later, "there's a dark, private aspect to it [which] is like playing with something that has not yet lost its sting."[3] It was a disturbing and revealing incident—and an indication of fundamental change for these obedient women who had come to think of themselves as equal participants in any crisis situation. For Katharine, the momentary flash of emotion was especially devastating, for she cherished Olmsted's good opinion above all things, regarding him as always with near-idolatry. Essayist Kristie Ross, writing of women in the transport service, noted this *contretemps* and remarked that Katharine "paid for her independence and ambition with feelings of shame that reminded her of her place and protected Olmsted from ever seriously considering her complaint."[4] This refusal to regard seriously the grievances of women was—and is—an effective tactic of male control which Olmsted did not hesitate to use here, despite his professed high regard for his female colleagues. In these moments something of their prized equality was snatched away, if only temporarily.

But more serious than the women's bruised sensibilities were the general malaise and growing realization of vulnerability which followed in the wake of Stuart's raid at White House. Patients on board the transports, no longer safe, now felt genuine fear; and although the nurses did all they could to calm them, Katharine noted at the close of that night that not until dawn "were the [wounded] all on board and comfortable . . .They are very sick; perhaps the worst set together I ever saw; scarcely any in their right minds, some are raving . . .They have been much shaken by the attack, which has, I think, aggravated their condition." Next morning she wrote of the harm that had been done and of the women's own fears during the night. "Our hearts beat for the railroad bridges (two distinct fires could be seen), and for a time we felt gloomy. It would have been a serious business to cut off even one day's supply to the army; it would have played into the enemy's hands—perhaps by forcing on a general engagement. Captain Sawtelle was arming every man—teamsters, etc.—and was preparing to burn everything, shipping and all, if necessary. . . . A battery of artillery was hastily got together of guns that had arrived the night before . . . and we learn now that the Bucktail Rifles, Colonel Biddle's regiment, has returned to guard the railroad bridges."[5]

Stuart's attack became a turning point in the fortunes of all those stationed at White House, and although the episode was not immediately followed by a second incursion, as feared, it was a portent none could ignore. On June 20, in a letter to her mother, Katharine shared a general sense of foreboding. "Orders have come to send the "Webster" and the "Spaulding" to Fortress Monroe immediately, and empty the hospitals there as fast as possible," she wrote. "We feel that something is impending; the clearing out of the hospitals, the arrangements thus decisively made for the wounded, all seem to point to a coming emergency. Oh! can we help dreading it?"[6]

The fears she expressed were well founded and soon confirmed. Within a week the Union position at White House was seriously threatened as Stonewall Jackson made haste from the Shenandoah and Lee's army prepared to engage McClellan on his front near Mechanicsville. On June 23, as the Seven Days battles lay just ahead, Katharine wrote of a visit paid the Sanitarians on board the *Small* by General Van Vliet, in command of the army quartermaster unit at White House. Describing him as a "jolly old gentleman, with his shock of yellow-white hair and his nice, old-fashioned *politesse* for 'the ladies,'" Wormeley reported that Van Vliet had dined at Fitz John Porter's headquarters "with some of the corps commanders yesterday, and [told us] it was 'generally agreed that Porter's position is no longer tenable and that our line is far too long." As always, such tactical details held

great fascination for Katharine's orderly mind, and she repeated the
general's conversation to her mother in precise detail:

> ". . .What [Lee] will do is try to turn our flank," Gen. Van
> Vliet said. "Perhaps he'll do it; perhaps not."
> "And what of us?" we cried.
> "'Oh you!" he said, with his jolly laugh, "*you'll* have to
> cut and run as best you can, and *we'll* go into Richmond!"
> "How are you going to get into Richmond—has Burnside
> got Fort Darling?"
> —But here the General looked impenetrable, and so
> profoundly wise that if he did not tell his secret, he at least
> told he had one.[7]

This news, though delivered with Van Vliet's customary good
humor, was hardly reassuring to the women. Especially disturbing
for Eliza was word just received that Joe was seriously ill with malarial fever even as the regiment prepared for action at the threatened sector near Mechanicsville. "I have put up a basket of stores for
him," she noted in her journal, " —bedsack, pillows, sheets, arrow-
root, etc., etc., to go with an orderly. Charley [has] telegraphed Generals Slocum and Franklin to know the truth, while Mr. Olmsted has
arranged with Captain Sawtelle for a pass to take me to Joe tomorrow morning. . . . General Van Vliet says that if I want to go to the
front at any time he will have his wagon meet me and take me to J.'s
camp."[8] But, eager as Eliza was to visit Joe and care for him herself, in
the end she did not make the trip. Perhaps her friends persuaded her
against it; perhaps she felt she was needed more where she was. In
any case she did not go—and this was fortunate. Had she accepted
Van Vliet's offer, she would have placed herself in a very dangerous
predicament. Next day Joe's position became a Confederate target,
and within two days—as Jackson arrived full force with his troops
from the Shenandoah—the first of the Seven Days Battles exploded
across the very terrain that Eliza would have traveled in the quartermasters' wagon.

Beginning on June 26, fierce confrontations followed one another,
spreading the opposing forces across a semicircular swathe of coun-

tryside east of Richmond in destructive engagements that erupted and subsided, one succeeding another, in a near-continuous conflagration in which each battle yet managed to retain its own devastating identity. Elements of the armies clashed at Beaver Dam Creek, Gaines' Mill, Savage's Station, Glendale and finally at Malvern Hill. McClellan, as he realized his command base at White House was rapidly becoming indefensible, ordered his army southward across the Chickahominy swamps, fighting as it fell back towards Harrison's Landing on the James. This overland retreat left the former base only minimally defended, and precipitated a corresponding removal of all Union vessels down the Pamunkey and York rivers, a monumental undertaking beset with problems of its own.

This emergency evacuation by river from White House —the "Skedaddle of the Pamunkey"—was an extraordinary maneuver virtually without precedent. Hastily organized under pressure, largely confused, with the spectre of Stonewall Jackson's advancing Confederates always at its back. Coordinated as much as possible by the Union army, who burned and slashed as they departed, the exodus itself was largely non-military. It included a widely assorted company of civilians, suttlers, fleeing slaves, medical personnel, and, inevitably, a multitude of casualties who traveled by river transport if possible or, if less fortunate, were painfully jostled across the Peninsula by ambulance. For the Sanitary Commission nurses this was an emotionally wrenching departure as well as a daunting logistical problem, for although they knew their destination lay somewhere on the James River, they had been officially advised of nothing else.

But, as so often during these weeks, the women's friends at the Quartermaster Department found time to ease their anxieties, at least to the extent of sorting through the masses of misinformation that inevitably circulated about White House as the evacuation became a certainty. Katharine trusted these officers to relay what little valid news they were free to share, and as preparations intensified she reassured her mother (and perhaps herself) that, "the truth is, this has been preparing for days. Captain Sawtelle told us this morning that seven hundred thousand rations and a large amount of forage were sent up the James River a week ago. This is doubtless a masterly strategic movement of MacClellan's, compelled by the want of reinforcements. As for what is going on in the army today . . . the wildest and most contradictory rumors are afloat. We lie at the wharf, and all about us are people eager to tell absurd and exaggerated stories. Yesterday there was an impression that Stonewall Jackson was coming down upon us to destroy this depot . . . I make it a rule to believe nothing that I do not pick up from Captain Sawtelle."[9]

But whether long planned or quickly thrown together, the evacuation became an overnight reality which all three women somehow found time to record in their letters and journals. On the day the transports' completed their final preparations, Katharine paused long enough to evoke a sense of loss and of events spiraling to climax as she looked out across the familiar landscape, now suddenly made barren: "All the trees have been cut down and toppled in the river," she wrote. "The gunboats are drawn up ready for action, with their guns pointed to sweep the plain laid bare by the felling of the trees. Every tent . . . is down. . . all articles of value, commissary stores, medical stores, etc., are on transports and barges and on their way down the river. . . . We saw our dear tent dismantled before our eyes, all its contents going on board the 'Elizabeth,'—Dr. Ware rescuing for me, at the last moment, my invaluable Lund's patent corkscrew. . . . On the 'Elm City' we are waiting and have had our steam up all day, ready to be off at a moment's notice; [now] *even as I write* comes the order to start."[10]

As they moved out into the stream, Katharine, still writing, reported that, "all our army is now across the Chickahominy: General Porter crossed at four this morning; only General Stoneman and the cavalry are on this side. The enemy are in force three miles from us; they have seized the railroad and cut the telegraph. The order which finally moved us was a message from General Stoneman to General Casey, which came by mounted messenger. It said, 'I hold the enemy in check at Tunstall's, and shall for a short time. Then I shall retreat by White House.' We privately hope to get a glimpse of them as we go down the river," she continued. "It would be something to say that we had seen the Confederate Army of Richmond."[11] Instead she described a "jolly panic" as shore people, contrabands, suttlers and an assortment of army hangers-on swarmed aboard any barge that could hold them, wading into the river and scrambling up the boats' sides. Georgy also recorded this colorful exodus:

> The most interesting thing was the spontaneous movement of the slaves. When it was known that the Yankees were running away, they came flocking from all the country about, bringing their little movables, frying pans, old hats, and bundles, to the river side. There was no sign of anxiety or confusion among them, and fortunately there was plenty of room . . . One of the forage boats we passed seemed filled with women only, in their gayest dresses and brightest turbans, like a whole load of tulips at a horticultural show. The black smoke rose from the burning stores on shore (fired to keep them from the enemy), and now and then the roar of battle came to us, but the slave women were quietly nursing their children, and singing hymns. The day of their deliverance had come, and they accepted this most wonderful change with absolute placidity.[12]

"The last I saw of the White House," wrote Katharine, "General Casey was sitting on the piazza, and the signal-men on the roof were waving their pretty signals, which were being answered by the gunboats. Then the great gun of the "Sebago" boomed out, and we all slipped our moorings. The gunboats were in line of battle; we passed between them and the shore; the men were beat to quarters, and standing at their guns—the great ferocious guns!" As the transport drew away from shore she remembered that "we saw clouds of dust, and General Stoneman's baggage-train came trotting in; and at the same moment a corral of invalid horses and mules kept here by the quartermasters' department, seven hundred of them, were let loose and driven towards Cumberland."[13]

Whether the evacuation was, indeed, a "masterly stroke" on McClellan's part or not, to *believe* that it was apparently eased Katharine's mind. As the exodus continued she wrote, " [We] go down the river to clear the way, order the transports and barges quietly down, and prevent confusion. All the steamers tow the sailing vessels. Imagine a fleet of several hundred vessels streaming down the shining river. The Pamunkey twists and turns so much that after passing the "Webster" on her voyage down, we meet her again, half an hour later, with only a narrow belt of trees between us."[14]

Eliza's journal recalled the same procession of vessels as somewhat less orderly: "Running away again down the Pamunkey as fast as we can go, escaping from Stonewall Jackson! All night the wood choppers were at work cutting down the woods at White House to give the gunboats a chance to command the land beyond, and just now as we passed the banks were shorn and the pretty little place laid bare. Our pickets had been driven in, and Jackson was supposed to be close at hand. Eighty wounded were brought down last night and put on board the *Knickerbocker*. Twelve more and a few sick came down this morning. . . .The rumor to-day is that all communications with the front are to be stopped, to conceal an advance of our army."[15]

But even as she wrote, at the moment of departure, the evacuation was made suddenly more devastating for Eliza. Just as the *Elm City* cast off her mooring and steamed into the channel, word was received by telegraph from McClellan's headquarters advising her that Joseph had been wounded—yet with no details of his condition. Frantic for more news, Eliza remembered her desperation as the vessel steamed slowly south, recalling that "we went as far as West Point, followed by a train of schooners and barges running away like ourselves. There we lay through the evening and night, watching for the flames of burning stores at White House which did not burn, and for booming of guns that did not boom—without news or orders until after dinner, when we ran up the river again in search of both. Near Cumberland we met the *Arrowsmith* with Surgeon Vollum on board, who hailed us and told us all we yet know of yesterday's action at the front."[16]

That action was, in fact, the battle of Gaines' Mill where, in the afternoon, Joe was wounded while leading his men as they assaulted, recaptured and later defended two critically placed Union batteries against a Confederate force under General D. H. Hill. The telegram with news of Joe's fate told merely of a "slight flesh wound," and, as it

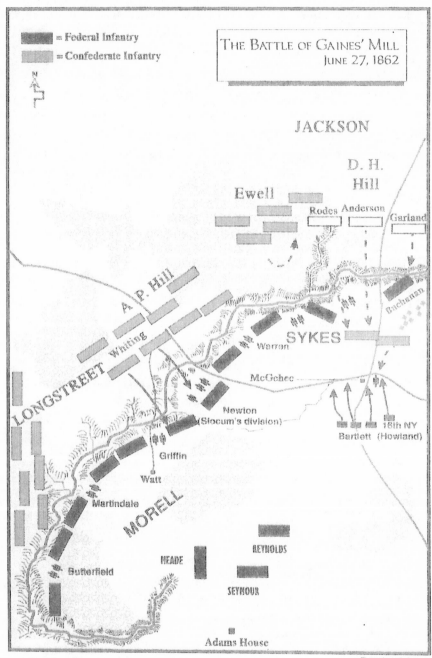

Theodore P. Savas

had been delivered just as communications from the front were cut off, no more details could be forthcoming. Describing the urgency of the moment, as well as her own alarm, Georgy wrote later, "the rebels were upon us. Stoneman sent down word that they were in sight. We went off into the dark, taking what comfort we could in that one word, "slight."[17]

Gaines' Mill, day three of the Seven Days' Battles before Richmond, was a bitter engagement and a defeat for McClellan. Beginning at 1:00 o'clock, it raged across farmland and surrounding forest through the early evening; and for Joe Howland, the high water mark occurred at mid afternoon. It was then that Fitz John Porter's division, heavily pressed and suffering severe losses, was seen to require immediate support—and to provide this, and stem the tide of D. H. Hill's advance, General Slocum ordered Bartlett's Brigade forward under extraordinarily heavy enemy fire. During a period of several hours, during which desperate attacks and counter-attacks were exchanged between the two armies, the Sixteenth became one of several regiments thrown into the perilous breach. Much of this action took place on a slope that rose gently 400 yards through open ground planted in corn, through which Hill sent five of his regiments to secure two crucially-placed Yankee batteries. It was as this struggle hung in the balance that the Sixteenth was ordered to attack, Joe leading and directing his men on horseback.

On that June day, as on all hot days, members of the regiment wore their signature white straw hats and were thus highly visible to all on the field. One of Joe's men remembered that, although some might have seen the hats as ready targets, in fact they may have offered life-saving diversions. "Most of the enemy firing was too high," recalled this soldier, "they must have aimed at our hats." This may have been a wishful conclusion, for it is true that many men of the Sixteenth *were* struck in the head or upper body. But as it happened, this particular soldier managed to do all his firing on one knee, thereby prudently ending the day unscathed. He recalled that "the air was too full of lead for standing room," a summation of this battle that has endured. Losses suffered by the Sixteenth New York at Gaines' Mill were among the heaviest for the Union on that day, reaching 40 percent.[18] Colonel Joseph Bartlett, Commander of Slocum's Second Brigade, was respectful as he described the regiment's conduct in his official report:

> The enemy were slowly but surely forcing back the right of the entire line of battle. At this point I ordered forward the 16th New York Volunteers, Colonel Howland commanding. It was necessary to change front forward under the most terrific fire of musketry, with the shells and round shot of two batteries raking over the plain, making it seemingly impossible for a line to withstand the fire a single instant. But with the calmness and precision of veteran soldiers the movement was executed. . . . To Colonel Joseph Howland I am indebted for maintaining the extreme right of my line, for nobly leading his regiment to the charge and retaking two guns from the enemy. Whatever of noble moral, physical and manly courage has ever been given by God to man, has fallen to his lot. Cheering his men to victory, he early received a painful wound, but with heroism worthy of the cause he has sacrificed so much to maintain, he kept his saddle until the close of the battle."[19]

A major on Howland's staff also recalled that Joseph was resolutely firm throughout; placing himself in the thick of action, personally directing the attack, encouraging his men and staying with them until at last he "conducted the regiment from the field" in an orderly retreat—the batteries so hotly defended now once more in enemy hands.

Stephen Sears has described the denouement of this bitter engagement in vivid language: "It was nearing 7:00 PM, and the sun low on the western horizon was glowing a dull red through the haze of battle smoke, giving the scene a hellish cast. . . . General Lee was making this final, supreme effort to win the day, with no margin to spare. . . .The climax of the battle was hardly a picture-book charge, with the entire Confederate line advancing in unison and seamless alignment. It was, instead, a matter of fits and starts, of rushes and repulses."[20]

But for the Woolsey women, as well as for the men of the Sixteenth, it was the aftermath of Gaines' Mill which in the end would
generate a more gentle memory—and this, though not as stirring as
the men's recollections of battle, would become regimental lore of a
different sort. The true tale, written by Eliza as Joe recounted it to
her, began as the evening faded, after the men had left the field, the
crisis now behind them. As they settled themselves to rest, exhausted
and spread across the ground in no particular order, Joe, whose horse
had apparently wandered away from the others, managed to dismount
and lie down under a tree. Falling asleep or perhaps losing consciousness, he drifted in and out of dreams for hours before finally waking
to find himself quite alone in silence and deep darkness. Yet as his
senses returned, he imagined that he was somehow *not* alone, and,
feeling a presence very near him, Joe realized that something soft
was nudging at his cheek insistently, as if to wake him. As Eliza described the experience in her journal, "Joe roused himself to find that
it was his war horse, old Scott, rubbing his nose against his face. The
horse had got loose from where he was tied and had looked for his
master until he found him. Joseph was not ashamed to say that he
cried like a child, as he put his arms around the dear old fellow's neck."
The tale of Scott, the faithful steed who would not forsake his battle
partner, remained a cherished legend to be recalled for years by members of the Sixteenth as well as by a generation of Woolsey friends and
relatives.[21]

As it happened, Joe Howland was quite fortunate despite the
pain he suffered and the fever which still wracked him. Although his
wound was disabling, it was not mortal, and he had been able to make
his way from the field independently. News of his mishap was telegraphed immediately to his wife, a privilege virtually unknown for
the average soldier in the Civil War. With other Union casualties from
Gaines' Mill, he was brought to the general hospital at Savage's Station on the Richmond and York River railroad. From there as many as
could be carried away were sent by ambulance across the Peninsula
to Harrison's Landing in the fighting retreat that marked the subsequent battles of the Seven Days. Joe, with another, more seriously

wounded officer, were transported in an ambulance sent from McClellan's headquarters for their use.

Others of his regiment did not fare as well. On June 29 Savage's Station itself became a battleground, and after the day's fighting had ended, the Union wounded from both engagements were necessarily abandoned in a general retreat. Newton Curtis wrote that, "about two thousand five hundred sick and wounded officers and men, with their attendants, were left at Savage's Station and fell into the hands of the enemy. Of this number, seventeen wounded, three sick and two nurses were members of the Sixteenth New York." One of these captives reported later that during the action "the Confederates brought up their artillery and opened on our troops stationed eighty rods south of the track [as] the wounded lay between the lines, *with their noses well down,* for an hour or more." After the firing ceased this prisoner also remembered that, "We of the Sixteenth, wearing our straw hats, received special attention from the Confederate officers and men who fought against us. They said, 'We have great respect for the members of the "straw hat regiment," they were a brave and stubborn lot who inflicted severe punishment on us.'"[22]

But despite such individual evidences of mutual respect, the engagement at Savage's Station was a defeat for the Union regiments involved, and although it proved ultimately successful as a delaying action which enabled McClellan's retreating forces safe passage south across White Oak Swamp, it was an occasion of great sadness for survivors of the Sixteenth who were forced to leave their wounded friends behind. Curtis wrote movingly that,

> It is impossible to describe the feelings of comrades wounded in action and left to fall into the hands of the enemy; and most difficult to portray those of the unscathed, who are compelled to march away to new conflicts without their old associates. . . . Brave men, who have unfalteringly approached belching cannon and driven away those who served them at the point of a bayonet, have trembled with grief and turned away speechless from the pleading countenances of those whom they have stood beside in battle, and now must leave to fall "into the hands of the enemy."[23]

Following the battle of Gaines' Mill, in which the Sixteenth New York suffered heavy losses, a second, and perhaps more severe test awaited them. Above, a photograph by James Gibson shows men of Joe Howland's regiment in their white straw hats crowded into the hospital yard at Savage's Station, soon to be overrun by Confederates and abandoned. Although Joe himself was removed, these men would soon be left behind. Below, Alfred Waud sketched survivors of the regiment as they joined other elements of Franklin's Sixth Corps bringing up the rear of the army as it retreated south to the James. Here again, straw hats can be seen silhouetted against furiously burning stores as the regiment moves on.

With all communications severed, none of these details could be known on board the transports as they steamed south, and the women were able only to conjecture what might have passed in the action before Richmond. But although they were largely without information themselves, they were besieged for news when at last they reached Fort Monroe: greeted with confusion and rumor on all sides and subjected to questions for which they had no answers. In their role as messengers, bringing dispatches from Captain Sawtelle to General Van Alen, the Sanitarians were assumed to enjoy a privileged confidence which amused Katharine, allowing her to indulge a mildly perverse superiority. "This [responsibility] gave us the special fun of being the first to come leisurely into the panic then raging at Yorktown," she wrote. "The 'Small' was instantly surrounded by terror stricken boats; the people leaning over the bulwarks to question us. Nothing could be more delightful than to be as calm and monosyllabic as we were—partly by choice, and partly under orders from Colonel Ingalls. . . . [here they] knew nothing, except that the enemy had possession of White House—it seems that General Van Alen, commanding at Yorktown, had telegraphed Colonel Ingalls *after* we had left White House, and received from our successors a polite request to 'go to ****!'"[24]

But pleasant as it was to be the bearers of important news, the unanswered questions and stressful nature of their position remained unchanged. Katharine would recall her emotions during those last nights on the York as the Sanitarians drew farther away from White House. "Our minds had been strained to the utmost, and the disappointment and uncertainty striking upon them were more than we could bear. . . . I could not sleep, but went out and sat on the deck and wrote by the light of my lantern, and wondered if my mind were leaving me, and whether it would right itself again."[25]

Olmsted also recalled the exodus sadly, and remembered the evening of their departure as a time of melancholy contemplation. "In the night we sat on deck," he wrote, "watching the fire-flashes above the trees toward White House; watching the fading of what had been, to us, through those strange weeks, a sort of home where we had worked together and been happy;—a place that is also sacred for its intense living memories of one who, through months of death and darkness, lived in and for the sufferings of others, and finally gave himself for them." Dr. Robert Ware, of whom Olmsted wrote, was greatly loved by all the transport personnel. It was he who had led his colleagues into the death trains of Fair Oaks, working through the dawn, inspiring all with his extraordinary moral and physical stamina. It was also Ware who, in rare moments of calm between the stressed demands of his calling, had been able to retain a capacity for levity, a ringleader whose gentle good humor had, as Katharine remembered, challenged others to "'be as funny as we could be,' full of fun - joining in cheerful concert together." After leaving Harrison's Landing in August 1862, Ware would choose active duty as surgeon of the Forty-fourth Massachusetts Volunteers, preferring such service to an appointment at the new Army General Hospital in Portsmouth Grove, Rhode Island. During the siege of Washington, North Carolina in March 1863, just seven months after leaving the Peninsula, Ware died at his post while caring for casualties of the Forty-fourth. He was twenty-seven years old.[26]

On June 30 the transports left Norfolk and headed cautiously up the James, reaching Harrison's Landing on July 1. On that same day, in a final desperate confrontation, the opposing armies met at Malvern Hill some ten miles distant. On July 2 Katharine wrote, "we came here yesterday to hear the thunder of battle and to find the army just approaching this landing. The feelings with which we came to the James River I can't describe, our anxiety, excitement, and breathless desire to know *something* were so great. Not a vessel was in sight after we left Newport News, except the Quartermaster's Department boat, which was just ahead of us. No one could guess what knowledge any moment might bring." Arriving at length at their destination she wrote, "We were just admiring a fine old colonial house, [Berkeley] when someone standing in the bows cried out: 'I see something white

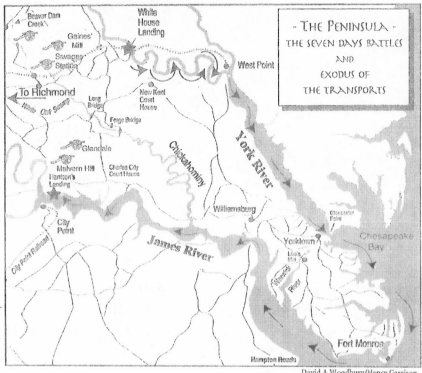

David A Woodbury/Nancy Garrison

The Army of the Potomac was sorely tested in its retreat south during the final week of June. The Seven Days battles—Beaver Dam Creek, Gaines' Mill, Savage's Station, Glendale and Malvern Hill—left it weakened and diminished, though still game, on its arrival at Harrison's Landing on the James River.

As the Army retreated, the armada of transports also made its escape from White House to Yorktown, around Fort Monroe and up the James to rendezvous at McClellan's new headquarters at Berkeley Plantation. The nurses' river journey and the battles of the Seven Days are indicated here.

Alfred Waud sketched two scenes of action as the Seven Days battles drew to a close and the Army of the Potomac continued its fighting retreat towards Harrison's Landing. Above, Union gunners at the crest of Malvern Hill fire over their own lines aiming at distant columns of advancing Confederate infantry. Below, at the Battle of Glendale, Union marksmen hold their line, firing through dense woods. The nurses, recently arrived from White House and waiting on board the "Wilson Small," listened to the guns throughout the day, imagining ,wondering and.conjecturing.

among the trees to the right!' and in a few minutes more we made them out to be army wagons. We had met our army! Never shall I forget the look of the first officers who came on board. . . .They were gaunt and haggard, their hair stood out from their heads stiffened with dust and dirt, their faces were nearly black, and to the waists they were literally molded in Virginia clay.

"'Oh what is this?' we cried. 'Is it a defeat?'

'Defeat! No; we have retreated, but we never turned our backs on them. We have faced and fought and beaten them for five days.'"[27]

"I never felt the slightest desire to witness a battle," Katharine wrote, "until I listened to the accounts they gave of Malvern Hill, where our whole artillery was massed on the hillside and hurled back a column of thirty thousand men as it debouched with three heads. I listened to the guns; and even where we were it was a mighty thunder." For one who had so constantly tended the human miseries of war, it seemed a curious desire, yet perhaps it was consistent with the heightened sense of angst and sadness that now preyed upon the women.[28] Allen Nevins also evoked images of Malvern Hill with awe, basing his description upon the account of a soldier who survived the battle:

> Participants never forgot the magnificence or horror of the scene. In the bright summer evening not a breath of wind stirred the air. From the artillery rose black columns of smoke, towering stately to the sky. The crash of musketry and the deeper roar and thud of cannon were deafening and continuous . . . while the troops on both sides sank exhausted . . .the sky grew overcast and inky darkness shut down. Toward dawn came a heavy downpour. "Such ugly wounds, sickening to the sight . . . as the rain beat upon them, washing them to a pale purple."[29]

Confederate General D. H. Hill would later describe this battle concisely: "it was not war—it was murder." [30]

On July 2, as the retreating army neared the end of its weary march to Harrison's landing, Joe Howland was brought on board the

Wilson Small suffering from an infection of his wound and danger-ously ill with malarial fever. His journey across the Peninsula with the procession of ambulances had been tortuous and slow, defined by the reverberations of nearby battles at Glendale, Malvern Hill and down the Charles City Road. "A very painful experience in itself," Georgy wrote of his ordeal, "—but he was safe now, and *with us!*" [31] Thankful that the wound, though serious, was less destructive than she had feared, and relieved that Joe could now receive treatment from Sanitary Commission doctors, Eliza immediately undertook her husband's care herself, and made plans to move him north with the first available transport leaving Berkeley. On July 5 the *Daniel Webster* sailed for New York with the Howlands on board—Eliza serving as superintendent of the nursing staff and Moritz assisting her as they cared for Joe together. The journey marked the end of her active ca-reer as a Commission nurse. She had come to the Peninsula to be near her husband; she had sought adventure and found much more. Now the Howlands left as they had come; as close together as it was possible to be in the violent disconnect of civil war.

With the move to Harrison's Landing, where all medical care was dispensed on shore by military personnel, the remaining nurses inevitably experienced a sense of denouement and loss. The realiza-tion that they were now superfluous, and that their services were no longer essential was a bitter truth that none seemed able to absorb easily. Vitally active at White House, they had been sustained by the necessity of work, living to their fullest capacity and assured that their contribution was important. Now all that was changed. Here, on the James, they became supernumeraries. Looking inland from the *Wilson Small* lying just offshore at Berkeley, Katharine described a scene of activity from which she was now excluded. "My eye can follow the lines within which our army lies," she wrote. "The immediate pros-pect is of a sandy shore up and down which the cavalry are ceaselessly passing to water and swim their horses in the river. . . .The long wharf is a moving mass of human beings: on one side, a stream of men un-loading the commissariat and other stores; on the other, a sad proces-sion of wounded, feebly crawling down from the Harrison House to go on board the [army] transports. The medical authorities are doing well by them. The Harrison House is made into a hospital, and the men are comfortable (or so say our gentlemen, who have been among them); the slight cases are lying on the lawn and under the trees. Today—thank God—is cloudy without rain. . . . We women are not permitted to go on shore, and I try to believe, as I am told, that it is impossible we should."[32]

This isolation on board their own vessels, while patients were cared for by others, was intensely frustrating to the women. Yet their new—and seemingly purposeless—position had come to be *because* the Sanitary Commission's efforts had met with increased acceptance, and for this they were grateful. The army was learning from them, and from its own mistakes, initiating new procedures and standards of readiness and becoming capable of caring for its own. It was precisely the result envisioned and planned by Olmsted. Yet for the women, even as they acknowledged positive change, the stress of evacuation and subsequent comprehension of their own uselessness fostered a sense of futility.

Exacerbating their distress was the fierce loyalty they still felt for their commanding general and the lack of faith they perceived from official Washington. Shortly after the *Wilson Small* reached Harrison's Landing, McClellan himself arrived by gunboat and Wormeley, proud of the part the transports had played in the evacuation, imagined the general "relieved in his anxious mind to learn the perfect success of our removal from White House, and to know that supplies were already here, and following us up the river for his exhausted army!"[33] The transport nurses, with many other civilian and military personnel on the Peninsula, blamed McClellan's failure on what to them was an incomprehensible lack of support at home. They saw their hero's problems—from McDowell's delayed arrival to the denial of massive reinforcements—as the grievous fault of indifferent politicians. Katharine reflected the righteous wrath of these loyalists in her letters from Berkeley.

"As I write I glance out from time to time at the Army of the Potomac, massed on the plain before me—an army driven from its position because it could not get reinforcements to render that position tenable; forced every day of its retreat to turn and give battle; an army just one third less than it was: and yet it comes in from seven days fighting, marching, fasting, in gallant spirits, and making the proud boast for itself and its commander that it has not only marched with its face backward to the enemy, but has inflicted three times the loss it has borne.

"And yet the sad truth cannot be concealed: our position is very hazardous. What I hear said is this: 'unless we have reinforcements, what can we do? Must McClellan fight another bloody battle in a struggle for life—or surrender? Give us reinforcements, and all is well. We have got the right base now. We could not have it at first; we made another; and that other the Government made it impossible for us to maintain. Day by day we saw it growing untenable. *Now* we have the true base of operations against Richmond. The sacrifice? Yes! *but who compelled it?* The nation *must* see that. The army and McClellan have done their part, and nobly have they done it. Let them now be strengthened, and all is well, or better than before.'

"This is the tone here. No wonder the men feel in [high] spirits; they have done their duty; and I look in their poor worn faces and feel that their deepest honor in life will be that they belonged to the beaten Army of the Potomac—and yet not beaten; everything that that is, except precisely the thing it is. . . . We look and hope and pray for reinforcements. Immediate levies should be made, the recruits used in garrisons, and the older troops sent here. The whole question is, are we in earnest? Is the nation in earnest? Or is it the victim of a political game? For God's sake, for the sake of humanity, let us strike one mighty blow now, and end this rebellion! . . . . Let it be done; and oh! do not sacrifice this noble army . . . this is not my opinion only, it is the sum of all I hear . . ."[34]

On July 4 Katharine's depression was scarcely lightened by an impromptu visit to Washington on which she accompanied Olmsted aboard the *Wilson Small*. Proposed by Col. Letterman, the senior medical officer on the scene, the mission was designed to acquaint the Surgeon General with hospital conditions on the James. The prospect of a restaurant meal in the capitol, to say nothing of a hot bath, were powerful incentives to travel, and Katharine approached the trip eagerly. But the reality was disappointing. "I can't tell you how Washington oppressed me," she wrote on her return. "Its bitter tone towards McClellan fell strangely on our ears, which yet rang with the cheers of the army." Perhaps worse, she noted, "we reached Washington on Saturday morning. Mr. Olmsted transacted his business, and we started on our return on Saturday afternoon bringing with us a cargo of tents for the army. This destroyed our blissful visions of a bath and bed at Willard's."[35]

Yet there *were* major diversions, even amidst the oppressive moods of Harrison's Landing. On July 8, soon after her return from Washington, Katharine wrote with great excitement that "for the last two hours I have been watching President Lincoln and General McClellan as they sat together, in earnest conversation, on the deck of a steamer close to us. I am thankful, I am *happy*, that the President has come,— has sprung across the dreadful intervening Washington, and come to see and hear and judge for his own wise and noble self.

"While we were at dinner someone said, 'Why, there's the President!' and he proved to be just arriving on the 'Ariel,' at the end of the wharf close to where we are anchored. I stationed myself at once to watch for the coming of McClellan. The President stood on deck with a glass, with which, after a time, he inspected our boat, waving his handkerchief to us. My eyes and soul were in the direction of the general headquarters, over which the great balloon was slowly descending. Presently a line of horsemen came over the brow of the hill through the trees, and first emerged a firm-set figure on a brown horse, and after him the staff and body-guard. As soon as the General reached the head of the wharf he sprang from his horse, and in an instant every man was afoot and motionless. McClellan walked quickly along the thousand-foot pier, a major-general beside him, and six officers following. He was the shortest man, of course, by which I distinguished him as the little group stepped on to the pier. When he reached the 'Ariel' he ran quickly up to the after-deck, where the President met him and grasped his hand. I could not distinguish the play of his features, though my eyes still ache from the effort to do so. He is stouter than I expected, but quicker and more *leste*. He wore the ordinary blue coat and shoulder-straps; the coat, fastened only at the throat, and blowing back as he walked, gave to sight a grey flannel shirt and a—suspender!

"They sat down together, apparently with a map between them, to which McClellan pointed from time to time with the tip of his cigar. We watched the earnest conversation which went on, and lasted till 6:00 P. M.; then they rose and walked side by side ashore,—the president, in a shiny black coat and stovepipe hat, a whole head and shoulders taller, as it seemed to me, than the General. Mr. Lincoln mounted a led horse of the General's, and together they rode off, the staff following, the dragoons presenting arms and then wheeling round to follow, their sabres gleaming in the sunlight. And so they have passed over the hill, and I have come to tell you about it. The cannon are firing salutes,—a sound of strange peacefulness to us, after the angry, irregular boomings and sharp screams of the shells to which we are accustomed . . ."[36]

The yearning for justification of her hero, for recognition and relief from the President, whom she clearly placed above the "dreadful intervening Washington," is palpable through Katharine's telling of this episode. Aware that she is recording history, her voice assumes new gravity. For her, and for the remaining faithful at Berkeley, the outcome of this meeting with Lincoln would be anticipated with fervent, if dwindling optimism.[37]

But away from the James, where reality might more easily be assessed, there were many who disagreed with Katharine and her immediate companions. Outspoken Abby Woolsey, at home in New York and working tirelessly with Louisa Schuyler at the WCAR, had already abandoned any heroic assumptions about McClellan and his generals. At the close of the Seven Days battles she reflected that,

> We shall never know all that this week of desperate fighting has cost us; our dead and wounded being left behind, or crawling painfully along in the trail of the retreating army. Our great beautiful Army of the Potomac dwindled down to an exhausted handful. . . . *Fifty thousand* in all destroyed by fever and wounds, in McClellan's brief campaign! No wonder the President has hesitated to send more troops to be used up in the swamps, when so little was being done to show for it.

> Any fool might have known that Beauregard and the bulk of
> his army had come to Richmond; but then our generals are
> not even fools, but something less, if possible. [38]

For Katharine and her colleagues at Harrison's Landing, the passionate partisanship and grief they felt for McClellan served to diminish their reserves of strength still further and fueled a sense of
discouragement. They had endured countless trials, fortified by nerve
alone; now that nerve was leaving them. Even before the tortuous
relocation from White House, the effects of their harsh life had begun
to tell upon the closely-knit group. Frederick Knapp, depleted by sleep-
less nights and inadequate food was sent home with typhoid fever,
hoping to return. Christine Griffin, suffering from "curious symptoms
of fainting and wandering" had also been sent north at Dr. Ware's
insistence. These absences seriously reduced Olmsted's core staff—
and now Eliza, too, was gone. Of the original quartet of nurses on
board the *Wilson Small*, only two remained.

It was a strange vacuum that these women now inhabited. Pro-
hibited from going on shore, they experienced restlessness and an
unfamiliar sense of ennui. In a letter to her mother Georgy noted that
"the last two weeks of waiting have been wearing on us all, and Miss
Wormeley is a fascinating wreck."[39] Katharine admitted to bouts of
depression as well as partial deafness caused by quinine, fatigue and
emotional stress. Begging out of an impromptu sightseeing excursion
she wrote, "[today] I did not go on board the 'Monitor' after all.
The others went, but I had fallen into a weary and disconsolate condition, in which the effort seemed too great. . . . I sat alone, while the
rest went rowing on the river."[40]

But this uncharacteristic lethargy did not prevail. On July 10,
somewhat defiantly, Katharine went on shore at last, urged on by
General Barlow's wife, Arabella "without orders and, indeed, without
permission." The two women toured the makeshift hospital, talked
with the men and wrote letters for them. This independent gesture
revived Katharine and left her much encouraged. "The influence of
the new Medical Director [Dr. Letterman] is already manifest," she

wrote. "It is too much to say that all the men's wants are met as they would be in our own boats . . . it would be absurd to expect as much as that in a temporary hospital hastily arranged, and after such an exhausting march; but I am satisfied that the men have every essential care." She approved of the surgeons, the nurses, and the hospital steward—even to the point of sharing with him the secrets of her milk punch and promising to send him her spirit lamp, kettles and a supply of beef extract and condensed milk. "I am glad I went ashore," wrote Katharine at the close of this day. "Now I am content to go home. Our work—I mean the women's work—is over. The Government is doing well by the sick and wounded. The Commission can justly claim that it has led the Government to this. But as for us, we ought to go; for to stay here doing nothing is a sarcasm on the work we have already done."[41]

The *Wilson Small*, and all its company, were now soon to depart. But although Katharine herself had declared their continued presence on the James a "sarcasm," there were those who would disagree, and who would miss the women sorely for many reasons—not all of them strictly humanitarian. Of this she would presently be assured in a letter from a special friend whom she identified simply as "that United States officer who did more than any other to make our work successful." Captain Charles Sawtelle, already mourning the lost days of mint juleps at White House, wrote with feeling, "'How I [shall] miss the dear ladies of the 'Wilson Small' and their freshening drinks,—animal that I am!—but how can I forget that which comforted me?'" Comfort had been provided by the Sanitarians, in large and small portions, to a multitude of Union soldiers on the Peninsula. In this effort, despite obstacles, the Sanitary Commission had been supremely successful. Like Sawtelle, there were many men who would remember the nurses with fondness as the Army of the Potomac moved on from Harrison's Landing to other battles in farther campaigns.[42]

In the wake of the Seven Days, as the women absorbed the significance of a slaughter which had accomplished little, and contemplated future battles that now appeared inevitable, there was, perhaps for the first time, a growing realization that this was to be a long and bitter war, waged against a formidable adversary. The imagined Union assault on Richmond, intended to deliver the mortal blow from which the South could not recover, had deteriorated instead to a scattered campaign ending in retreat. The mood among the nurses remaining at Harrison's Landing was echoed by Abby Woolsey in one of her frequent letters to Georgy during the Sanitarians' last days on the Peninsula:

> It is infinitely sad, all this desperate fighting and struggling; this piecemeal destruction of our precious troops, only to keep the wolves at bay. . . . I suppose the poor innocent, confident new [recruits] will be in the thickest of the fight at once. They will have their wish! be put to the immediate use for which they enlisted. . . . I grow stony and tearless over such a mass of human grief. I am lost in wonder, too, at the generalship, the daring and endurance of the Southern army. We are to fight now, even if it becomes extermination for us and them.[43]

The move to the James had, in effect, defined the close of the Peninsula Campaign. Lee had failed in his attempt to split the Union army in half, but McClellan had failed more seriously, and with his failure there came disillusionment for all who had hailed him. The young general's fall from favor was profoundly saddening to the Sanitarians, for they were now forced to accept that, although their own mission had achieved its immediate goals, the campaign itself, to which they had committed their hearts and energies, had ended ingloriously. Some regiments would now be posted back to Washington; others would remain. McClellan himself would linger on the James for some weeks more with remnants of his weakened force before being recalled. His goal of conquest had been frustrated; the public perception of him as a Messianic hero was on the wane, and the Antietam campaign of the coming fall would see his reputation further eclipsed and his status reduced to the level of a moderately competent career officer.

In mid-July Katharine Wormeley was superintendent-in-charge of the *Daniel Webster* as it made its last northward journey with patients from Harrison's Landing. On the night before her departure she sat with Georgy and their Chief on board the "home ship" *Wilson Small*, talking until dawn, "as people will who know that on the morrow they are to separate widely." As the sky lightened behind the trees of Berkeley, Wormeley reflected that "from first to last there has been perfect accord among us, and I can never look back to these months without feeling that God has been very good to let me share in them and see the human nature under such aspects. It is sad to feel that it is all over." In the emotion of the moment Katharine even acknowledged the softening of her memory of Stuart's raid: "Did I say somewhere that Mr. Olmsted was severe? Well, I am glad I said it, that I may now unsay it. Nothing could be more untrue; every day I have understood and valued and trusted him more."[44]

Later that morning Katharine sailed for New York with Olmsted, leaving Georgy to follow on a later voyage—and it was there, as the vessel docked next day, with the proprieties and signatures of a previous life once more about her, that Katharine faced the finality of her adventure. "The last I saw of Mr. Olmsted he was disappearing down the side of the 'Webster' clad in the garb of a fashionable gentleman," she wrote. "I rubbed my eyes, and felt that it was indeed *all over*. I rose to the occasion myself by putting on a black lace tablespoon (such were the bonnets of the period) in which I at once became conventional and duly civilized."[45] The days of flannel shirts—the beloved "Agnews"—and all they had come to symbolize to the transport nurses were now, irrevocably, part of the women's pasts.

Chapter VIII

LEGACIES .

Occasionally a scholar has speculated on certain aspects of the women's wartime sojourn, isolating them, dissecting them and interpreting them provocatively to support one argument or another. Nina Bennett Smith has suggested that, in what may have been an uneasy negotiation, women who went to the war devised an acceptable "ideology of justification" upon which they built their self-perceptions, defined their motivations, and survived demeaning treatment from authoritarian males. This justification had much to do with their identity as *special* women in terms of ability and in terms of class. Conversely, Kristie Ross has questioned the adequacy of such a negotiation and argued that, at least for Katharine Wormeley, it was ultimately unsuccessful and that the tensions created by her conflicting emotions proved debilitating.

Perhaps more than her companions, Wormeley had wrestled with the contradictions and limitations of inclusion

in the war based on the privileges and proscriptions of class
and gender. Her experience left her depressed and exhausted.
She had been invited on board the transports because she
was a lady, and yet the war and the work itself had begun to
push and pull at the rules, preoccupations, and qualities which
defined her as a member of that class. Wormeley could not
bear the leftover turmoil from the Peninsula and later . . .
retreated from the open-mindedness, the personal stamina,
the bonding, and sheer enthusiasm that had sustained the
women volunteers through the summer of 1862.[1]

One could well fault the dismissiveness of this analysis, for although Wormeley did indeed experience some temporary depression
and physical debilitation during the last days at Harrison's Landing,
such an image of melancholic retreat seems at odds with the record of
her subsequent accomplishments. Within weeks of leaving the Peninsula, Wormeley, with every appearance of vigor and enthusiasm, assumed an important administrative position through which her own
immediate ambitions would be realized. Yet Ross's argument is valuable in that it suggests and intersects with another enduring para-
dox: the conflict between acquiescence and autonomy which was a
basic dilemma for women of Wormeley's era and continues today as a
classic theme affecting women's professional confidence and sense of
personal worthiness. If Katharine was somehow "pulled and pushed"
by her experience on board the transports, she was also alternately
encouraged to show initiative, and then forced to submit to Olmsted's
notions of control. The messages of Sanitarian ideology were often
mixed, specifically as they affected women. The record of how the lady
nurses of the Peninsula would reconcile these sorts of contradictions
for themselves after the war, and how they would utilize the expertise
they had labored to acquire, reveals much about them as individuals
and as members of their class. The transport experience not only
brought them to new levels of fortitude and self-awareness, it opened
specific areas of concentration and methodology which would affect
their lives and the lives of others. The example set by the Sanitary
Commission of an administrative body and working institution had
been deeply instilled. For these women, it would be a long-lasting and
far-reaching legacy.

Most of the transport nurses left the Peninsula with their reserves of physical and spiritual energy tested but essentially strengthened. Women who had arrived in Virginia with little more than eagerness and a talent for organization departed with a profound sense of vocation. Katharine Wormeley, who had at first felt diffidence toward others she deemed braver and more accomplished, left with her courage proved, and confident of her own abilities. Previously untried women whose task it had been to receive men "shattered and shrieking, in every condition of horror" adapted to those demands and devised fresh ways to deal with suffering and despair. One result was a passionate dedication to the theory and practice of good nursing. The realization that nurses' training and hospital environment might be vastly improved became a crusade for many of these women, as it had for Florence Nightingale.

But if the elite transport nurses were profoundly altered in some ways, in others they remained virtually static. While they had witnessed the relaxation of certain conventions and been introduced to new possibilities through their work and relationships, their overall outlook remained curiously consistent with their early training and privileged backgrounds. Their choices in the postbellum years would reflect this consistency. The women's war experience had shown them their own strengths through a process of ministering to others, sharpening their sympathies and defining their priorities, but it had *not* weakened their faith in their class or their justifications of the dominant culture. The ways in which Olmsted's core group would use their keener vision would confirm those patterns. The epiphany of the Peninsula was only partial. It did not, despite its potential for discovery, lead these women to question or rethink the absolutes which governed their lives. If this is disappointing, it is at least not surprising.

When they came to the Peninsula they brought with them their upbringing as "ladies," who could "master the principles of order and retain the inner strength to endure privation and danger uncorrupted."[2] Their belief was that, unlike men and lower-class women, these strengths pertained specifically to elite women like themselves. As well as patrician fortitude, they brought a "lady's delicacy" to their work with men in extremis; as Katharine Wormeley wrote, "it is not too much to say that delicacy and refinement and the fact of being a gentlewomen could never *tell* more than they do here." Their faith in the power of genteel endurance explained why Wormeley and her colleagues considered themselves essential—even immune—in an environment where they were often resented. Required to justify or explain their presence as they sought to enter (or invade) the medical and military territories of men, they were *sure* of what they brought, and this assurance rendered them unassailable in their own eyes. They attributed their perseverance to class. Delicacy coupled with strength—the steel hand in the kid glove: these were the dual requirements of their wartime service *and* the legacy they carried forward to their postbellum efforts in reform.[3]

There may have been good reason, as Kristie Ross has suggested, for the transport veterans to question the "contradictions and limitations" of class and gender in the light of their new-found freedoms. From the evidence, however, this confusion, if indeed it existed, seems to have been manageable. When Katharine Wormeley left the Peninsula her letters disclosed little alteration in her essential world-view. She seems not to have questioned the ultimate necessity or morality of war, or the "rules and qualities" that defined her as a member of her class. Yet she *had* crossed a life-changing divide—one which would affect her future significantly.

From the very first days of her transport service, Katharine had regularly confronted appalling examples of medical and organizational unpreparedness. As her experience increased, she was able to analyze and identify a series of underlying problems and resolve them— at least theoretically—to her own satisfaction. Faulting those hospital administrators who complained the loudest, she recognized them as the authors of their own failure—and knew that *she*, given the opportunity, could operate a hospital far more competently than they. In June, with the voice of a natural leader frustrated by the bungling of others, she wrote, "I should like to have charge of a hospital *now*. I could make it march, if only I had hold of some of the administrative *power*."[4]

But that power was presently beyond her reach—or the reach of any woman. Pondering the deficiencies of the army's system of care

provision, Wormeley imagined the well-managed hospital as an institution of centralized authority, with the integration of multiple departments, a revolutionary concept at the time. Her plan would entail
supervision of all the infrastructure needed to support a large institution: the power to approve or disapprove *all* personnel, male or female; the dispensing and purchasing power for all non-medical supplies; the mandate for all non-medical decision-making. It was an
ambitious vision, and one which presumably would never open for
her.

In mid-July, newly-returned to Newport and enduring the role of
a reluctant celebrity, Katharine remembered that "the town called on
me at home, beginning, like a Fourth of July procession, with the
mayor and the clergy"—and concluded that a woman home from the
war was a public curiosity for all to marvel upon.[5] Yet the desire to be
back at work was far more compelling than glorification, and within
days she was considering a startling new venture proposed by Surgeon General William A. Hammond who visited her from Washington
to plead his case. The opportunity he put before her was the director-
ship of a large general hospital, soon to open at Portsmouth Grove
near Newport, an offer which, even in her secret imaginings, she had
never seriously anticipated. Now that it *had* been presented she delayed her decision long enough to consult with Olmsted and Woolsey
before making a commitment. In August, letters were exchanged
among the three friends, and with the encouragement of both colleagues Katharine at last accepted.[6]

From the outset she was very firm in her requirements for the
hospital's staffing. She specifically requested appointments for *women
in key positions* and insisted that she be given sufficient power to disapprove staff positions for any doctors who would not work harmoni-
ously with female nurses and superintendents. Georgy, elated at her
friend's success, noted that the opportunity was "too good a chance to
miss, and was certainly a great compliment from the Surgeon
General."[7] Olmsted agreed. Soon, with all arrangements made to her
satisfaction, Katharine herself wrote enthusiastically that "no ladies
have *ever been allowed* to come into a U. S. General Hospital in this
way—much less warmly requested and thanked, and confided in as

we are. It is General Hammond's first cordial reception and experiment of ladies in hospital, and is in [recognition] of what we did at
White House."[8] Katharine's imagined hospital had become reality, and
her opportunity for full executive power had miraculously arrived.

Yet despite impressive support, the position at Portsmouth Grove
was not without its problems. As Katharine drew up organizational
charts and assembled her staff she once again confronted the old, familiar resistance from those who scorned women in positions of authority or who refused to accept more than a token complement of
female nurses. She remembered "a surgeon who was inclined to one
woman for each ward (twenty-eight barracks, of sixty men in each)," a
balance that was unacceptable. "I soon hunted him out of that idea,"
she wrote, and now, assured of her own authority, she assumed command at last. Officially designated "Lady Superintendent," she controlled "everything in the domestic management of the hospital" but
conceded that she would only *gently* avail myself" of this sweeping
new mandate until men of her staff became acclimated to the administration of a woman. From then on her judgment prevailed in all
decisions affecting patient care at Portsmouth Grove.[9]

Professional relationships at the new hospital proved especially
happy for Katharine. She soon came to regard its chief medical officer,
Dr. Lewis A. Edwards, with much of the same veneration she had felt
for Olmsted on board the transports. In fact, when Edwards was
unexpectedly recalled to Washington, Wormeley entreated Olmsted
to muster whatever influence he could bring to bear on the Surgeon
General to cancel the doctor's transfer. Impressed with Wormeley's
success, and happy to accommodate her, Olmsted told his wife at the
time, "I like to have the gratitude and friendship of such a high strung
and thoroughbred woman, even at a small cost." The warm bond between the two friends was apparently undimmed, despite Olmsted's
controlling behavior during the last days on board the transports. But
though it would remain close, Katharine's friendship for him would
become increasingly dependent as time passed, and Olmsted would
see the "small cost" of her affection multiply with the years.[10]

At Portsmouth Grove Katharine's working relationship with her
women associates was also successful. As assistant superintendents,

Katharine chose Georgy, Georgy's elder sister Jane, and their cousin Sarah Woolsey, an experienced nurse. "Tall, symmetrical" Harriet Douglas Whetton of the transports joined her former colleagues as the fourth and final assistant superintendent. Delighted to be back at the work she loved, Georgy remembered that "we were all hankering for our active life in the thick of the fight"—and though a Rhode Island hospital could never match the Pamunkey in terms of front-line action, it *did* offer an opportunity to serve Union soldiers as these women had been trained to do.[11] Wormeley assumed her post on September 1, 1862 and moved soon afterward with her staff into the new quarters which had been prepared for them.

Hammond's "experiment" was a clear success. Portsmouth Grove under Katharine Wormeley's supervision lived up to its promise. With her efficient staffing nearly completed, the hospital was equipped and functioning before the battle of Antietam, and later accommodated its share of the wounded from Fredericksburg. Katharine proved a forthright and resourceful leader, described admiringly by Jane Woolsey: "Kate Wormeley, our chief, is clever, spirited and energetic in the highest degree. . . a great capacity for business and not a single grain of mock-sentiment about her. [She] has been made agent of the Sanitary Commission here, with sole authority to draw and issue supplies." Jane, a fiercely efficient nurse herself, also remembered with evident satisfaction that, *"bad men are turned out* and good ones put in."[12]

Unhappily, the tenure of Katharine's elite corps of nurses was prematurely cut short by circumstance. In February, 1863 a virulent strain of smallpox broke out among the patients which, at the urgings of their families, precipitated the departure of all three Woolseys. For these women, who had braved the rigors of "Pamunkey Fever" and an array of other exotic ills unscathed, with only quinine and an occasional drop of whisky to sustain them, it was a bitter disappointment. Wormeley herself persevered throughout that spring and summer, serving until at last her own health failed in September. Later in the autumn, as Portsmouth Grove was converted from a general hospital into an Army convalescent camp, her career at the facility quite naturally came to an end.

Above, Bellows late in life.
Below, the Washington headquarters of the United States Sanitary Commission.

Katharine's experience had affirmed her administrative capacities and achieved a personal and professional goal. Her success had also confirmed the tenuous notion that trained women could function effectively in positions of authority previously dominated by males. In so doing she had helped to lower a specific barrier of prejudice. Wormeley, driven by a vision of efficient management and spurred by her own ambition, was among the first to pioneer a system of care which would set brave precedents and initiate new standards in the field of hospital management.

In the waning days of the Peninsula Campaign, as transport nurses parted from their colleagues at Harrison's Landing, the Sanitary Commission itself continued to press forward on other fronts. Throughout the remaining war years it would play its part with energy despite a succession of mis-steps within, and recurrent problems from without, often not of its own making. The Commission assumed major importance after the battle of Antietam, when government medical supplies had either been used up or left behind in the retreat. Its vast store of replacement goods proved essential to the survival of the battered army. That same year the Commission also successfully introduced two new services: a volunteer inspection corps of distinguished physicians to visit military hospitals and recommend changes and a hospital directory to aid families wishing to learn the location of sick or wounded relatives. By November 1862 the Commission had established a directory for military hospitals in Washington, and in 1863 extended the system countrywide to respond to all inquiries. Many of these successful innovations could be credited to Olmsted's management.[13]

But a major setback for the Sanitary Commission developed soon after the Peninsula Campaign when conflicting loyalties of regionalism among its distant branches threatened to undermine its original system of centralized distribution. As early as the fall of 1862, a move toward independent localism was on the rise throughout the Commission's network. Difficulties accumulated when some midwestern and eastern states empowered their agents to channel aid exclusively to their own regiments without going through the collection and distribution system mandated by the Commission in Washington.

Although such regional demands did not seriously cripple the Commission's operation, they provided underlying sources of friction which would ultimately hamper overall effectiveness and create divisiveness within the Executive Committee. Still clinging to his vision of a central coordinating authority, Olmsted found the drift toward regionalism especially troubling, for he saw it as "the selfish pettiness and the states rights doctrine which had directly given rise to secessionism" and considered it a dangerous counter-movement within the Commission itself.[14] He was outspoken in his support of the centralist methods originally proposed by the founders, and his keen sense of orderly process rebelled at any threat to the efficiency of his machine. Autocratic as always, Olmsted was frequently discouraged by the response of Executive Committee members who swayed to accommodate positions he found unacceptable.

The winter of 1862-63 was a highly stressful period for Olmsted, with administrative pressures placing increased demands on his physical stamina and peace of mind. In November he moved his wife and young children from New York to Washington in hopes of leading a more regular life, but domesticity did little to ease his burden. Late in December, seriously overworked and plagued by the problems which would soon distance him from the Commission's Executive Committee, Olmsted wrote to Bellows complaining that "my brain simply vomits all the business that I bring to it. I can lay hold of nothing right end foremost. I have my way of carrying on business, and it plainly is not your way."[15]

Here was a dangerous rift between President and Secretary which would not only strain the personal relationship between them, but would compromise the effectiveness of the Commission itself. Conscientious to a fault, here Olmted's perpetual state of over-commitment worked against him. By January George Templeton Strong, observing Olmsted's work schedule with distaste, noted that the General Secretary maintained "the most insanitary habits of life," working until four in the morning, sleeping in his clothes on a cot in the Commission offices, and breakfasting there on coffee and pickles before starting the day anew.[16]

Early in1863 Olmsted's differences with the Executive Committee became more defined and consequently more difficult to resolve. His grievances hinged upon an awkward division of administrative authority which rendered his position as General Secretary ambiguous in terms of responsibility and accountability. Resenting the limits imposed upon him, he chafed under the necessity of writing reports and justifications for his administrative decisions, and repeatedly petitioned for a free rein—which the Directors were loath to grant him. Anxiety, aggravated by overwork, made concentration difficult. Especially distressing was a conflict with Cornelius Rea Agnew over the alleged misdoings of two Commission agents, rumored to have been intemperate and derelict in their duty. Agnew, a strict churchman, accused Olmsted of being lax in his personnel policies and berated him for not discharging the disorderly agents. Angered by Agnew's charges, Olmsted complained to Bellows in an emotional letter:

> I positively cannot have any responsibility for the general management [of the Sanitary Commission] at present. . . . Agnew gives me the severest task in averages that I ever had. . . . Satan himself could not be as indifferent to a man's rights without consciousness of self-reproach. [Agnew's] letter in fact proves to me that my worst anticipations of what would result from the complication of responsibility between the Exec. Com. & the Genl Sec'y are realized.[17]

Concerns for the Sanitary Commission were not Olmsted's only preoccupation during these months, for in addition to his responsibilities as Executive Secretary he was involved in two other significant projects. With Wolcott Gibbs he was laying plans for an organization dedicated to the principles of patriotic nationalism and the suppression of states rights sentiments which would, in time, evolve as the Union League. And with Edward Godkin he was designing editorial policy for a periodical which would later take shape as *The Nation*.

But unhappily for Olmsted, neither of these ventures would prove entirely satisfying, for although he was influential in the formulation of both, neither one would turn out quite as he originally hoped and imagined. Jane Turner Censer has noted that, "the Union League Club did not adopt the explicitly nationalistic and educational platform he had advocated, and realization of the *Nation* lay with Godkin in the future, although the statement of purpose drafted by him with Olmsted's help in 1863 described the periodical that began publication in 1865."[18]

For Olmsted and the Sanitary Commission, a parting of the ways now seemed inevitable, and it came to pass in the summer of 1863. Exhausted from administrative conflict, and physically weakened by the lingering effects of his Peninsula service, Olmsted made the decision to resign. In August he accepted the offer of a more lucrative position as superintendent of the Mariposa Estate, a mining and business venture developed by Eastern interests in California which, he hoped, would bring him a measure of peace as well as the challenge of a new environment. The prospect was appealing: management of a "principality of seventy square miles, lying in the western foothills of the Sierra Nevada, within sight of the rising precipices rising out of the Yosemite Valley." For Olmsted, it seemed the ideal solution.[19]

Bellows, unwilling to lose his Secretary despite the mounting differences between them, attempted to dissuade him from accepting the Mariposa offer, suggesting that his decision to leave was financially motivated—which indeed it was, in part. Olmsted remained unmoved, however, and resigned as General Secretary on September 10, 1863, sailing for California four days later. Considering all that had passed between them, his letter of resignation to the Executive Committee was magnanimous: "Looking at the whole field of the present," he wrote, "the disappointment and failure in my official department is of small moment, and the grounds for satisfaction preponderate so largely that I must regard the time [spent] with the Commission as the most fortunate period of my life. I close that period with hearty congratulations and deep gratitude."[20]

Of the two years Olmsted spent as the Commission's Administrative Secretary, the intense weeks of the Peninsula Campaign had

By 1864 and 1865, when these photographs were taken, noticeable improvements were evident in hospitals, field stations and rest houses. Above, a convalescent hospital, much like the one at Portsmouth Grove, is festively decorated with flags and garlands as patients await their discharge to resume soldiering or return to their homes. Below, a Sanitary Commission field station closer to the front provides medical and non-medical services to Union soldiers. The presence of women, now apparently welcomed as nurses and care-givers in these settings, was for a large part the result of Sanitarian methods.

proved most satisfying. The discoveries, accomplishments and relationships offered him during that period were perhaps his finest and most personally rewarding wartime experiences. Olmsted's ability to anticipate problems, and his meticulous control of detail under chaotic conditions, were little short of miraculous, given the circumstances and the technologies of his time. He recognized his own contribution in crisis management and took comfort in it, his emotion apparent in many of his written recollections. Those who served with Olmsted sensed how deeply the transport interlude had motivated and moved him, and shared with him a sense of loss at what had passed. In August of '62, restless in an interval of idleness between Harrison's Landing and Portsmouth Grove, Georgy Woolsey remembered her chief's words, using them to express her own longing for sustained action and engagement, and mourning the dissatisfactions of civilian life. In a letter to Katharine she allowed herself a rare moment of nostalgia as she quoted Olmsted writing,"'my heart's still in the Pamunkey.'"[21]

Commenting on Olmsted's contribution to the Sanitary Commission, Jane Turner Censer noted the deterioration which ensued with his departure. "Never again did the Commission have a general secretary so powerful or so forceful as Olmsted. The trends that he had decried continued: the branch societies continued to display considerable independence and the Executive Committee retained its primacy in decision making. . . . Without Olmsted's strong leadership factionalism soon erupted at the Washington office [with] even the usually gentle Knapp participating in recurring quarrels."[22]

The administrative duties which the Secretary had handled so admirably at the beginning now devolved upon John Foster Jenkins, a physician and former hospital inspector who, in 1861, had been made the Commission's associate secretary for the East. His tenure was short lived, and during that time tensions between the national Commission in Washington and its local organizations became further strained. In September, 1863 a generous donation of two hundred thousand dollars from the California branch of the Commission was received in Washington with restrictive stipulations insisting that the money be designated primarily for the benefit of Western soldiers.

This and other conflicts of regionalism continued to smolder unresolved at the same time that persistent, and potentially more serious, problems erupted in another quarter. These related to the Christian Commission, whose politically charged fundraising campaigns now threatened the Sanitarians' financial base. Making matters worse, were widely circulated charges now being brought by returning veterans who claimed that when hospitalized in the line of duty they had never benefited from the Sanitarian's donated stores. These allegations could not easily be traced or deflected, and they fueled damaging rumors of opportunism and profiteering within the Commission which Bellows could not entirely shake off.[23] Finally, in 1864, the Sanitarians were seriously embarrassed when William A. Hammond, the surgeon general for whom they had enthusiastically lobbied in 1862, was convicted by court martial and dismissed. This well-publicized event further strained relations with the Army Medical Bureau and caused Bellows and his associates considerable loss of prestige.

Yet in spite of these and other problems, the Sanitarians continued to take on new projects and function effectively. The Commission expanded its important supplemental role in all theaters of battle and, as an effective aid to Union soldiers in their transition from military service to civilian living, set up Army-Navy claim offices for veterans seeking military pensions. During the war years, in all its endeavors, the Commission was regarded with esteem throughout the North. Yet, as Censer noted, "it was a tragedy that it proved unable to transmit its organizational achievements to a successor. At war's end, self-conscious about its place in history, the Sanitary Commission slowly wound up its affairs, putting its archives in order and commissioning its own authorized histories."[24]

In 1866 Henry Bellows became president of the American Association for the Relief of the Misery of Battlefields, a short-lived organization which hoped to gain ratification of the Geneva Convention— a set of qualifications designed to grant protection and the privileges of neutrality to wounded soldiers and medical workers on the battlefield. Although Bellows' group attempted to work with the International Red Cross Committee, its efforts to gain credibility proved ineffective, and the Association was disbanded in 1872. Ironically, the participation of the United States in the International Red Cross would at last come about through the efforts of Clara Barton, the enterprising nurse who had consistently disparaged the Sanitary Commission's institutional model of centralized relief to operate her own independent aid system during the war years. Her concept, which would provide peacetime disaster relief as well as battlefield aid in time of war, ultimately led to the ratification of the Geneva accords in 1882.[25]

The United States Sanitary Commission had accomplished much and had become a watershed effort in public responsibility by private citizens. Although it died "unmarked and unmourned," its legacies were nonetheless far-reaching; and as it faded from view it succeeded in passing on its own vision of public service linked with authoritarian control exercised in terms of class. Of this continuity George Fredrickson noted,

> A final effect of the Sanitary experience was to give the conservative activists of the upper class . . . a stronger sense that philanthropy and reform could be carried on for practical, nonutopian, even profoundly conservative purposes.[26]

Many female Sanitarians would transfer that philosophy of leadership—along with their talents and considerable energies—to a new constellation of reform organizations yet to be conceived. These efforts would focus upon primarily conservative goals and they would bear the unmistakable stamp of their elitist predecessor. As a result, in their adherence to this legacy, many of the female Sanitary Elite would deny, even ignore, one of the most visible initiatives of the late nineteenth century: the postbellum resurgence of the Women's Movement. Of this denial Nina Bennett Smith noted, "there were those [veteran nurses] who showed ingenuity and energy . . . but somehow missed the connection between what they had done and what it might mean for the status of women. Katharine Wormeley, oddly enough, belongs in this category, despite her formidable intelligence and skill."[27] Among her colleagues of the Peninsula and WCAR, Katharine's clouded vision in this instance would prove more typical than not.

EPILOGUE

In August, 1862 Joseph Howland was promoted to the rank of Brigadier-General by brevet for his heroism at Gaines' Mill. Impatient at the inaction forced upon him, and exerting strong self-discipline, he would allow himself only a few week's recuperation with Eliza at Mrs. Woolsey's home in New York, then, against his doctor's advice, would rejoin his regiment before being fit to travel. But although Joe's return to Harrison's Landing was met with rejoicing— each officer and man visiting his quarters to welcome and care for him—the reunion was necessarily short-lived. Renewed stress and the debilitating humidity of the Peninsula brought on a fresh bout of malaria, and within days of his arrival Joe was sent home once again— this time for good. His active service with the Sixteenth was now at an end, and in September, accepting the painful reality that his usefulness to the regiment was finished, Joe tendered his resignation to General Franklin. In October his discharge from the army was granted with regret.

The Howlands settled once again at Tioronda, the estate in Fishkill which they had left summarily in the spring of '61. It was a return of mixed emotions, little more than a year since they had departed—gratitude for surviving the challenges of the Peninsula; disappointment that Joe could no longer serve the regiment to which he had committed himself, his loyalties and prospects. Eliza, too, missed the life of fierce engagement she had known on board the transports. "I think of you all, all the time, and pine for you," she wrote to Georgy on her return to New York. "Give my love to Miss Wormeley and dear Mrs. Griffin, who should be with you by now. Write me *all* the details, all you want. . . . I hate to be clean while you go dirty." And then, wistfully, knowing that her discomfort could not match theirs, "Today is hotter than *any* we had on the Pamunkey!" Jane Woolsey, nursing at an army convalescent hospital in Virginia, remembered that Eliza, like a former Zouave she had known, "seemed a little stunned by the silence . . .the bands and the music had marched so far away."[1]

Tioronda, with its peaceful fields and formal gardens, remained the Howland's home for many years; Joseph supervising work on the land, Eliza, active in the WCAR during the war years, and other benevolent causes thereafter, welcoming streams of visiting family, and immersed in the concerns of tenants on the estate. Physically removed from the violence of a continuing war, the Howlands did not retreat from their duty, nonetheless. During the three years following his resignation from the Sixteenth, Joe would serve as adjutant general for recruitment in the state of New York, a position which may have assuaged his disappointment by providing an outlet through which he could share his strong sense of patriotism. At war's end he turned his attention once again to the Christian ministry—not as a candidate, but as mentor and benefactor to ministerial students. Joe's unfailing courtesy, good humor and dry wit endeared him to all who knew him, not the least the families who worked the land at Tioronda. In the years after the war he and Eliza would travel again, returning to Europe as they had done before. But Joe never wholly recovered from the "slight" wound received at Gaines' Mill, nor from the recurring fevers of the Pamunkey. He died in France, at Mentône, on April 1, 1886 at the age of 54, his life shortened by the rigors of the Peninsula. At the time of his death, Newton Curtis remembered his friend and commanding officer as he had known him during the summer of 1862:

Faithful to the discharge of every duty, he exacted prompt compliance from others. Conscious of the advantages to be derived from a strict observance of military etiquette, a dignified bearing, and an erect, soldierly carriage, he cultivated . . . those habits which promoted self respect and an *esprit de corps* among his men. . . . Young himself, and fully recognizing the aggressive and irresistible power of youth, he roused it and led his men forward to accomplishments which the conservatism of middle age would never have undertaken.[2]

Joseph and Eliza Howland would never have children of their own, but in 1893, mindful of leaving a record of the war years for their nieces and nephews, Eliza collaborated with her sister Georgy to collect, compile and edit the large collection of wartime letters exchanged between Woolsey and Howland cousins in uniform and their relatives at home. A small number of these volumes would be published privately as *Letters of a Family During the War for the Union, 1861 - 1865*, a remarkable compendium of experience and reflection by articulate aristocrats in intimate correspondence during a time of national crisis.

By late July of 1862, when Joe Howland took final leave of his regiment, it had become clear that McClellan's attempt to subdue Richmond via the swamps of the Peninsula had proved a dismal failure not to be prolonged. At the order of General Henry W. Halleck, now McClellan's senior in command, the transfer of the army back to Washington began in earnest soon afterward. On the 16th of August, a sweltering day, the Sixteenth New York left its camp at Harrison's landing and marched to Charles City where it bivouacked overnight. Next day it crossed the long pontoon bridge near the mouth of the Chickahominy, and in the next few days made its way to Newport News and thence by transport up the Potomac to Alexandria.

Describing this final march in a letter to his mother, Lieutenant Robert Wilson of the Sixteenth may have evoked the discouragement of many soldiers in all regiments of the once-great Army of the Potomac.

Six days march to Newport News, choking with dust, parched with thirst, melting by day and freezing by night, poorly fed and with nothing but the sky to cover us. You can judge of our exhausted condition when I tell you that six miles before we reached Newport News the 16th Regiment, N. Y. Vols., numbered only 184 men in the ranks, though men straggled in, so there were 400 in the morning, *and the 16th is no straggling regiment!* Next day embarked on the transports and arrived at Alexandria, sorrowful and humiliated when looking back over a year and finding ourselves on the same ground as then. The debris of the Grand Army had come back to its starting place with its ranks decimated, its morale failing, while thousands who sleep their last sleep on the Peninsula demand the cause of their sacrifice.[3]

During the next eleven months the Sixteenth would see action or serve in a supportive capacity at Second Bull Run, at Fredericksburg, and throughout the Antietam and Chancellorsville campaigns. The men's last battle would be fought at Salem Heights, Virginia on May 3, 1863, only days before their period of enlistment was to expire. Curtis wrote with forgivable pride of that engagement, "Never was the Sixteenth put into a hotter fight, and never did it show more valor and fortitude than in the battle of Salem Heights, where it contended against overwhelming numbers. The official reports set forth in glowing terms the meritorious conduct of rank and file, and no additional evidence is necessary to signalize their devotion to duty."[4] It was a satisfying closure which may have mitigated the sense of discouragement expressed by Lt. Wilson at the denouement of the Peninsula Campaign. Although the Sixteenth had lost not a man in action until the battle of West Point in May 1862, at which time its allotted time was nearly half spent, the regiment concluded its two years of service with aspirations and honor intact; a fighting unit to the end.

In May 1863 the regiment broke its home camp at White Oak Church, Virginia and began its journey home by transport and train. Arriving at Albany three days later, the men were treated to a hero's welcome of feasting, parading and a reunion with their recovering

Sunday Service at Harrison's Landing

Alfred Waud sketched McClellan seated, between trees, with his officers, listening
to prayers at Berkeley headquarters during the last weeks on the Peninsula.

colonel who had come, with Eliza, from Fishkill to join the celebration
and to be honored with ceremonial gifts. In a scene reminiscent of the
presentation of Colors in Washington Square just two years earlier,
these tributes were received and acknowledged with deep emotion,
and departing members of the regiment were encouraged by their
former leader to re-enlist; a hope which many would promptly fulfill.
In all, six hundred and forty men of the Sixteenth New York Volunteers would serve the Union army after 1863, persevering until war's
end.[5]

For Georgeanna Woolsey, departure from the Peninsula and Portsmouth Grove did not signify endings, merely changes of venue. Her
role as an active nurse would continue throughout the conflict. Characteristically, she chose the role of an unencumbered, free-lance spe-
cialist, going wherever the need arose, often answering a personal
call from Olmsted as long as he retained his position with the Sanitary Commission. On July 4, 1863 she arrived at Gettysburg as Lee's
forces retreated south and casualties from both armies still lay upon

the battlefield. Georgy was accompanied on this journey by her mother, a woman whose compassion, humor and endurance seem to have matched those of her children.[6] Mother and daughter adapted to the rigors of heat and rain, spent nights in makeshift tents, often begging door-to-door for their food. They remained at Gettysburg for three weeks, nursing Union and Confederate casualties alike, and did not leave until all the wounded who could be moved had been sent north, and adequate hospitalization had been arranged for any who remained.[7]

In June 1865, soon after the war's end, Georgeanna became engaged to Francis Bacon and was married to him the following year. Bacon, the son of a prominent New Haven family, had long been an intimate friend of the Woolseys. During the war he had served initially as regimental surgeon with the Second Connecticut Volunteers and later as a doctor assigned to go wherever the need for his services was deemed most critical. His name appears frequently in the Woolsey sisters' collected wartime letters, and he was accepted as Georgy's special friend whenever he visited the family in New York. Georgeanna did, after all, marry her army surgeon, though the two never pursued a vagabond-like medical career together in the western territories as she had once whimsically imagined. Instead Bacon was for many years a professor of surgery at Yale. The couple, who were childless, lived their long lives in New Haven close by the university campus, supporters of cultural causes and respected members of the academic and medical communities.[8]

For other Woolsey sisters, as for a number of female Sanitarians, the immediate postwar years formed a hiatus between careers. Jane returned to New York and began work on her book, *Hospital Days*. Abby resumed church and charity work. In 1872, with their active service far behind them, the sisters immersed themselves in the "new" training of nurses and hospital reform—movements which gathered momentum through the efforts of well-connected women like themselves who had seen service with the Sanitary Commission and had absorbed its methods and philosophy. In 1873 a group of these ex-Sanitarians initiated plans for the first Nightingale-inspired nurses' training schools in the United States. Three opened almost simultaneously in Boston, New York and New Haven. Jane and Abby served on the boards of both Bellevue and Presbyterian Hospitals in New York, while Georgeanna became one of the founders of the Connecticut Training School for Nurses at New Haven. Through the Woolseys' influence, and the influence of other patrician reformers, Nightingale's model of nurses' training was implemented in a growing number of urban American hospitals. The sisters were central to this new vision and they expended great energy in its promotion—their rationale based on the lessons learned from wartime experience.

But nursing reform was not the only cause to occupy the transport veterans during the 1870s, and in fact the principle focus of the Woolseys' later lives was not upon nursing per se, but rather upon Charity Organization Reform. In this they conformed with a broader pattern of elite activism. The postbellum years saw a transition from wartime patriotism to a succession of social causes in which upper-class Protestant women would once again work side by side with their male peers. Charity organization reform societies, as envisioned by their founders in the 1870s and '80s, would establish a "scientific" order of philanthropy quite unlike the paternalistic, church-based almsgiving of the past, and would focus upon self-discipline, self-help and sobriety, measures the poor were to adopt as antidotes against their own poverty.[9] George Fredrickson, in linking the theories of charity reformers with Sanitary Commission philosophy, argued that the new instigators of reform sought to transform civilian benevolence and its needy recipients in much the same way that the Sanitary elite had urged obedience and re-education upon the common soldiers of the Union army:

> It was a group of former Sanitarians, mostly women, who brought about a revolution in the philosophy and methods of charity work, especially in the area of urban poor relief. Louisa Lee Schuyler turned her energies to organizing the New York State Charities Aid Association. This organiza-

tion, modeled after the Sanitary Commission, was a semi-official group of prominent citizens who inspected public institutions such as poor houses and work houses—much in the way the Sanitary Commissioners had inspected camps—and made recommendations based on "scientific" principles. Like the Commission, it placed members of the upper classes in positions of influence which were immune from the pressures of democratic politics.[10]

This "new model" would secularize and de-sentimentalize the concept of charity, and would place the burden of recovery upon needy members of society themselves. It would also define which categories of poverty were "worthy" or "unworthy" to receive aid. These designations were highly conservative, arbitrary, and typically based upon middle- and upper-class Anglo-Saxon notions of propriety. Some critics would question the system as unnecessarily draconian, but its appeal to former Sanitarians is not surprising.

For Katharine Wormeley, life after the Peninsula returned quickly to its familiar pattern. During the later years of the war she continued her volunteer service in Newport and cared for her mother, who was in declining health. In the winter of 1863, as she regained her own strength following the months spent at Portsmouth Grove, she wrote and published an artful propagandist tract, *The United States Sanitary Commission: A Sketch of its Purposes and Work* characterized by one reviewer as a "charming volume, graceful in style, direct in detail, plain in statement and logical in argument."[11] This book, which passionately defended the Commission (and, by implication, Olmsted) at a time when its operations were being openly criticized in some quarters, netted "some hundreds of dollars" for the Boston Sanitary Fair of that year. Quite naturally, it became one of the "approved" histories welcomed by the Sanitarians. After her mother's death in 1872 Katharine did not marry, but instead embarked upon an independent life, soon to be reinforced by a move to her own house, "Red Beech Cottage," a gem of high-Victorian cottage design executed for her by Charles Follen McKim.[12]

But life did not proceed entirely without pain for Katharine. In 1878 her long and rewarding correspondence with Frederick Olmsted, cherished by both for many years, came to an abrupt end. This distressing disconnection, which may very possibly have been precipitated by Katharine herself, caused both friends considerable grief and has never been satisfactorily explained. Laura Roper in Olmsted's biography noted that, "there would seem to have been an emotional parting" and cited Olmsted's words to Katharine at the time of their split: *"remember*, whatever comes in life, nothing can ever make me lose my perfect confidence in you"—a reassurance presumably elicited by severe angst on Katharine's part.[13]

During the sixteen years since the Peninsula, Olmsted and Wormeley had taken great comfort in their correspondence. She had stood by him loyally through the vicissitudes of the Sanitary Commission, and later, when Tammany Hall politicians eliminated his position with the ongoing Central Park and Riverside projects, she had sympathized and supported him. "On her side the relationship had been ardent and confidential," wrote Roper. "She appealed for advice on personal and business matters . . . She confided to him the unhappiness of her childhood, blighted by the forbidding religiosity of the older sister who reared her, and the grief in her middle years when a friendship of seventeen years' standing 'that had nothing to do with a marriage, but took the place of a marriage' was brutally and gradually broken up so that she fled Newport for a time."[14]

Through all this, Olmsted had valued their shared bond, and, if his friend's emotional dependence upon him was sometimes burdensome, at the same time he realized that her claim to understand and appreciate him was true—and affectionately supportive. Roper remarked of Wormeley that, "her worshipful attitude may have embarrassed him; it irked his wife." Mary Perkins Olmsted was not worshipful by nature. But careful civility seemed always to prevail in the relationship, and the two women maintained an appearance of cordiality for many years.[15]

Katharine's estrangement from Olmsted remains something of a mystery. She herself referred cryptically to "circumstances" as its cause. It does seem clear, however, that she suffered some sort of malaise or breakdown in 1878 and '79 which was quite possibly physiological as

A Translator's Retreat

Characterizing her work as "frightfully tough," and wishing to find a peaceful setting in which to write, Katharine Wormeley began her search during the 1880s, staying first at country hotels in the White Mountains of New Hampshire and eventually settling on this hillside meadow as a perfect environment. Requiring simplicity as well as quiet, she commissioned Charles Follen McKim to design a house which, in completion, was smaller and less elaborate than many Victorian mountain "cottages." Today it is thought that the house may comprise approximately one half of McKim's projected design, and it remains an unassuming and graceful refuge.

well as emotional. At the time, in an effort to understand and explain the abruptness of their alienation, Olmsted described her behavior to Dr. Mary Putnam Jacobi, a noted woman physician, who, without examining, or even meeting Katharine, suggested that her symptoms indicated "a type of hysteria—'pitiful, troublesome and dangerous'— not uncommon in women her age." Wormeley was then nearing fifty. In any event, Katharine destroyed all of Olmsted's letters to her—a great loss—and the rift seems to have lasted for some years; a sad postlude to the mutual esteem forged on the Peninsula.[16]

During the 1870s, like Louisa Schuyler, Christine Griffin and other colleagues of the war years, Katharine involved herself in charity reform work, using her considerable executive skills as founder, initial secretary and general agent of the Newport Charity Organization Society. In 1887 she broadened her social responsibilities still further to found a girls' industrial school offering classes in the domestic arts and sciences.

Yet it is not as a reformer that Katharine is principally remembered, but rather as a translator and literary figure of considerable skill. During the 1880s, her writing accomplishments and lifelong fluency in French led her to undertake a succession of translations from eighteenth- and nineteenth-century French letters, histories, works of fiction and biography which would establish her reputation among sophisticated readers of European literature.[17] This new work necessitated a change in routine, and as she immersed herself further in it, a change of venue as well. She found increasingly that she required a more tranquil working environment than Newport had so far provided, and so in 1891 Katharine built her own summer house near North Conway, New Hampshire—a secluded refuge looking out across a broad valley toward Mount Washington and the massed peaks of the Presidential Range. Here, surrounded by watercolors and books, with congenial friends close at hand, she accomplished much of her best work, becoming the first American scholar to interpret the complete works of Honoré de Balzac.[18] Her elegant translations embody not only a remarkable linguistic proficiency, but the ability to translate the *spirit* of an author whose emotional and philosophical world was foreign to most American readers of the day. One review, written soon after the publication of Wormeley's new edition of *Père Goriot*, the first of a proposed series of Balzac's novels, was praised by *The New York Tribune* which noted that "the time should now be ripe for the introduction of English-speaking people to an author who by right of genius stands alone among his contemporaries. The translation is very good, and Balzac is not the easiest to translate. The publishers cannot do better than to entrust the succeeding volumes to the same capable hands."[19] These translations had presented stern challenges, and their success must have been especially satisfying. For Wormeley, these were extraordinarily productive years.

When she died at her summer home in August 1908, Katharine left a wide circle of fond connections, among them her colleagues of the Peninsula; yet it is uncertain what her relationship with Olmsted may have been at the time of her death. Roper has noted that "he remembered her long and kindly," drafting an especially friendly letter to her in 1893—and, this being so, we may hope that the two made up their differences. In her last years Katharine still described Olmsted as "one of the two men I had loved best in life out[side] my own family." Theirs had been a long, and for a time, a uniquely fulfilling friendship.[20]

In 1862 Katharine Wormeley, Georgeanna Woolsey and Eliza Howland shared a potentially soul-changing adventure, an adventure from which they returned to lead full and useful lives. These were also, without exception, notably conservative lives—and it is this conservatism which marks the real, and for some, the puzzling finale to their Peninsula sojourn.

These women, through patriotism, or sense of duty, or longing to be involved, or love of adventure—or all of these motivations together— had, in one summer, slipped the bonds of Victorian convention to serve gloriously. But although the courage and adventurousness of that early interlude were not forgotten or ignored by the associates of the women's later years, it was upon highly conventional values that one newspaper journalist focused in an obituary written soon after Katharine Wormeley's death. Glorifying her subject through a comparison with Queen Victoria, this writer noted that Katharine, like the British Queen, belonged to a generation "untroubled to any serious extent, if troubled at all, by revolutionary conceptions of woman's proper sphere." She also, with great confidence, identified Katharine with an arch-conservative, even stuffy, vision of womanhood, praising her traditionally feminine outlook as a commendable antidote which "strong-minded women" might well emulate.

To memorialize Katharine in such terms is disappointing when we consider the liberating nature of her Peninsula experience, and puzzling when we realize the individual legacies of strength which she and her colleagues brought away from that experience. But, if the eulogist was astute in her analogy, and if we are to accept her accolade as an accurate assessment of Katharine in maturity, then it would seem relevant to ask how, if at all, the lady-nurses of the Peninsula considered the feminism of their suffragist contemporaries in the years after the war. We might also inquire *why* it was that Katharine and her friends chose to remain aloof from the burgeoning women's movement of their time.[21]

During the '70s, '80s and '90s, as these former Sanitarian women submerged themselves in charity organization and other "uplifting" reforms, it became apparent that they had little inclination to consider any cause which advocated *change* in the condition of women beyond the basic education of working-class women to "take their place" in society as it then existed. Instead, they favored projects which "sought to instill principles of order and stability" on those less fortunate than themselves, utilizing indoctrination tactics of various kinds. The idea of transforming society in a progressive, let alone feminist, direction was clearly not a priority of the transport nurses' postbellum years. Intelligent, forthright, articulate, they might well have occupied the front lines in women's march toward suffrage. Their own experiences of "liberation" had, after all, positively affected their careers and had strengthened them as autonomous individuals. Yet with few exceptions, the elite veterans of the Sanitary Commission shunned feminist activism, allying themselves with the most conservative areas of volunteerism and reform.

The simple truth may well be that they did not *need* the women's movement, or so they thought. For upper-class women like Katharine and the Woolsey sisters, the reforms they espoused *automatically* translated into positions of status and quasi-professionalism without the requirement of a political voice. That this did not hold true for less privileged women seemed to cause them little concern—a curious blindness, quite possibly deliberate. Identifying with men of their own class *rather* than with women in the larger sense, they joined their male peers in disparaging the "strong-minded" cause of women's suffrage as unworthy and unwomanly. Because they were themselves assured a measure of effective public involvement *without* feminist activism, they seemed untroubled that other women did not enjoy similar access.[22]

For these reasons, despite a deep admiration for the Sanitarians' wartime careers, it becomes difficult to credit the "lady nurses" with a legacy which has helped advance the state of *all* women to a significant degree; and there remains an intrinsic dilemma in any attempt to reconcile their arch-conservatism or elitist views with the feminist thinking of their time—or of ours. Much in the philosophy of these privileged women simply cannot be justified when we compare their priorities with the progressive convictions of feminist contemporaries who fought and survived in the cause for suffrage.

Yet even as we question the female Sanitarians' aloofness towards women's rights, (and some may not do so at all,) it is important to separate their Establishment views and personal choices from their more tangible gifts to us. These women—who preferred not to call themselves "strong minded"—*were* strong, adventurous individuals who carried their gifts of character and ability into the public arena. They honored the source, as they perceived it, of their strength and usefulness, and this was deeply ingrained: the moral obligation of old wealth and Protestant duty. "From those to whom much has been given, much is expected"—an oft-quoted maxim with which they identified. They were wholehearted in their fulfillment of that obligation—as they interpreted it—both during and after the war, and they saw no reason to adjust their priorities to accommodate a cause for which they, personally, saw little need.

The ladies of the Peninsula were a unique group whose adventurous resolve left a legacy of female professionalism and social responsibility which cannot be denied, despite its elitism—a pattern which many women have since chosen to emulate and adapt to their own aspirations. If this was not a legacy of inclusive feminist solidarity, it *was*, as Nina Bennett Smith has noted, "individual, based on self-worth, pride, and the consciousness of personal achievement"—motivational satisfactions enjoyed, without apology, by many of today's women professionals.[23]

But the aristocratic Sanitarians personified a great deal more than professionalism, and they embodied virtues which no amount of feminist commitment could, of itself, change or improve. Katharine Wormeley and her friends were brave, compassionate and idealistic. Born to privilege, they were unafraid to stand firmly for convictions they believed were peculiarly their own, and to defend these with a resolve exceptional in their own time and vanishing in ours. Correctly assessing their strengths, and deliberately eschewing the perquisites of their position, these women offered themselves unstintingly during a period of crisis—to serve all and risk all in a cause they rightly perceived as greater than themselves. It is for this exemplary endeavor that we remember them.

NOTES

CHAPTER I NOTES: PAGES 1 - 7

1. William Quentin Maxwell, *Lincoln's Fifth Wheel: The Political History of the United States Sanitary Commission*, (New York: Longmans, Green & Co. 1956), vi.

2. In 1952 Quentin Maxwell published *Lincoln's Fifth Wheel*, a work which embodied most of a large body of primary source material which had long remained un-tapped. Although Maxwell's work is generous in its praise of the Commission, it maintains a degree of objectivity which sets it apart from two other valuable histories which frankly valorize the Commission and all those connected with it. Charles Janeway Stillé's *History of the United States Sanitary Commission* appeared in 1866, and was intended as an "official" history. Katharine Prescott Wormeley's *The United States Sanitary Commission: A Sketch Of Its Purposes And Its Work* was published anonymously in 1863 as supportive publicity for one of the great Sanitary Fairs, a series of massive fund-raisers which, as the war progressed, raised thousands of dollars for the cause. The authors of these earlier works, who were closely associated with the Sanitary Commission and highly conscious of its place in history, chose to memorialize it with a certain sense of awe.

3. Ginzberg, Lori D., *Women and the Work of Benevolence*, (New Haven: Yale University Press, 1990), 133.

4. Carroll Smith-Rosenberg, "Writing History: Language, Class, and Gender" *Feminist Studies: Critical Studies*, Teresa deLauretis, Ed., (Bloomington: Indiana University Press, 1986), 33.

5. Nina Bennett Smith, *The Women Who Went to the War: The Union Army Nurse in the Civil War*, Ph. D. Dissertation, Northwestern University, 1981, (Ann Arbor: UMI Dissertation Services, 1993), 36.

6. Nevins, Allan, *The War for the Union: The Organized War 1863-1864 - Vol. I*, (New York: Charles Scribner's Sons, 1971), 416.

CHAPTER II NOTES: PAGES 9 - 39

1. Kring, Walter D., *Henry Whitney Bellows* (Boston: Skinner House Books - Unitarian Universalist Association, 1979), 221.

2. Seven Southern states (South Carolina, Georgia, Louisiana, Mississippi, Florida, Alabama, and Texas) seceded from the Union in November 1860 following the election of Abraham Lincoln as President of the United States. These states joined together to become the Confederate States of America and set up a provisional government at Montgomery, Alabama. They drafted a constitution which resembled the U.S. Constitution, but which embodied important provisions establishing a policy of States Rights and maintained the institution of slavery.

One of the Confederacy's first endeavors in the early months of 1861 was to secure all Federal arsenals and forts lying within its borders, an initiative which they had nearly completed by mid-April, with only three sites still remaining in federal hands. An important one of these was Fort Sumter, located in the outer harbor at Charleston, South Carolina. On the day after Lincoln's inauguration, Major Robert Anderson, commanding Sumter, advised the President that he could only hold the fort if he was sent immediate reinforcements of twenty thousand men and a large naval force, together with a cache of adequate supplies. Lincoln's dilemma was to supply the fort peacefully without provoking incident, and to this end he notified South Carolina authorities that he would supply Sumter *without* the additional military or naval reinforcements requested by Anderson. This decision left the onus of aggression on the South, but it also made it possible for Sumter to remain a Union fortification in the mouth of the Confederacy's best harbor, a choice the Confederates would not allow. When Charleston authorities requested Major Anderson to surrender Sumter before Union supply ships were due to arrive, he promised to do so by April 15 unless ordered to remain. Pressed for a decision, the Confederates opted not to risk this delay.

Civil War began as Confederate batteries on shore fired upon the fort on April 12, initiating a thirty-four hour bombardment and causing Anderson to surrender on April 14. This opening round at Sumter precipitated Lincoln's immediate call for 75,000 Union troops on April 15, and on April 19 his implementation of a blockade on all Southern ports, effectively diminishing vital exports and incoming aid to the South.

By May these actions had servd to spur on the secession of four more slave states from the Union: Arkansas, North Carolina, Virginia and Tennessee. Four indecisive slave states, Kentucky, Missouri, Maryland and Delaware would eventually remain in the Union. Richmond, Virginia became the capital of the Confederacy, with Jefferson Davis and A.H. Stephens serving as its elected president and vice president.

3. Kring, *Bellows,* 29, 222.

4. This meeting and the one which followed are documented in Maxwell, Kring, Ginzberg, Stillé and others, as is the direct connection with, and influence of, Florence Nightingale upon the formation of the Sanitary Commission. All of these sources, in turn, relied upon the records of the U. S. S. C. which reside in New York's Public Library.

5. The Crimean War, 1853-56, was fought between Russia and the allied powers of Turkey, England, France, and Sardinia. Russia was aggres-

sively attempting to expand and to acquire warm-water ports accessible to the Mediterranean. The other powers, especially Great Britain, were intent on thwarting Russia's ambitions. The war's underlying cause was the ongoing "Eastern Question" of expansion; its immediate pretext was a quarrel between Russia and France over guardianship of Palestinian holy places. Turkey declared war on Russia; England, France, and Sardinia joined with Turkey later. Today, the war is principally remembered for the work of Florence Nightingale and for the battle of Balaklava in which thousands of British soldiers were sacrificed due to what is now seen as seriously flawed leadership on the part of senior officers. (See Cecil Woodham-Smith *The Reason Why.*) This engagement was memorialized and romanticized in Tennyson's poem, *The Charge of the Light Brigade.*

Although much of the military action took place on the Crimean Peninsula at Sebastopol and adjacent terrain on the northern shore of the Black Sea (now Ukraine,) the principal hospital to which British wounded were transported by ship was located at the Turkish town of Scutari, just across the Bosporus from Istanbul.

For details of Nightingale's service in the Crimea, see Cecil Woodham-Smith, *Florence Nightingale 1820-1910,* (New York: McGraw-Hill, 1951). Hospital conditions at Scutari are specifically discussed on pages 83 through 90.

6.   Henry Wadsworth Longfellow's poem, *Santa Filomena*, depicts a saintly nurse who passes through the wards of a dark hospital, easing suffering merely by her presence and by the light that shines from her lantern. Wounded soldiers kiss the hem of her skirt or touch her shadow as it falls across their beds and on the wall. Nightingale is said to have been the poet's inspiration. Katharine Wormeley later parodied this poem in her own ironic version.

7.   Woodham-Smith, *Nightingale,* 85.

8.   Woodham Smith, *Nightingale,* 90.

9.   Olmsted described Bellows thus in a letter to his wife, Mary Cleveland Olmsted, October 14, 1860. In Laura Wood Roper, *FLO: A Biography of Frederick Law Olmsted,* 51.

10. Three resolutions of purpose proclaimed the WCAR goals:

1. Resolved, that it is highly expedient to concentrate & methodize the spontaneous & varied efforts now making [sic] by women of New York in behalf of the sick and wounded of the approaching campaigne—the better to secure proportion, economy & efficiency in their benevolent labors.
2. Resolved, that to accomplish this end, it is desirable to form a Women's Central Association of Relief.
3. Resolved, that a committee of three ladies and three gentlemen be appointed by the chair to report a plan of organization to this meeting. Kring, Bellows, 229.

Although the Sanitary Commission was formed to aid Union soldiers, its benefits were also felt by countless Confederate officers and men captured in battle and brought to Commission facilities for medical care.

11. Ginzberg, *Benevolence,* 155.

12. Ginzberg, *Benevolence,* 159. Jane Turner Censer notes that "[Schuyler's] tireless energy, organizational skill, and tactful yet firm diplomacy in relations with the Association's local tributary aid societies steadily increased her importance and power."Jane Turner Censer, ed., *The Papers of Frederick Law Olmsted. Vol. IV: Defending the Union: The Civil War and the U. S. Sanitary Commission, 1861-1863,* (Baltimore: The Johns Hopkins University Press, 1986), 625-626.

13. Marjorie Latta Barstow Greenbie, *Lincoln's Daughters of Mercy,* (New York: G.P. Putnam's, 1944) 66.

14. See Anne L. Austin, *The Woolsey Sisters of New York; A Family's Involvement in the Civil War and a New Profession 1860-1900* (Philadelphia: American Philosophical Society, 1971) Chapters I and II detail Georgy's and her sisters' childhoods. For a genealogy and further details of this remarkable family, see Jane E. N. Woolsey, *Woolsey Family Records,* Microform #85/7059, Library of Congress, Washington, D. C., hereafter L.C.

The sisters' mother, Jane Eliza Newton Woolsey, was widowed prematurely when her husband, Charles William Woolsey, was drowned in a shipwreck while crossing Long Island Sound, a route often used in the nineteenth century by travelers between Boston and New York. At the time of her husband's death Mrs. Woolsey was left with seven daughters all under the age of eleven. Charles Woolsey's posthumous son, Charles Jr., was born two months after his father's death.

15. Georgeanna Muirson Woolsey and Eliza Woolsey Howland, *Letters of a Family During the War for the Union, 1861-1865,* (New Haven, Conn., Tuttle, Morehouse & Taylor 1899) Vol. I, 78-82.

16. Bacon & Howland, *Letters,* Vol. I, 79.

17. Austin, *The Woolsey Sisters of New York,* 34-37. Bucklin, Massey, Oates and Wormeley have also detailed the dress, appearance, and personality conventions observed by would-be nurses.

18. Bacon & Howland, *Letters,* Vol. I, 82.

19. Bacon & Howland, *Letters,* Vol. I, 85, 86.

20. Austin, *Sisters,* 39.

21. Smith, *The Women Who Went to the War,* 8.

22. Smith, *The Women Who Went to the War*, 8, 10.

23. Censer, *Papers*, 324.

24. J. A. Mangan and James Walvin, Eds., *Middle-Class Masculinity in Britain and America, 1800-1940* (New York: St. Martin's Press, 1987) 38.

25. See Austin, *Sisters*, and Woolsey, Jane E. N. *Woolsey Family Records* for details of this family's history and genealogy.

26. Bacon and Howland, *Letters*, Vol. I, 63.

27. Austin, *Sisters*, 22.

28. Curtis, Newton Martin, Brevet Major-General, U. S. Volunteers. *From Bull Run to Chancellorsville: the Story of the Sixteenth New York Infantry Together with Personal Reminiscences* (New York: G. P. Putnam, The Knickerbocker Press, 1906.) 28.

29. Curtis, *Bull Run to Chancellorsville*, 29.

30. Curtis, *Bull Run to Chancellorsville*, 29 & 30.

31. Livermore, Mary Ashton Rice, *My Story Of The War*, (New York: Arno Press, 1972 American Women: Images and Realities Series). Mary Livermore was a home-front organizer and hospital supervisor who worked with auxiliary WCAR and Sanitary Commission organizations. Her memoirs spanning the Civil War period were published in 1889.

32. Livermore, Mary Ashton, *My Story of the War*, 122.

33. Kring, *Bellows*, 230 - 231.

34. Kring, *Bellows*, 230 - 231.

35. Bellows to Charles Janeway Stillé, Nov. 15, 1865. MHS.

36. Maxwell, *Fifth Wheel*, 6-7, Greenbie, *Lincoln's Daughters*, 72. Dorothea Dix (1802-87) was at the height of her reputation and influence in 1861. During her career she was responsible for a number of reforms which improved the inhuman conditions in insane asylums and prisons, reforms which she spearheaded both in the United States and abroad. The legacies of her reforms include the practice of parole and other 20th-century innovations such as psychiatric aid and vocational training aimed primarily at rehabilitation.

37. Howe was the husband of activist-poet Julia Ward Howe, author of "The Battle Hymn of the Republic." He was the sole member of the Sanitary Commission group who could possibly be considered a "reformer" in terms of

the antislavery movement. Howe would eventually find his work with Negro freedmen to be a more fulfilling vocation than his Commission duties, and would separate himself from the nucleus of conservative New York founders once the organization became a systematized machine. Fredrickson, *Inner Civil War,* 102.

38. Fredrickson, *Inner Civil War,* 23.

39. Fredrickson, *Inner Civil War,* 24; David Herbert Donald, *Liberty and Union,* (Lexington, MA, D. C. Heath & Co., 1978), 219.

40. Fredrickson, *Inner Civil War,* 8.

41. Fredrickson notes that Bellows' remedy for the political ills he perceived "was to compel the President 'to call about him men of middle age with business confidence, the moral approval, and the patriotic reliance of the nation. He must throw overboard all the mere politicians . . .' As an immediate step Bellows considered 'inviting together two or three hundred men of standing, moral weight and courage to form a sort of volunteer congress . . .' [In effect] a kind of enlarged Sanitary Commission which would prepare itself for taking power from incompetent and corrupt politicians. In these proposals [Bellows] revealed his basic distrust of democracy and his hope of restoring a dispossessed upper class." *Inner Civil War,* 109.

42. Fredrickson, *Inner Civil War,* 103.

43. Maxwell, *Fifth Wheel,* 8.

44. Henry Bellows to Eliza N. Bellows, June 13, 1861, MHS.

45. Katharine Prescott Wormeley, *The Cruel Side Of War: Letters from the Headquarters of the United States Sanitary Commission During the Peninsula Campaign in Virginia in 1862.* (Boston, Roberts Bros., 1888) First published as *The Other Side of War,* 63.

46. Fredrickson, *Inner Civil War,* 100.

47. Censer, *Papers,* 4.

48. Bellows to Cyrus A. Bartol, June 22, 1861. MHS.

CHAPTER III NOTES: PAGE 41 -60

1. On April 19, 1861 the Sixth Massachusetts Volunteers, crossing the city of Baltimore to the Washington Station, were attacked by a mob of rebel sympathizers and pelted with stones and brickbats. Four Massachusetts in-

fantrymen were killed and thirty-six others were wounded. Historian David Donald writes that, "the riot emphasized the importance for the Lincoln administration of keeping Maryland and the other border states in the Union." Donald, David Herbert. *Liberty and Union,* 87.

2. Curtis, *Bull Run to Chancellorsville,* 33.

3. Bacon and Howland, *Letters,* Vol. I, 86.

4. See Bacon, *What We Did at Gettysburg.* In 1863 Georgy was seemingly energized by the stark conditions at Gettysburg, where she (and her mother) were forced to sleep in a small tent, ask door-to-door for food, and in general do without amenities. At that time, as in similar stressful situations on the Peninsula, she was charged with vitality, nursing the wounded of both armies, working long hours without rest. She volunteered to go wherever she was most needed, often placing herself in disagreeable, even dangerous, environments from which she seemed to emerge strengthened and unscathed.

5. References to the atmosphere of Washington during the summer of '61 abound. See Woolsey and Howland, Nevins, Austin, Olmsted's letters, Bellows' letters, Leech, and Strong's diary of 1861. Contemporary illustrations show an unfinished capital building and Washington Monument.

6. Strong, George Templeton, *Diary of George Templeton Strong,* selections edited by Allan Nevins and Milton Halsey Thomas (New York: Macmillan, 1952), 164.

7. Curtis, *Bull Run to Chancellorsville,* 37.

8. Austin, *Sisters,* 42. Bacon and Howland, *Letters,* Vol. I, 145.

9. Austin, *Sisters,* 42.

10. Austin, *Sisters,* 46.

11. Moritz was devoted to Eliza Howland and her husband, remaining at her side throughout the Peninsula Campaign until he departed with her for New York early in July following the wounding of Joseph Howland at the battle of Gaines' Mill.

12. Bacon and Howland, *Letters,* Vol. I, 145-146.

13. Censer, *Papers,* 5.

14. Wormeley, *Cruel War,* 62-63.

15. Although the Commission itself still lacked official power, at least its surroundings were regal. Strong described them with characteristic humor: "[I] visited our very grand official room in the Treasury Building, with

its long, official, green-covered table and chairs ranged in official order around it, and official stationery in front of each chair. One could not sit there a moment without official sensations of dignity and red-tapery." Strong, *Diary,* Nevins & Thomas, Eds., 164. Later, the Commission moved into a building of its own, where, if the offices were perhaps less elegant, at least a volume of productive work was accomplished. (See illustration page 178.)

16. Maxwell, *Fifth Wheel,* 45.

17. Olmsted to Mary Perkins Olmsted, July 2, 1861. Censer, *Papers,* 125; Olmsted to John Olmsted, August, 1861 in Roper, Laura Wood. *FLO: A Biography of Frederick Law Olmsted.* (Baltimore: The Johns Hopkins University Press, 1973), 169.

18. Olmsted to Mary Perkins Olmsted, June 28, 1861. Censer, *Papers,* 121-122.

19. Paul E. Steiner, *Disease in the Civil War: Natural Biological Warfare in 1861-1865* (Springfield, Ill.: Charles C. Thomas, Pub. 1968), 6.

20. George Worthington Adams, *Doctors in Blue: The Medical History of the Union Army in The Civil War* (Dayton, Ohio: Morningside Press, 1985), 17.

21. The cursory nature of these army physical examinations, which often did not even require enlistees to strip, helps explain why an estimated 400 women were able to enter the ranks during the Civil War and to serve undetected for long periods of time—often until wounded and hospitalized. Adams, *Doctors,* 13.

22. Adams, *Doctors,* 12; Margaret Leech, *Reveille in Washington 1860 - 1865* (New York: Harper & Brothers, 1941), 214.

23. Censer, *Papers,* 153, "Report on the Demoralization of the Volunteers."

24. Censer, *Papers,* 13.

25. Maxwell, *Fifth Wheel,* 17. Allan Nevins also describes the weaknesses implicit in this policy of political dispensation at the state level, demonstrating its shortcomings as they affected the commissioning of incompetent, often vicious, officers. Nevins, *The War for the Union, Vol. I,* 274-282.

26. Adams, *Doctors,* 18-19.

27. Maxwell, *Fifth Wheel,* 51.

28. Adams, *Doctors,* 146-147. For all their good intentions, the Sanitary Commission would be unable to eradicate or improve the incidence of disease

in any significant manner with the tools and knowledge currently at hand. Paul Steiner has noted that "field sanitation and hygiene were ineffective because they were based on physical and chemical concepts of cleanliness rather than on microbiological ones. Contamination occurred under subvisible conditions, and dilution did not eliminate infection. In 1861, the existence and importance of the pathogenic microbes was still unknown. The concept of living, subvisible, self-multiplying, invasive organisms, some of them . . . ubiquitous, as the cause of disease had not been accepted." Steiner, *Disease in the Civil War,* 4-5.

29. For the designations of the lesser hospitals from which sick and wounded soldiers were sent to the general hospitals, see Maxwell, *Fifth Wheel,* 50 and Adams, *Doctors,* 149.

30. Adams, *Doctors,* 149. For a vivid account of the deplorable conditions in one of these general hospitals located in the Georgetown section of Washington, see Louisa May Alcott, *Hospital Sketches,* (Bedford, MA: Applewood Books, 1987). In it Alcott describes her experiences as a nurse during the winter of 1862-1863 following the battle of Fredericksburg when incoming wounded were crammed into every corner of a dark, unsanitary requisitioned hotel. Alcott's tour of duty there was cut short by a bout of typhoid fever contracted while nursing infected soldiers. This illness, coupled with the side effects of calomel medication, left her severely debilitated, affecting her health for the remainder of her life.

31. Censer, *Papers,* 138-139.

32. Fredrickson, *Inner Civil War,* 102.

33. Censer, *Papers,* 12.

34. Wormeley, *Sketch of the Sanitary Commission,* 253-254.

35. Fredrickson, *Inner Civil War,* 102-104. The Commission believed that an elite cadre of medical inspectors could superimpose the values of a conformist ideology upon the "raw material" of American soldiers for whose dignity as human beings some Commissioners seemed to hold little respect. George Templeton Strong characterized the working classes from which those soldiers were recruited as "blind masses [and] swinish multitudes, that rule us under our accursed system of universal suffrage." Strong, *Diary,* Nevins & Thomas, Eds., Vol. III, 272.

36. Censer, 97; Nevins, ed. in Strong, *Diary,* Nevins & Thomas, Eds., Vol. III, 218-219.

37. William Alexander Hammond (1828-1901) received the post of surgeon general in April 1862 after six months of concentrated lobbying and support by the Sanitary Commission. Hammond introduced a number of positive changes, reforming and revitalizing many departments of the military

medical establishment, and in so doing made numerous enemies which indirectly led to his court-martial conviction in 1863. This ruling did little to diminish his professional standing, however, and he "enjoyed a long, successful postwar career in the newly emerging field of neurology." Censer, *Papers,* 96-98.

38. Donald, *Liberty and Union,* 110; Bruce Catton, *This Hallowed Ground; the Story of the Union Side of the Civil War,* (Garden City, N.Y.: Doubleday, 1956), 43.

39. Catton, *Hallowed Ground,* 43.

40. Curtis, *Bull Run to Chancellorsville,* 37.

41. Bacon and Howland, *Letters,* Vol. I, 285-286.

42. Adams, *Doctors,* 24 - 25.

43. Maxwell, *Fifth Wheel,* 20. There are many detailed accounts of this battle, and of the rout which ensued when fleeing soldiers and picnicking civilian spectators converged in a terrifying meleé, trampling one another on the road back to Washington. Bruce Catton has noted that some of the best contemporary reports of the event were filed by William Howard Russell (the crusading journalist of the Crimea) to *The Times* of London. Note from Joseph Howland to Eliza Woolsey Howland, July 21, 1861. Austin, *Sisters,* 44.

44. Adams, *Doctors,* 25.

45. Maxwell, *Fifth Wheel,* 20.

46. Censers, *Papers,* 129.

47. Nevins, *War for the Union, Vol. I,* 224-225.

48. Bacon and Howland, *Letters, Vol. I,* 255.

49. Strong, *Diary,* Nevins & Thomas, Eds., Vol. III, 181.

CHAPTER IV NOTES: PAGES 61 - 93

1. Mark Nesbitt, *Rebel Rivers: A Guide to Civil War Sites on the Potomac, Rappahannock, York and James,* (Mechanicsburg, PA, Stackpole Books, 1993), page 1.

2. The principle sources I have relied upon for military and logistical analyses are Stephen Sears, *To the Gates of Richmond: The Peninsula Campaign,* (New York: Ticknor and Fields, 1992); Alexander Stewart Webb, *The*

Peninsula: McClellan's Campaign Of 1862, (New York: Scribner, 1882); Allan Nevins, *War for the Union,* Vol. II, and David Miller, Ed., *The Peninsula Campaign of 1862: Yorktown to the Seven Days,* Vol. II, (Mason City, IA: Savas Savas Publishing Co., 1995.) Of special interest as a contemporary view which included official reports and reminiscences was Curtis, Newton Martin, Brevet Major-General, U. S. Volunteers. *From Bull Run to Chancellorsville: the Story of the Sixteenth New York Infantry Together with Personal Reminiscences.* Also useful were the books, pamphlets, and audio-visual materials available at the museum of the National Park Service National Battlefield Park in Richmond, VA. Their self-guided audio-taped tours were especially valuable in visualizing terrain and determining distances between points.

3. Nevins, *War for the Union,* Vol. II, 46 and 57-58.

4. Nevins, *War for the Union,* Vol. II, 48.Nevins cites as a source for this description the N. Y. *Weekly Tribune* of April 12, 1862.

5. Bacon and Howland, *Letters,* 285-286.

6. Bacon and Howland, *Letters,* 285-286.

7. Curtis, *Bull Run to Chancellorsville,* 94 & 95.

8. Censer, *Papers,* 317.

9. Bacon and Howland, *Letters,* 312.

10. Austin, *Sisters,* 55- 56.

11. Wormeley, *Cruel War,* 42.

12. Smith, *Women Who Went to the War,* 49.

13. Eliza Woolsey Howland to Joseph Howland, April 28, 1862, in Bacon & Howland, *Letters*, 312 & 313.

14. Roper, *FLO,* 192.

15. Wormeley, *Cruel War,* 15.

16. Roper, FLO, 196; Ann Townsend Zwart, "Katharine Prescott Wormeley," *Notable American Women, 1607-1950: a Biographical Dictionary,* Edward T. James, ed., Janet Wilson James, associate ed., Paul S. Boyer, assistant ed., (Cambridge, MA: Belknap Press/ Harvard University Press, 1971.)

17. Zwart, "KPW," *Notable American Women,* Edward T. James, ed.

18. Roper, *FLO,* 196.

19. Roper, *FLO,* 83, 196, 365.

20. L. P. Brockett and Mary C. Vaughan, *Women's Work in the Civil War: A Record of Heroism, Patriotism and Patience,* Introduction by Henry W. Bellows (Philadelphia: Ziegler, McCurdy & Co., 1867), 318.

21. Wormeley, *Cruel War,* 16.

22. Sears, *To the Gates of Richmond,* 60.

23. Nevins, *War for the Union,* Vol. II, 62.

24. Wormeley, *Cruel War,* 19.

25. Wormeley, *Cruel War,* 18-20.

26. Wormeley, *Cruel War,* 18.

27. Wormeley, *Cruel War,* 19.

28. Wormeley, *Cruel War,* 20-21. ·

29. Wormeley, *Cruel War,* 22.

30. Wormeley, *Cruel War,* 22, 23 and 25.

31. Wormeley, *Cruel War,* 22.

32. Wormeley, *Cruel Side War,* 26-27.

33. Wormeley, *Cruel War,* 32.

34. Wormeley, *Cruel War,* 69-70.

35. Wormeley, *Cruel War,* 23-24.

36. Wormeley, *Cruel War,* 23-24.

37. Wormeley, *Cruel War,* 25.

38. Austin, *Sisters,* 40.

39. Webb, *The Peninsula,* 82.

40. Curtis, *Bull Run to Chancellorsville,* 104.

41. Curtis, *Bull Run to Chancellorsville,* 104.

42. Newton M. Curtis, author of *From Bull Run to Chancellorsville* (the regimental history cited frequently herein) remembered that Wormeley cred-

ited him with one extra inch. In fact he measured "only" 6'6".

In his memoir of the Sixteenth, Curtis noted that unusually tall soldiers were often easy targets and were not considered worth training for that reason. During his first weeks with the regiment, a visiting senior officer had advised the young Captain's colonel to defer any promotion because he would be picked off early in the very first engagement. Curtis was apparently undaunted by such warnings. He survived his wounds at West Point and was later promoted by brevet to Major-General after acquitting himself valorously at Fort Fisher in 1863. He served through the end of the war and went on to undertake a successful career in the law.

43. Wormeley, *Cruel War,* 27, 33-34.

44. Wormeley, *Cruel War,* 30; 137-138.

45. Wormeley, *Cruel War,* 49-50.

46. Wormeley, *Cruel War,* 50.

47. Wormeley, *Cruel War,* 52.

48. Wormeley, *Cruel War,* 52-54

49. Of course, the Sanitary Commission was not the only agency to bring women to the Peninsula. Religious orders like the Roman Catholic Sisters of Charity, the Protestant-based Christian Commission, and Dorothea Dix's corps of army nurses were all represented in Virginia during the summer of 1862. Clara Barton, working independently as was her wont, was also on the scene at White House. In fact, she had little use for the Sanitarians, for she deplored their elaborate system of organization, preferring to procure her own supplies and to make her own arrangements.

It is the issue of class and privilege, and the ways in which these affected and influenced their perceptions of work, which sets the female Sanitarians' experience apart and makes their story particularly intriguing. See Nina Bennett Smith, Brockett and Vaughan, Bucklin, Dannett, Oates and Ropes for details of a richly diverse group of Civil War nurses.

50. Wormeley, *Cruel War,* 52.

51. Wormeley, *Cruel War,* 49; 50-51.

CHAPTER V NOTES   PAGES 95 - 117

1. Sears, *Gates of Richmond,* 104.

2. Miller, *Yorktown to the Seven Days,* 149.

3. Steiner, *Disease in the Civil War,* 133.

4. Steiner, *Disease in the Civil War,* 10-11.

5. Wormeley, *Cruel War,* 43; 70.

6. Wormeley, *Cruel War,* 92.

7. Wormeley, *Cruel War,* 78-79.

8. Wormeley, *Cruel War,* 160.

9. Wormeley, *Cruel War,* 61, 93.

10. Smith, *Women Who Went to the War,* 58.

11. Smith, *Women Who went to the War,* 47.

12. Wormeley, *Cruel War,* 58.

13. Wormeley, *Cruel War,* 54-55.

14. Wormeley, *Cruel War,* 56.

15. Censer, *Papers,* 351.

16. Nevins, *War for the Union, Vol. II,* 121.

17. Bacon & Howland, *Letters,* Vol. II, 379.

18. Curtis, *Bull Run to Chancellorsville,* 110-116.

19. Nevins, *War for the Union, Vol. II,* 123; Webb, *The Peninsula,* 114.

20. Nevins, *War for the Union,* Vol. II, 123.

21 Woolsey and Bacon, *Letters,* Vol. II, 381.

22. Woolsey and Bacon, *Letters,* Vol. II, 382-383.

23. Censer, *Papers,* 363.

24. Wormeley, *Cruel War,* 11-114.

25. Smith, *Women Who Went to the War,* 61.

26. Brockett & Vaughan, *Woman's Work,* 309. A slightly different version appears in Wormeley, *Cruel War,* 102-104.

27. Wormeley, *Cruel War,* 104-108.

28. Smith, *Women Who Went to the War,* 43-44.

29. Wormeley, *Cruel War,* 27; Smith, *Women Who Went to the War,* 45.

30. Smith, *Women Who Went to the War,* 45.

31. Wormeley, *Cruel War,* 114.

32. Livermore, *My Story of the War,* 187-197.

33. Carmichael, Peter S.,*"The Merits of this Officer Will Not Go Unrewarded": William R. J. Pegram and the Purcell Artillery in the Seven Days Battles,* William J. Miller, ed., *The Peninsula Campaign: Yorktown to the Seven Days,* 192.

34. Wormeley, *Cruel War,* 114-115.

CHAPTER VI PAGES 119 - 140

1. Wormeley, *Cruel War,* 32-33.

2. Wormeley, *Cruel War,* 27.

3. Wormeley, *Cruel War,* 32.

4. Wormeley, *Cruel War,* 42-43.

5. Wormeley, *Cruel War,* 35-36.

6. Wormeley, *Cruel War,* 165.

7. Wormeley, *Cruel War,* 164

8. Bacon & Howland, *Letters, Vol. II,* 410. *Maud* was a popular opera of the period famed for its "mad song" to be sung dramatically in *coloratura*.

9. Bacon & Howland, *Letters,* Vol. II, 414.

10. Smith, *Women Who Went to the War*, 45.

11. Ginzberg, *Benevolence,* 146.

12. Wormeley, *Cruel War,* 148-49.

13. Wormeley, *Cruel War,* 147

14. Curtis, *Bull Run to Chancellorsville,* 288.

15. Curtis, *Bull Run to Chancellorsville,* 289.

16. Miller, William J., *Logistics, Friction, and McClellan's Strategy for the Peninsula Campaign, Yorktown to the Seven Days: the Peninsula Campaign of 1862,* William J. Miller, ed., 135.

17. Wormeley, *Cruel War,* 113.

18. Wormeley, *Cruel War,* 163.

19. Wormeley, *Cruel War,* 134.

20. Bacon & Howland, *Letters,* Vol. II, 411-412.

21. Wormeley, *Cruel War,* 77.

22. Wormeley, *Cruel War,* 102.

23. Smith, *Women Who went to the War,* 73.

24. Smith, *Women Who Went to the War,* 74.

25. Brockett & Vaughan, *Women's Work,* 62.

26. Wormeley, *Cruel War,* 164.

27. Bacon and Howland, *Letters,* Vol. II, 424.

28. Wormeley, *Cruel War,* 164-165. Henry Wadsworth Longfellow's poem *Santa Filomena* is said to have been inspired by Florence Nightingale, the "Angel of the Crimea." These are his stanzas that Wormeley parodied. Wormeley often referred to Woolsey as "Santa Georgeanna" in humorous reference to this poem.

> Lo! in that house of misery
> A Lady with a lamp I see
>   Pass through the glimmering gloom,
>   And flit from room to room.
>
> And slow, as in a dream of bliss,
> The speechless sufferer turns to kiss
>   Her shadow as it falls
>   Upon the darkening walls.

29. Sylvia Dannett, ed., *Noble Women of the North,* (New York, T. Yoseloff:

1959), 88-89. Smith, "Women Who Went to the War," 15. Smith continues by pointing out that, "the pre-war society had ironically helped to bring this [necessity] about. By forbidding women to leave the household, it had given women a monopoly of control over the skills surrounding cleanliness, order, diet, and health. The scope of the national emergency rapidly made it obvious that these skills would be essential in maintaining the effectiveness of the Army."

30. McPherson, James M., *For Cause and Comrades: Why Men Fought In The Civil War.* (New York, Oxford University Press: 1997), 63.

31. Bacon and Howland, *Letters,* Vol. II, 385-386.

32 .Censer, *Papers,* 113.

33. Wormeley, *Cruel War,* 28 and 44.

34. *Louisa May Alcott, Her Life, Letters and Journals,* Ednah D. Cheney, ed., (Boston: 1930), 115.

35. Bacon and Howland, *Letters,* Vol. II, 501.

36. Smith, *Women Who Went to the War,* 18.

37. In the opening lines of *Hospital Sketches,* a true account of her work as a nurse, Alcott alludes to her own restlessness to "do something," while in *Little Women,* a fictional version of a family's wartime experience, she adopts a more conventional tone in her descriptions of women's efforts on the homefront.

38. Bacon & Howland, *Letters,* Vol. I, viii.

39. Smith, *Women Who Went to the War,* 10

40. Smith, *Women Who Went to the War,* 10-12.

41. Wormeley, *Cruel War,* 160-161.

42. Wormeley, *Cruel War,* 161.

43. The episode of Stuart's raid was very troubling to the women, and it figures prominently in all their memoirs.

44. Wormeley, *Cruel War,* 128.

45. Brockett & Vaughan, *Women's Work,* 437.

CHAPTER VII   PAGES 141 - 171

1. Woolsey & Howland, *Letters,* Vol. II, 412.

2. Wormeley, *Cruel War,* 139-40.

3. Wormeley, *Cruel War,* 142.

4. Kristie Ross, *Arranging a Doll's House,* in *Divided Houses,* Catherine Clinton & Nina Silber, Ed, (New York: Oxford University Press, 1992), 111.

5. Wormeley, *Cruel War,* 140-145.

6. Wormeley, *Cruel War,* 158.

7. Wormeley, *Cruel War,* 162-163.

8. Bacon & Howland, *Letters,* Vol. II, 427.

9. Wormeley, *Cruel War,* 168.

10. Wormeley, *Cruel War,* 167-169.

11. Wormeley, *Cruel War,* 171.

12. Bacon & Howland, *Letters, Vol. II,* 433.

13. Wormeley, *Cruel War,* 171.

14. Wormeley, *Cruel War,* 167.

15. Bacon & Howland, *Letters, Vol. II,* 430.

16. Bacon & Howland, *Letters, Vol. II,* 428-429.

17. Bacon & Howland, *Letters, Vol. II,* 432.

18. Sears, *Gates of Richmond,* 236. Sears cites Private Cyrus Stone of the Sixteenth.

19. Bacon & Howland, *Letters,* Vol. II, 430.

20. Sears, *Gates of Richmond,* 236-237.

21. Bacon & Howland, *Letters, Vol. II,* 431, Curtis, *Bull Run to Chancellorsville,* 126. Eliza noted that the faithful horse, Scott, was in due course brought home to Tioronda to be ridden by Joe for many years. When

he was deemed too old for further use as a saddle horse, his shoes were removed and he was turned out to pasture. But it did not suit Scott to be idle, and in the end he was re-shod and used on the farm doing light work and pulling the lawn-mower, happy to be active again. After his death the shoes he had worn as a saddle horse were mounted and hung in a place of honor at Tioronda.

22. Curtis, *Bull Run to Chancellorsville,* 131.

23. Curtis, *Bull Run to Chancellorsville,* 132.

24. Wormeley, *Cruel War,* 174.

25. Wormeley, *Cruel War,* 175.

26. Wormeley, *Cruel War,* 173.

27. Wormeley, *Cruel War,* 176-177.

28. Wormeley, *Cruel War,* 199.

29. Nevins, *War for the Union, Vol. II,* 137.

30. This remark by General D. H. Hill was widely quoted. The general's words now appear on a plaque which overlooks the field at Malvern Hill from the elevated position where Union guns fired down range at Confederate forces as they advanced up the slope.

31. Bacon & Howland, *Letters, Vol. II,* 434.

32. Wormeley, *Cruel War,* 180

33. Wormeley, *Cruel War,* 175.

34. Wormeley, *Cruel War,* 179 & 188.

35. Wormeley, *Cruel War,* 183-184.

36. Wormeley, *Cruel War,* 189-191.

37. Lincoln's July 8 visit to Harrison's Landing initiated a series of important events which presaged the close of the Peninsula Campaign and directly affected the Army of the Potomac.
  Already disturbed by McClellan's predicament and the ongoing conflict over the defense of Washington, Lincoln had consolidated several commands from other sectors to form an Army of Virginia under General John Pope. This force, combined with McClellan's remaining army withdrawn from Harrison's Landing, might, the President reasoned, undertake a more successful overland offensive.
  During Lincoln's meeting, in consultation with McClellan's general staff,

he learned that there were mixed opinions as to the merits of remaining on the James. Generals Keyes and Franklin advised withdrawal, while others felt that this would seriously decrease morale. It should also be noted that, although Katharine Wormeley expressed guarded optimism about the medical facilities at Harrison's Landing at the time of her departure, the incidence of fever would prove devastating as the summer progressed. Not surprisingly, McClellan insisted he be allowed to remain and finish the campaign—reinforced by 100,000 men.

Assessing the situation on the Peninsula, Lincoln, on his return to Washington, recalled General Henry W. Halleck from the West and named him general-in-chief of the Union Armies, thus giving him overall control of strategy. So it was to Halleck that McClellan presently proposed a highly questionable plan to resume his march on Richmond, and, alarmed by the dangerous logic of this (and other) schemes, Halleck soon made the decision to withdraw the Army of the Potomac from the James. Although McClellan protested bitterly, Halleck remained firm and the evacuation was begun during the second week in August.

A famous footnote to the meeting between President and General which Katharine witnessed was the presentation to Lincoln of what would come to be known as the "Harrison's Landing Letter." This letter contained a litany of McClellan's own opinions as to how the war should proceed, including policy, management and strategy. Among other things the letter advised against confiscation of Southern property, against emancipation, and warned of other "radical" measures which smacked of abolitionist thinking. Lincoln accepted the letter with thanks but without comment, much to the general's chagrin. (For more on the July 8 meeting and its aftermath, see Sears, *Gates of Richmond,* 350-355, and Sears, *Lincoln and McClellan* in Borrit, Gabor S., ed, *Lincoln's Generals* (New York: Oxford University Press, 1994) 38, among other sources listed herein.)

38. Bacon & Howland, *Letters, Vol. II,* 441.

39. Bacon & Howland, *Letters, Vol. II,* 459.

40. Wormeley, *Cruel War,* 197-199.

41. Wormeley, *Cruel War,* 193.

42. Wormeley, *Cruel War,* 206.

43. Bacon & Howland, *Letters, Vol. II,* 478.

44. Wormeley, *Cruel War,* 205.

45. Wormeley, *Cruel War,* 206.

CHAPTER VIII PAGES 171 - 187

1. Ross, *Arranging a Doll's House*, 112-113.

2. Smith, *Women Who Went to the War*, 11.

3. Smith notes yet another conviction by which elite women justified their wartime service—though not their work in postbellum reform: they had created a " moral image of the Union Army. . . . This moral image served a dual purpose. It gave the nurses ideality by association; they had not served soldiers, rough and bloody, but immortal heroes. In addition, those heroes were citizens, and the nurses claimed that they had been kept citizens largely through the feminine influence. The separation of a young man from his home and regular religious privileges, exposing him to the 'temptations of camp life,' was seen by his mother, wife and sister as a dire moral emergency at least equal to the national one." *Women Who Went to the War,* 14.

4. Wormeley, *Cruel War,* 136.

5. Bacon & Howland, *Letters, Vol. II*, 464; Wormeley, *Cruel War,* 202. Wormeley to Woolsey, July 21, 1862, *Letters, Vol. II,* 465.

6. Brockett & Vaughan, *Women's Work,* 321-322.

7. Woolsey to Howland, August 26, 1862, *Letters, Vol. II,* 479.

8. Wormeley to Woolsey, August 29, 1862, *Letters, Vol. II,* 481.

9. Brockett and Vaughan, 322; Bacon & Howland, *Letters, Vol. II,* 495-496; Wormeley to Woolsey, September 5, 1862, *Letters, Vol. II,* 480.

10. Roper, *FLO,* 216.

11. Bacon & Howland, *Letters,* Vol. II, 478.

12. Bacon & Howland, *Letters,* Vol. II, 502.

13. Censer, *Papers,* 33.

14. Censer, *Papers,* 34.

15. Censer, *Papers,* 47.

16. Strong, *Diary,* Nevins & Thomas, ed., 291.

17. Olmsted to Bellows, April 25, 1863. Censer, *Papers,* 615-617.

18. Censer, 60. For analyses of the Union League Clubs and the *Nation*, respectively, see Censer, 39-41 and 630-637. For discussions of the Union League only see Fredrickson, *Inner Civil War,* 131-135 and Nevins, *The War for the Union: The Organized War 1863-1864,* Volume VII, 164.

19. Roper, *FLO,* 233.

20. *Papers,* 704-709.

21. Bacon & Howland, *Letters, Vol. II,* 478.

22. Censer, *Papers,* 59.

23. The charges that soldiers did not benefit from the Commission's stores distressed and infuriated Wormeley. Her 1863 *Sketch of the Sanitary Commission* specifically addressed and attempted to refute all such damaging allegations.

With the *Sketch*, she entered the fray with characteristic vigor to defend the Commission's integrity. She argued persuasively that ill and severely wounded men were necessarily unaware of changed sheets and moistened bandages; that they did not consider who cooked their soup or who had sewn the donated clothes in which they completed their convalescence. Although Wormeley forgave the soldiers for not fully understanding the origin of the food, stimulants and blankets which had saved their lives, she made clear to her readers how and from whom this largesse had been forthcoming. Wormeley, *Sketch of the Sanitary Commission,* 242-245.

24. Censer, *Papers,* 59-60.

25. Censer, *Papers,* 60. For a complete summary of Olmsted's career with the Sanitary Commission after the Peninsula, see Censer, *Papers,* 33-60.

26. Frederickson, *Inner Civil War,* 112.

27. Smith, '*Women Who Went to the War,* 62.

EPILOGUE NOTES   PAGES 189 - 203

1. Woolsey, Jane Stuart, *Hospital Days,* (New York: New York: D. Van Nostrand, 1868, 5-6.

2. Curtis, *Bull Run to Chancellorsville,* 140-143.

3. Bacon & Howland, *Letters, Vol. II,* 471.

4. Curtis, *Bull Run to Chancellorsville,* 265.

5. Curtis, *Bull Run to Chancellorsville,* 306-310.

6. Mrs. Woolsey traveled to Gettysburg after receiving news that her son Charley had been wounded in the battle. In early 1863, after his service on the transports, Charley had been commissioned a lieutenant in the 16th New York Volunteers, Joe Howland's old regiment. Happily for Georgy and her mother, when they arrived at Gettysburg they found Charley to be only slightly wounded. Austin, *Sisters*, 93; Bacon & Howland, *Letters*, Vol. II, 494. See also. Georgeanna Muirson (Woolsey) Bacon, *What We Did At Gettysburg,* (unpublished: E. O. Jenkins, Printer, 1863.)

7. Bacon, *Gettysburg*, 12.

8. Austin, *Sisters*, 115.

9. During the first three decades of the nineteenth century the concept of public charity in America continued much the same as it had been in colonial years: primarily a moral commitment based on religious principles and often connected with churches. The poor were, as the New Testament reminded Christians, "always with us," and it was the moral duty of the good man to give alms to his unfortunate neighbor. Walter Trattner has noted that "disparities in wealth and condition existed not to separate men but to make them have more need for each other—to bind them closer together 'in the bond of brotherly affection,'" as the Puritan cleric John Winthrop had expressed it.
The Great Awakening, principles of Enlightenment thinking, and the American Revolution itself had reinforced the humanitarian impulses of Americans, while the separation of church and state encouraged voluntary associations and institutions for the relief of indigence. Walter Trattner, *From Poor Law to Welfare State: a History of Social Welfare in America,* (New York: Free Press; London: Collier MacMillan, ¡1989), 16.

10. Fredrickson, *Inner Civil War,* 211-212.

11. Brockett & Vaughan, *Women's Work,* 323.

12. This house remains occupied and preserved in good condition on one of Newport's side streets. Not to be confused with the elaborate, gilded age palaces of the next decades which came to be known as Newport "cottages," Wormeley's house is of medium size, discreet, and rather whimsical, with a domed gilded tower and fish-scale shingles.

13. Censer, *Papers*, 113-114; Roper, *FLO*, 365

14. Roper, *FLO*, 365.

15. Roper, *FLO*, 365.

16. Roper, *FLO*, 365-366.

17. A recent computer search of Harvard's Widener Library brought up 94 works of Wormeley's translation. They are comprised of historical treatises, letters and recollections authored by, or describing, a wide variety of French historical and literary figures. As well as her major Balzac project, Wormeley translated a number of other works which focus upon personalities and circumstances connected with the regicide period of the French Revolution known as "The Terror."

18. In an 1888 letter to a fellow trustee of The Newport Industrial School for Girls, Anna F. Hunter, Katharine revealed tension between the demands of work and literary scholarship. Following a detailed analysis of vexing administrative problems Katharine wrote, "My new book comes out next week, *Modeste Mignon,* and I am now doing *La Peau de Chagrin* and find it *frightfully tough.*" Completion of this translation brought her temporarily to the point of collapse. K. P. W. to A. F. H., NHS.

19. Honoré de Balzac, *The Magic Skin,* (Boston: Roberts Brothers, 1894), 1. "Balzac in English". Publisher's promotional notes from the *New York Tribune.*

20. Censer, *Papers*, 113-114.

21. The unidentified clipping in which this eulogy appears is part of a collection of family memorabilia belonging to Henry C. Longnecker of Jackson, NH.

22. See Ginzberg, *Benevolence*, 189-199 for a discussion of how the legacy of the Sanitary Commission, the emergence of the Charity Reform Organizations and the Suffrage Movement intersected, diverged and related to one another in the years after the war.

23. Smith, *Women Who Went to the War,* 158.

BIBLIOGRAPHY

(Works Cited; Works Consulted)

Adams, George W. *Doctors in Blue: The Medical History of the Union Army in The Civil War.* Dayton, Ohio: Morningside Press, 1985.

Alcott, Louisa May. *Hospital Sketches.* Bedford, MA: Applewood Books, 1987. Originally published, Boston, MA: J. Redpath, 1863.

_____, *Louisa May Alcott, Her Life, Letters and Journals,* Ednah D. Cheney, ed., (Boston: 1930).

Annual Report of the Adjutant General of the State of New York for the year 1899: Registers of the 12th, 13th, 14th, 15th, 16th, 17th, 17th Veterans and 18th Regiments of Infantry, Serial # 19. Albany: James B. Lyon, State Printer, 1900

Ashburn, P. M. *A History of the Medical Department of the United States Army.* Boston: Houghton Mifflin Company, 1929.

Attie, Jeanie. "Warwork and the Crisis of Domesticity in the North".¡ *Divided Houses,* Clinton, Catherine & Silber, Nina editors. New York: Oxford University Press, 1992.

Austin, Anne L. *The Woolsey Sisters of New York; A Family's Involvement in the Civil War and a New Profession 1860-1900.* Philadelphia: American Philosophical Society, 1971.

_____. "Woolsey" [Abby, Georgeanna and Jane]. Edward T. James, editor., Janet Wilson James, associate editor, Paul S. Boyer, assistant editor, *Notable American Women, 1607- 1950: a Biographical Dictionary.* Cambridge, MA: Belknap Press, Harvard University Press, 1971.

_____. *History of Nursing Source Book.* New York: Putnam 1957.

Bacon, Georgeanna Muirson (Woolsey) and Howland, Eliza Newton (Woolsey). *Letters Of A Family During the War For the Union 1861-1865*. New Haven, Conn: Tuttle, Morehouse & Taylor,1899.

Bremner, Robert Hamlett. *American Philanthropy*. Chicago: University of Chicago Press, 1960.

Borrit, Gabor S., ed. *Lincoln's Generals* (New York: Oxford University Press, 1994

_____. *The Public Good: Philanthropy and Welfare in the Civil WarEra*. New York: Knopf, 1980.

Brockett, L. P. and Vaughan, Mary C. *Women's Work in the Civil War: A Record of Heroism, Patriotism and Patience*. Philadelphia: Ziegler, McCurdy & Co., 1867.

Bucklin, Sophronia E. *In Hospital and Camp: A Woman's Record of Thrilling Incidents Among the Wounded in the Late War*. Philadelphia: J.E.Potter and Company, 1869.

Bullough, Vern L., & Bonnie. *History, Trends, and Politics of Nursing*. Norwalk, Conn.: Appleton-Century-Crofts, 1984.

Burgess, John W. *The Civil War and the Constitution: Vol. II*. New York: Charles Scribner's Sons, 1901.

Catton, Bruce. *This Hallowed Ground: the Story of the Union Side of the Civil War*. Garden City, N.Y.: Doubleday, 1956.

Censer, Jane Turner, Ed. *The Papers of Frederick Law Olmsted. Vol. IV: Defending the Union: The Civil War and the U. S. Sanitary Commission, 1861-1863*. Baltimore: The Johns Hopkins University Press, 1986.

Cope, Zachary. *Florence Nightingale and the Doctors*. Philadelphia: J. B. Lippincott, 1958.

Curtis, Newton Martin, Brevet Major-General, U. S. Volunteers. *From Bull Run to Chancellorsville: the Story of the Sixteenth New York Infantry Together with Personal Reminiscences*. New York: G. P. Putnam, The Knickerbocker Press, 1906.

Dolan, Josephine A., M. Louise Fitzpatrick, Eleanor Krohn
    Herrmann. *Nursing in Society: a Historical Perspective.*
    Philadelphia: Saunders, 1983.

Dannett, Sylvia D. L., ed. *Noble Women of the North.* New York, T.
    Yoseloff: 1959.

Donald, David Herbert. *Liberty and Union.* Lexington, MA, D. C.
    Heath & Co.,1978.

Farrell, Betty. *Elite Families: Class and Power in Nineteenth-
    Century Boston.* Albany: State University of New York
    Press, 1993.

Ehrenreich, Barbara & English, Deirdre, Eds. *Complaints and Dis-
    orders: The Sexual Politics of Sickness.* New York: The
    Feminist Press, City University of New York, 1973.

Fredrickson, George M. *The Inner Civil War: Northern Intellectuals
    and the Crisis of the Union.* New York: Harper & Row, 1965.

Ginzberg, Lori D. *Women and the Work of Benevolence.* New Haven:
    Yale University Press, 1990.

Greenbie, Marjorie Latta Barstow. *Lincoln's Daughters of Mercy.*
    New York: G.P. Putnam's, 1944.

Holland, Mary A. Gardner. *Our Army Nurses: Interesting Sketches,
    Addresses and Photographs.* Boston: M. Wilkins & Co.,
    1895.

Huggins, Nathan Irvin. *Protestants Against Poverty: Boston's
    Charities, 1870-1900.* Foreword by Oscar Handlin.
    Westport, Conn., Greenwood Pub. Corp. 1971.

Kring, Walter D. *Henry Whitney Bellows.* Boston: Skinner House
    Books-Unitarian Universalist Association, 1979.

Leech, Margaret. *Reveille in Washington 1860 - 1865.* New York:
    Harper & Brothers,1941.

Levine, Bruce. *Half Slave and Half Free: The Roots of Civil War.*
    New York: Hill & Wang, 1992.

Livermore, Mary Ashton Rice. *My Story Of The War.* New York: Arno Press, 1972. American Women: Images and Realities Series.

Mangan, J. A. and Walvin, James, Eds. *Middle-Class Masculinity in Britain and America, 1800-1940.* New York: St. Martin's Press, 1987.

Massey, Mary E. *Bonnet Brigades.* New York: Alfred A. Knopf, 1966.

Maxwell, William Q. *Lincoln's Fifth Wheel: The Political History of the United States Sanitary Commission.* New York: Longmans, Green & Co.1956.

Mayer, Henry. *All On Fire: William Lloyd Garrison and the Abolition of Slavery.* New York: Saint Martin's Press, 1998.

McPherson, James. *Ordeal By Fire: the Civil War and Reconstruction.* New York: Knopf, 1982.

_____. *For Cause and Comrades: Why Men Fought In The Civil War.* Oxford; New York: Oxford University Press, 1997

Melosh, Barbara. *The Physician's Hand: Work, Culture and Conflict in American Nursing.* Philadelphia: Temple University Press, 1982.

Miller, William J., ed. *The Peninsula Campaign of 1862: Yorktown to the Seven Days, Vol. Two.* Mason City, IA: Savas Publishing Co., 1995.

Neely, Mark E. Jr. *The Last Best Hope of Earth: Abraham Lincoln and the Promise of America.* Cambridge, Harvard University Press, 1993.

Nesbitt, Mark. *Rebel Rivers: A Guide to Civil War Sites on the Potomac, Rappahanock, York and James.* Mechanicsburg, PA, Stackpole Books, 1993.

Nevins, Allan. *The War for the Union: The Organized War 1863-1864 -Volumes I, II & VII.* New York: Charles Scribner's Sons, 1971.

Oates, Stephen B. *A Woman Of Valor : Clara Barton And The Civil War.* New York: Free Press; Toronto: Maxwell Macmillan Canada; New York: Maxwell Macmillan International, 1994.

Olmsted, Frederick Law. *The Cotton Kingdom: A Traveller's Observations On Cotton and Slavery in the American Slave States, 1853-1861.* (Edited.) New York: DaCapo Press, 1996.

Reverby, Susan. *Ordered to Care: the Dilemma of American Nursing, 1850-1945.* Cambridge: New York: Cambridge University Press, 1987.

Roper, Laura Wood. *FLO: A Biography of Frederick Law Olmsted.* Baltimore: The Johns Hopkins University Press, 1973.

Ropes, Hannah Anderson. *Civil War Nurse: The Diary and Letters of Hannah Ropes.* John R. Brumgardt, Ed. Knoxville: University of Tennessee Press 1980.

Ross, Kristie. "Arranging a Doll's House: Refined Women As Union Nurses". *Divided Houses.* Clinton, Catherine & Silber, Nina, editors. New York: Oxford University Press, 1992.

Sears, Stephen W., ed. *The Civil War Papers of George B. McClellan: Selected Correspondence, 1860 - 1865.* New York: Ticknor and Fields, 1989.

_____. *To the Gates of Richmond: The Peninsula Campaign.* New York: Ticknor and Fields, 1992.

Smith, Nina Bennett. *The Women Who Went to the War: The Union Army Nurse in the Civil War.* Ph. D. Dissertation, Northwestern University, 1981. Ann Arbor: UMI Dissertation Services, 1993.

_____. "Men and Authority: The Union Army Nurse and the Problem of Power." *Minerva: Quarterly Report on Women and the Military* Vol. 6. No. 4. Arlington, VA: L. G. DePauw, 1988.

Smith-Rosenberg, Carroll. "Writing History: Language, Class, and Gender". *Feminist Studies: Critical Studies.* Teresa deLauretis, ed. Bloomington: Indiana University Press, 1986.

Steiner, Paul E. *Disease in the Civil War: Natural Biological Warfare in 1861-1865*. Springfield, Ill.: Charles C. Thomas, Pub. 1968.

Stillé, Charles Janeway. *History of the United States Sanitary Commission: Being the General Report of its Work During the War of the Rebellion*. Philadelphia: J.B. Lippincott & Co., 1866.

Strong, George Templeton. *Diary of George Templeton Strong*. Selections edited by Allan Nevins and Milton Halsey Thomas. New York: Macmillan, 1952.

Trattner, Walter I. *From Poor Law to Welfare State: a History of Social Welfare In America*. New York: Free Press; London: Collier MacMillan, 1989.

_____. *Social Welfare or Social Control?: Some Historical Reflections on Regulating the Poor.* Knoxville: University of Tennessee Press,1983.

Webb, Alexander Stewart. *The Peninsula : McClellan's Campaign Of 1862*. New York: Scribner, 1882.

Welter, Barbara. *Dimity Convictions : The American Woman in the Nineteenth Century*. Athens, Ohio: Ohio University Press, 1976.

Woodham-Smith, Cecil. *Florence Nightingale 1820 - 1910*. New York: McGraw-Hill, 1951.

Wormeley, Katharine Prescott. *The Cruel Side Of War: Letters from the Headquarters of the United States Sanitary Commission During the Peninsula Campaign in Virginia in 1862*. Boston, Roberts Bros.,1898.

_____. *The United States Sanitary Commission: A Sketch Of Its Purposes And Its Work*. Boston, Little, Brown and Co. 1863.

Zwart, Ann Townsend. "Katharine Prescott Wormeley". Edward T. James, ed., Janet Wilson James, associate ed., Paul S. Boyer, assistant ed. *NotableAmerican Women, 1607-1950: A Biographical Dictionary*. Cambridge, MA: Belknap Press, Harvard University Press, 1971.

MANUSCRIPT SOURCES

The Houghton Library, Harvard University, Cambridge, Massachusetts

Bacon, Georgeanna Muirson (Woolsey) and Howland, Eliza Newton (Woolsey). *Letters Of A Family During the War For the Union 1861-1865.* Two Volumes. New Haven, Conn: Tuttle, Morehouse & Taylor 1899. Privately published.

Library of Congress, Washington, D. C., Manuscript Division

Bacon, Georgeanna Muirson (Woolsey). *What We Did At Gettysburg.* Unpublished. E. O. Jenkins, Printer, 1863.

Bellows, Henry Whitney. "Report Concerning the Women's Central Association of Relief at New York, to the U. S. Sanitary Commission at Washington, Oct. 12, 1861". New York: W. C. Bryant & Co., printers, 1861.

_____. "Duty and Interest Identical in the Present Crisis." A Sermon. New York: Wynkoop, Hallenbeck & Thomas, printers,1861.

Olmsted, Frederick Law. *United States Sanitary Commission: Report Of The Secretary* "with regard to the probable origin of the recent demoralization of the volunteer army at Washington, and the duty of the Sanitary commission with reference to certain deficiencies in the existing army arrangements, as suggested thereby". Washington: McGill & Witherow, printers, 1861.

_____. *United States Sanitary Commission:* "Report of a preliminary survey of the camps of a portion of the volunteer forces near Washington".Washington, McGill & Witherow, printers, 1861.

_____. *United States Sanitary Commission:* "An account of the executive organization of the Sanitary commission". Washington: McGill & Witherow printers, 1862.

_____. *United States Sanitary Commission:* "Provision for the soldiers disabled in the war". New York, 1862.

Woolsey, Jane E. N. *Woolsey Family Records.* Unpublished. Micro-form 85/7059.

Woolsey, Jane Stuart. *Hospital Days.* New York: D. Van Nostrand, 1868.

Henry C. Longnecker, Jackson N. H.

Katharine P. Wormeley, letters, clippings and memorabilia

Massachusetts Historical Society, Boston, Massachusetts

Henry Whitney Bellows Papers

Newport Historical Society, Newport, Rhode Island

Katharine P. Wormeley, letters; biography of Ralph Randolph Wormeley; photographs of Newport house designed by Charles Follen McKim in 1876.

ILLUSTRATION SOURCES

Library of Congress, Washington, D. C.
Print and Photograph Division

National Archives II, College Park, MD
Still Picture Collection

National Library of Medicine, Bethesda, MD
Images from the History of Medicine

U. S. Army Military History Institute, Carlisle Barracks, Carlisle, PA
MOLLUS Collection, Mass. Commandery

National Park Service
Frederick Law Olmsted National Historic Site
Brookline, Massachusetts

David Hewitt & Anne Garrison
Architectural Photography
San Diego, California

INDEX

Adams, George W., 52, 56-57

Agnew, Dr. Cornelius R., 34, 68, 111, 181

Alcott, Louisa May, 134-135, 213, 221

Alexandria, Virginia, 46, 53, 65-68, 70, 191-192

American Association for the Relief of the Misery of Battlefields, 185

American Sanitary Commission, 3

Anderson, Maj. Robert, 206

Antietam, battle and campaign, 27, 168, 177, 179, 192

Ariel (steamer), 164

Army Medical Bureau, 4, 31, 57, 67, 185

Army Medical Department, 103

Army of the Potomac, 2, 58, 60, 63, 70, 84-85, 89, 126, 141, 162-163, 165, 167, 191, 223-224

Army of Virginia, 223

Arrowsmith (steamer), 149

Bache, Alexander D., 31

Bacon, Francis, 194

Baltimore, Maryland, 41, 133

Barlow, Arabella, 166

Bartlett, Col. Joseph, 104, 152, and his brigade, 106, 151

Barton, Clara, 131, 186, 217

Beauregard, Gen. Pierre G. T., 55-57, 166

Beaver Dam Creek, Battle of, 146

Bellevue Hospital, 195

Bellows, Rev. Henry W., 2, 9-11, 13-15, 30-31, 34-36, 38, 47, 53-54, 60, 111, 138, 180-181, 185, 210, photo, 178

Biddle, Col. Chapman, 144

Blackwell, Dr. Elizabeth, 11-12, 14, 18, 46

Brady, Mathew, 13

Burnside, Gen. Ambrose E., 145

Butler, Gen. Benjamin, 38

Butler, Rosalie, 81

Cameron Run, 45, 56, 90, 92

Cameron, Simon, 31

Casey, Gen. Silas, 147-148

Censer, Jane Turner, 47, 182, 184-185

Centreville, Virginia, 62

Chancellorsville, Battle of, 27, 192

Charity Organization Reform, 195

Cheesman's Creek, 69-70

Chickahominy River, 62, 97, 105-107, 109-110, 141, 191

Christian Commission, 217

Connecticut Training School for Nurses at New Haven, 195

Connecticut Troops; *2nd Infantry,* 194

Corps, Federal Army; *VI,* 104

Crimean War, 3, 12-13, 31, 52, 58, 207, 220

Cumberland Landing, 86-87, 90

Curtis, Gen. Newton M., v, 26-28, 85-86, 107, 120, 125, 154, 190, 192, 217

Daniel Webster (steamer), 68-69, 75, 77-78, 103, 128, 144, 149, 161, 168, photo, 80
Daniel Webster II (steamer), 66, 68, 77
Davies, Col. Thomas A., 26, 28, 42, 44, 65
Davis, Jefferson, 50, 95, 206
Dix, Dorothea, 18, 21, 31, 82, 217, photo, 33
Donnelly, Col. —, 26
Drewry's Bluff, 105

Ebbitt House, 44-45
Edwards, Dr. Lewis A., 176
Elizabeth (steamer), 78, 147
Elm City (steamer), 77, 79, 87, 104, 124, 147, 149
Eltham's Landing, 84-86
Emerson, Ralph W, 35

Fair Oaks, Battle of, i, 91, 98, 101, 104-105, 107, 109- 114, 117, 122, 126-127, 141, 157
Forts: Darling, 145; Fisher, 217; Monroe, 63, 75, 103, 138, 144, 156; Sumter, 10-11, 14, 55, 206;
Franklin, Gen. William B., 59, 68, 84, 86, 90-91, 104, 128, 145, 189, 224, and his division, 85-86
Fredericksburg, Battle of, 87, 177, 192, 213
Fredrickson, George, 186, 195, 210
Free Soil Party, 35
Fugitive Slave Law, 133

Gaines' Mill, Battle of, 153, 146, 149, 151, 189-190, 211
Garrison, William Lloyd, 35
Geneva Convention, 185
Gettysburg, Battle of, 193-194, 211, 227
Gibbs, Oliver W., 34, 181
Glendale, Battle of, 146, 161
Gloucester Point, 75
Godkin, Edward, 181-182
Griffin, Christine, 68, 70, 72, 77-78, 83, 104, 114, 125, 166, 190
Grymes, Dr. James M., 68, 75, 77, 103, 128

Halleck, Gen. Henry W, 191, 224
Hamilton, Alexander, 16
Hammond, Surgeon General William A., 55, 175-177, 185, 213
Hansen, Dr. Jacob, 31
Harris, Dr. Elisha, 31, 34, 47, 50
Harrison's Landing, 146, 153, 157, 160-162, 164, 166-168, 172, 179, 184, 189, 191, 223-224
Harrisonburg, Virginia, 42
Heintzelman, Gen., Samuel P. 109
Hill, Gen. Daniel H., 149, 151, 160, 223
Hone, Robert S., 28
Hopkins, Capt. Woolsey, 128
Howe, Dr. Samuel G., 34
Howe, Julia Ward, 209
Howland, Eliza, v, 4-6, 15, 19, 23-24, 26, 28-29, 41-46, 52, 56-58, 65-66, 68-70, 72, 75, 77, 81-82, 84, 90, 92, 104, 106-107, 109, 115, 120, 122-123, 127-130, 133, 136, 142, 145, 149, 153, 161, 166, 189-191, 193, 200, 202, 211-222
Howland, Col. Joseph, vi, 22-23,

25-26, 28, 41-44, 52, 56-58, 65-
66, 68-70, 84-85, 87, 89, 104,
106-107, 109, 128, 145, 149,
151-153, 160-161, 189-191,
211, 222, 227

Ingalls, Col. Rufus, 126, 128, 142,
156
International Red Cross, 185-186

Jackson, Gen. Thomas J., 63 87,
144-147, 149
Jacobi, Dr. Mary Putnam, 199
James River, 4, 61-63, 105, 146-
147, 157, 161, 163, 165, 167-
168, 224
Jenkins, John Foster, 184
Johnston, Gen. Joseph E., 57, 74,
109, 141

Keyes, Gen. Erasmus D., 109, 224
Knapp, Frederick, 68, 77-78, 103,
114, 166, 184
Knickerbocker (steamer), 78-79,
81-82, 149

Lane, Caroline, 68
Lee, Gen. Robert E., 91, 110, 141-
142, 144-145, 152, 168, 193
Letterman, Jonathan, 163, 166
Liberty Party, 35
Lieber, Francis, 34
Lincoln, Abraham, 3, 11, 14, 23,
31, 35-36, 47, 58, 60, 62-63, 87,
164-165, 206, 211, 223-224
Lint and Bandage Association, 31
Livermore, Mary A., 30, 209
Longfellow, James W., 220

Maine Troops; *5th Infantry,* 104
Malvern Hill, Battle of, 157, 223,

146, 160-161
Manassas, First Battle of, 27, 55,
57-59
Manassas, Second Battle of, 192
Massachusetts Troops: *6th Infan-
try,* 210; *44th Infantry,* 157
Maxwell, William Q., 51, 57
McClellan, Gen. George B., i-ii, 2,
58-59, 60-63, 67, 74, 77, 82-87,
89, 91, 97, 104-107, 109-110,
126, 141-142, 144, 146-149,
151, 154, 162-166, 168, 191,
223-224
McDowell, Gen. Irwin, 44, 55-57,
87, 89, 107, 141, 162
Mechanicsville, Virginia, 62, 144-
145
Mechanicsville, Battle of, 107,
photo, 106
Medical Reform Bill of April,
1862, 54
Merrimac, USS, 75
Mississippi River, ii
Monitor, USS, 105, 166
Morgan, Gov. Edwin, 27
Moritz (man-servant), 46, 69, 120-
121, 161, 211
Morrell, Gen. George W., 91

New York State Charities Aid Association, 195
New York Troops: *1st Cavalry,*
107; *7th Infantry,* 107; *16th Infantry,* vi, 2, 22, 26-29, 41-42,
44, 52, 56-57, 65, 67, 84-87, 92,
104-107, 129-130, 151-154,
189-193, 217, 227, photo of
casualties, 155; *18th Infantry,*
44; *27th Infantry,* 104, 106; *28th
Infantry,* 26; *31st Infantry,* 44;
32nd Infantry, 44

Newport Charity Organization Society, 199

Newport News, Virginia, 103, 157, 191-192

Newport Woman's Union Aid Society, 73

Newton, Gen. John, and his brigade, 85

Nightingale, Florence, 4, 12-13, 98, 125, 132, 173, 206-207, 220

Norfolk, Virginia, 61, 157

Ocean Queen (steamer), 77

Olmsted, Frederick Law, v, 2, 4, 13, 21, 36-38, 47, 50-53, 55, 57, 59-60, 68-70, 72-73, 77-78, 90, 103-104, 110-111, 113-114, 120, 124, 127, 138-140, 142-143, 145, 156-157, 162-164, 166, 169, 172-173, 175, 179-182, 184, 193, 196-197, 199-200, photo, 49

Olmstead, Mary Perkins, 197, 199

Pamunkey River, ii, 4, 61, 84, 87, 90, 97, 105, 127, 129, 146, 149, 177, 184, 190

Peninsula Campaign, i, 2, 4, 43, 54, 60-63, 87, 132, 179, 182, 187, 192, 211, 223

Pennsylvania Troops: *96th Infantry*, 104

Physicians and Surgeons of New York Hospital, 31

Pinkerton, Allen, 63

Pope, Gen. John, 223

Porter, Gen. Fitz-John, 59, 91, 144, 147, 151, and his division, 91

Portsmouth Grove, Rhode Island Hospital, 157, 175-177, 184

Potomac River, 43, 44, 50, 61, 63, 65, 68, 75, 87, 191

Presbyterian Hospital, 195

Rappahannock River, 62, 84

Richmond and York River Railroad, 84, 105, 142, 153

Richmond, Virginia, ii, 62-63, 84, 89, 104-107, 142, 145-146, 156, 163, 166, 168

Roman Catholic Sisters of Charity, 217

Ross, Kristie, 171-172, 174,

Russell, William Howard, 13, 214

Salem Heights, Engagement at, 192

Samuel S. Spaulding (steamer), 77, 104, 144, photo, 80

Sanitation Commission, see United States Sanitary Commission

Savage's Station, Battle of, 146, 154

Sawtelle, Capt. Charles, v, 126-127, 144-147, 156, 167

Schuyler, Louisa L., 15, 17, 29-31, 165, 195, 199, photo, 32

Schuyler, Gen. Philip, 16

Seven Days' Battles, 27, 89, 105, 127, 144-145, 151, 153, 165, 167

Seven Pines, Battle of, 107, 109-110, 114, 126

Shenandoah Valley, 63

Slocum, Gen. Henry W., 104, 145, 151, and his brigade, 85, 152

Smith, Nina B. 6, 102, 115-116, 129, 133, 137, 139, 171, 186, 203, 221, 225

Soldiers' Aid Society, 11

Stanton, Edwin M., 38

Stephen, Alexander H., 206

Stoneman, Gen. George, 107, 147-148, 151
Strong, George Templeton, 2, 34, 43-44, 47, 54, 59, 68, 78, 138, 180, 211-213, photo, 48
Strong, Mrs. George T., 104
Stuart, Gen. James Ewell Brown (JEB), 141-144, 169, 221
Sumner, Gen. Edwin V., 109-110
Superintendent of Contraband Labor, 38

Tunstall's Station, 142, 147

Union League, 181-182
The United States Sanitary Commission: A Sketch of its Purposes and Work (publication), 196
United States Sanitary Commission, i-ii, iv, vi, 1-2, 6, 11, 16-17, 22, 30-31, 67, 70, 72-74, 78, 122, 131, 138, 146, 161-162, 167, 196-197, 205-206, 209-210, 212-213, 226; access to generals, 91, ambitious plans become reality, 60, Army Medical Department, 103, Army Quartermaster Corps, 126, camp and hospital improvement, 47, catering on ships, 102, concept, 14, control of epidemics, 53, departure of Olmstead, 182, description, 7, discontinue training of nurses, 140, evolution, 9, example set, 172, Fair Oaks, 110-111, First Manassas, 57, fleet of boats, 68-69, 86, 97, formed to aid all soldiers, 208, founders' determination to construct, 35, goals, 34, 37, headquarters on

Wilson Small, 78, 84, hospital transports, 62, ideas of camp cleanliness, 52, ideology, 5, 139, legacy, 186, Medical Reform Bill of April, 1862, 54-55, mission of, 3, operational model, 4, paradigm, 12, philosophy, 195, post Peninsula Campaign, 179-181, 185, 193-194, 217, relationship with government, 114, role of, 38, struggles against volume of casualties, 114, temporary headquarters in Washington DC, 45, veterans of, 201, view of the army, 54, Washington DC hospitals, 46, worthy endeavor, 36
Urbanna, Virginia, 62, 84

Van Alen, Gen. James H., 82, 156
Van Buren, Dr. W.H., 31, 34
Van Vliet, Gen. Stewart, 126-127, 144-145
Vollum, Col. Edward P., 137-138, 149

Ware, Dr. Robert, v, 77, 101, 111, 113, 120, 147, 157, 166, photo, 76
Washington, D.C., 41-44, 46, 52, 56, 58, 66-67, 70, 77, 87, 139, 164-165
Washington, NC, siege of, 157
Webb, Gen. Alexander, 85, 110
West Point, Virginia, 61, 84-86, 149
Whetton, Harriet D., 83, 177
White House Landing, i-ii, 61, 84, 86-87, 89, 92, 95, 97-98, 101-102, 104-105, 123, 126, 141-144, 146-148, 156-157, 161-

162, 166-167, 176, 217, photo, 96

White Oak Swamp, Battle of, 154

Willard's Hotel, 45, 47, 164

Williams, Gen. Seth, 58-59, 91-92

Williamsburg, Battle of, 62, 74, 79, 82, 84, 86, 89

Wilson, Lt. Robert, 191-192

Wilson Small (steamer), 77-79, 82, 84-86, 89, 103, 124, 127, 143-144, 156, 161-163, 166-167, 169

Wissahickon, USS, 78, 128

Woman's Central Association of Relief in New York, 7, 14-18, 22, 29-30, 73, 122, 131, 133, 165, 187, 190, 207, 209

Woolsey, Abby, 17, 123, 133, 165, 168, 194-195

Woolsey, Charles, 68, 227

Woolsey, Eliza, (see Howland, Eliza)

Woolsey, Georgeanna, v, 4-6, 15-19, 21, 23, 26, 29, 42-43, 45-46, 52, 56, 58, 65, 68-70, 72-73, 75, 77, 79, 81-83, 90, 101, 104, 110-111, 113, 115, 121-124, 126, 133, 135-137, 140, 142, 148, 151, 153, 161, 168, 175, 177, 184, 190-191, 193-195, 200, 202, 211, 220, 227, photo, 20

Woolsey, Jane, 123, 133, 177, 190, 194-195

Woolsey, Sarah, 177

Wormeley, Caroline, 72

Wormeley, Katharine P., iv-vii, 2, 4-6, 15, 37, 47, 53, 70, 72-73, 75, 77-79, 81-83, 86, 89-92, 95, 98, 101, 103-104, 113-117, 119-122, 124-128, 130, 134-140, 142-148, 156-157, 160-169,

171-177, 179, 184, 187, 190, 196-197, 199-203, 207-208, 216, 220, 224, 226-228, photo, 71

York River, 4, 61, 63, 70, 74, 82, 84, 105, 146

Yorktown, Virginia and Battle of, 61, 63, 70, 74-75, 77, 82, 86, 103, 128, 38, 156